Calm Before The Storm

Calm Before The Storm

DAVE HAYES

dhayesMEDIA

DEDICATION

We dedicate this book to the board owners, volunteers, anons, and Q—all of whom have demonstrated undying devotion to the cause of freedom.

ACKNOWLEDGMENTS

My wife Denise and I would like to thank the thousands of anonymous patriots on 4chan, 8chan, and 8kun for dedicating their time to researching Q's messages. The world has greatly benefitted from your labor, your talent, and your commitment in the face of substantial opposition. Denise and I have been blessed by those who have helped support us while we set aside our usual work to research Q's messages. We also thank and recognize the indispensable prayer warriors behind the scenes. We acknowledge and thank those researchers who have struggled personally for this mission—losing relationships and jobs; they've received no benefit apart from the satisfaction of remaining true to themselves and their country. Others have paid the ultimate price; we honor them.

TABLE OF CONTENTS

INTRODUCTION

On December 21st, 2017, Donald Trump signed an Executive Order authorizing the U.S. Treasury Department to seize the assets of people and organizations known to be involved in human rights abuse, human trafficking, and corruption. That same day, Eric Schmidt stepped down as CEO of Google's parent company Alphabet. According to CNBC, the year 2018 saw a record number of CEOs leave their companies. The same source reported that the month of October, 2019, set a record for monthly CEO resignations and that 2019 was on pace to break the record set the previous year. It may seem like a coincidence, but I suspect that Trump's Executive Order is directly related to the record number of CEO resignations.

In October of 2017, due to allegations of sexual abuse, the famous film producer Harvey Weinstein was dismissed from his company and expelled from the Academy of Motion Picture Arts and Sciences. By October 31st, over 80 women had made allegations against him. The allegations sparked the #MeToo social media campaign, which resulted in similar sexual abuse allegations against powerful men around the world.

In early 2018, Keith Raniere and his associate, actress Allison Mack, were arrested and indicted on charges of racketeering and sex trafficking related to NXIVM. The organization was proven to be a cult that used mind control to coerce young women into becoming sex slaves. As of April 2019, five people associated with NXIVM—Mack, co-founder Nancy Salzman, Lauren Salzman, Seagram heiress Clare Bronfman, and bookkeeper Kathy Russell—had pleaded guilty to various federal charges.

Jeffrey Epstein was convicted in 2008 of procuring an underage girl for prostitution and of soliciting a prostitute. Although investigators identified 36 girls whom Epstein had abused, he pled guilty to the two charges related to one victim and served a 13-month sentence. Victims were outraged when Epstein was allowed to serve most of his sentence on work release. On July 6th, 2019,

Epstein was again arrested on federal charges of sex trafficking of minors in Florida and New York. He died in his jail cell on August 10th, 2019. Due to Epstein's death, all pending charges against him were dismissed. However, the U.S. Department of Justice announced that it is seeking testimony from witnesses and victims of Epstein and his accomplices.

Epstein's arrest led to dozens of new stories about two of his alleged accomplices, Ghislaine Maxwell and Prince Andrew. On November 5th, 2019, Project Veritas released a story about an investigation by ABC News into Jeffrey Epstein. The story contained a leaked video where Good Morning America host Amy Robach said she interviewed Virginia Roberts (now Virginia Guiffre), who came forward to discuss her knowledge of Epstein's crimes. "She had pictures, she had everything. She was in hiding for twelve years. We convinced her to come out. We convinced her to talk to us." Robach said. "I've had this story for three years... (ABC) would not put it on the air... "the Palace found out that we had her whole allegations about Prince Andrew and threatened us a million different ways." The Epstein scandal has rocked the British royal family. Following a televised interview in November of 2019, Prince Andrew announced that he was stepping down from all public duties.

The purpose of this series of books is to explain how, until recently, there existed a two-tiered system of justice that allowed rich and powerful people to commit crimes and avoid prosecution. It is my belief that this two-tiered system of justice is being dismantled, and a system of equal justice is being set in its place. The cases I've just described demonstrate this point.

A report has been released by the U.S. Department of Justice's Office of Inspector General, exposing the criminal acts committed by employees of government agencies, not just in the U.S. but around the world. These crimes were part of a coordinated effort to prevent Donald Trump from being elected President and after his election, to remove him from office. As a Presidential candidate, Trump vowed to "drain the swamp." By that, he meant that he intended to remove corrupt people from power. The purpose of opposing Trump's ascent to the oval office was to allow corrupt people to remain in power.

Corruption is more pervasive than we know. Most people suspect it exists in government and in the corporate world, but it has invaded Hollywood, the media, academia, and even the church. The scheme to remove Trump from office failed. Although an attempt to remove him by impeachment is underway, it will likewise fail. An old proverb warned, "If you try to kill the king, you'd better not miss." Trump's enemies missed. Their day of reckoning is coming.

I believe we will soon see the arrests of thousands of corrupt people in every part of society. If the arrests happen, many of Q's predictions will be validated.

Q has provided information on many other subjects. These books will explain in layman's terms what he has had to say. Q (or Qanon, if you prefer) has become a global internet sensation. If you're active on social media, it's hard to avoid conversations about this mysterious figure. In this book, when I refer to Q as "he" or "him," it is strictly for ease of writing. I do not know if Q is a male or female, an individual or a group. We'll discuss what Q has said about himself in chapter 10.

I've spent most of the last five years working full-time as an author. In December of 2017, I put all pending book projects on hold to devote my time to researching Q. Since then, I've averaged 50 hours a week reading Q posts, exploring relevant news articles, and discussing Q with other researchers.

Although many people have offered commentaries on Q, some have never researched Q's posts. While we are all entitled to our opinions, uninformed opinions are responsible for much of the confusion that exists regarding Q. I do not claim to be the *ultimate* expert on Q. I have, however, studied his posts exhaustively, and I enjoy teaching others about the nuances of Q's messages. Those who follow my decodes on social media enjoy my teaching, and many have expressed their gratitude. I am also grateful to them; were it not for their encouragement, this task would be far less enjoyable.

At the time this book was published, Q has posted more than 3,700 messages on 4chan, 8chan, and 8kun. I've read every message more than once. The subjects that have been mentioned are too numerous and too complex to be adequately covered in a single volume. (I've published more than 170 videos on Q's posts so far). Because of the great depth and breadth of Q's messages, I've decided to write a series of books that will chronicle Q's posts from beginning to end.

But even if this series contained ten volumes, there wouldn't be adequate space to cover all of Q's posts and explain each one in detail. Instead of covering every post, each volume in this series will examine a sample of posts over a span of time and explore the main subjects discussed during that time period. Whenever possible, details of those discussions will be examined from the time they were first mentioned until the time of publishing.

There are posts of every kind to be considered, including links to news articles, videos, and photographs. Research from relevant news articles is provided where appropriate. I've done my best to describe relevant images and provide commentary on them, however copyright laws, privacy concerns, and space constraints make it difficult for the images themselves to be included in this book.

Many of Q's posts contain cryptic abbreviations, acronyms, and diagrams, as well as the initials of people and government agencies with which you may not be familiar. I've included a glossary at the back of the book to help explain them.

Formatting in this Book

Please note that the formatting of Q's posts when they appear in this book will adhere to the following guidelines:

- If there were typos in a post by Q or an anon, the typos will also appear in this book. *Note: Some of Q's "typos" are intentional and convey a message.*

- In some cases, an original post by Q or an anon may contain blank lines between sections of text. We have tried as much as possible to preserve original use of paragraph returns, but occasionally, they may be removed due to space constraints.

- Dates will always be provided when I display a post by Q if they are relevant. I will occasionally break a long post into multiple sections and explain each part individually. In those cases, the date will appear at the top of the first section, but the sections that follow will not have a date because they're part of the same post.

- I will occasionally explain a conversation thread between two people that occurs on a single day. In those cases, the date of the first post will be displayed but the dates of the responses may be omitted.

- To limit distracting data, I've opted in most cases to omit the timestamps and user IDs from Q's posts. That information usually isn't relevant to the discussion. In the few cases where it is, timestamps and user ID's will be included.

- I've chosen at times, to cut out certain parts of Q's posts while including other parts because, from a teaching standpoint, it's best if we focus on the part of the post that's relevant to the subject we're discussing. Some Q posts cover many subjects and it's easy to become confused or distracted by off-topic information. When I need to display only a section of a post, you'll see three diamonds like this ♦♦♦ to indicate where part of the original message has been omitted.

Q's Purpose

Mainstream news outlets publish articles every week, each claiming to know Q's purpose, and yet, each has completely missed the point of Q's operation. In order to help you understand Q's mission, I'd like to provide a simple analogy.

Imagine a place named Westopia. Imagine that Westopia's government is corrupt, but they've managed to hide it from the public. Westopia's governing body, for example, approves contracts based on bribes that it receives from contractors. A contract to build a low-income housing project worth $250 million was awarded to Blue Sky Construction (no relation to any real company), which paid $25,000 in bribes to key government officials in exchange for the contract.

Let's imagine that Westopia has a paid military, and I'm a high-ranking member who specializes in intelligence. Our military conducts both foreign and domestic surveillance. The corrupt activities of politicians have been captured on video and stored on secure servers. Nothing has been done about corruption because the officials who have the power to make things right have always gone along with it. Until now.

Westopia has now elected as its Executive, an outsider who knows about the corruption but has managed to avoid being involved in it. A plan was developed to expose these crimes. Because Westopia's law enforcement is also involved in corruption, alerting them isn't a good option. Instead, a decision was made to make citizens aware of the corruption and help them take back control of their government.

Westopia has an anonymous internet messaging board that protects the identity of users, and it's free of censorship. Rather than disclose corruption directly, military leaders will inform the public by posting clues on the message board that, when decoded, will allow citizens to discover the truth for themselves. We've planned out a series of messages that will be posted over the course of a year. This is our first message:

Some of us come here to share the truth.
There are dark things going on behind the scenes in Westopia that must be exposed.
The highest levels of government are involved.
Who knows their secrets?
What is a contract?
How are contracts awarded?
Highest bidder?
What is the salary of a public official?
What is the net worth of JP, for example?
Does he own a yacht?
How is that possible?
Sometimes a Blue_Sky foretells a storm.

If you were a citizen of Westopia and you read this message, what would you think of it? The first few messages posted by the military would seem irrelevant to most people. But if, as time went on, the messages continued in the same manner, suggesting that illegal activities were taking place, more people would take them seriously. What would happen if photos were posted that hinted at corrupt activities? What would happen if the insiders answered questions and provided proof after proof that they had access to highly sensitive information?

If you understand this illustration, you have some idea of the purpose of Q's mission and the way in which it is being carried out.

My research has led me to conclude that Q is, primarily, an open source intelligence operation. In our society today, there is, in fact, public corruption. Although some people are suspicious that such corruption exists, the full extent of the corruption and the negative effect it has on society have been hidden from the public's consciousness. Q provides open source information (intelligence) that can be used by average people to uncover the truth about corruption.

Q has addressed hundreds of subjects with varying degrees of disclosure. Some subjects have been discussed at length, and Q has provided confirmation of theories about them, giving us a clear understanding of their meaning and relevance. Q has not provided detailed information on other subjects—preferring to leave them shrouded in mystery. He has repeated some posts frequently and called attention to certain topics, stressing their importance. The following post illustrates this point.

Nov 4 2017
When big news drops please re-read entire graphic.
This is so critical and why information is provided in a certain order and why some topics are continually emphasized more than others as those will be the recent happenings.
This is the purpose of this new thread (re-organize).
Snow White
Wizards & Warlocks.
Q

Q intends to reveal as much information as practically possible, but some subjects pose a risk if too much is said about them. National Security laws present one obstacle to disclosure. Some information, if released, could do irreparable harm to allies, which could precipitate war, causing worldwide (WW) suffering.

Feb 11 2018
Understand one simple fact - the US is connected to the rest of the world.

Knowing that, understand, by default, if certain intel is released it would cause a WW/mass suffering. We share the idea of open source but value life and must make decisions base decisions on outcomes and containability.

Q

If Q were interested in providing a one-way flow of information, he could simply set up a website and publish his information on it. Q posts on message boards because he wants a two-way dialogue. He asks questions of followers and confirms their research or points them in a different direction when needed. Fine-tuning research is critical to Q's mission.

A subject's relevance and its full meaning are never revealed before the appointed time. For that reason, Q provides generous information on some subjects and almost nothing on others—at least initially. When a subject is first mentioned, whether a series of images or statements, if, after a few days of people guessing about its meaning, Q has not confirmed any of them or he hasn't suggested a different line of thinking, it's safe to conclude that the subject will be explained at a later date.

Many people provide decodes and commentary on Q's posts. I've learned a great deal from other researchers. The commentary I provide is a mix of what I've learned from others and what I've found during my own research. I try to avoid excessive speculation except when Q specifically asks us to speculate. I try to stick to the information that Q has already confirmed.

Readers who follow Q are given pointers on various subjects and encouraged to research and assign meaning to them as they see fit. This allows them to come to their own conclusions. Once a conclusion is reached, the meaning becomes personal. A personalized understanding of a subject leads to diversity of thought among peers. Each of us emphasizes the things we feel are important, while diminishing the importance of things someone else might value. With such diversity of opinion, discussions can become messy. Diversity of thought is a different dynamic from the groupthink that exists in much of society today.

These chronicles describe the way Q has impacted my life, personally. I make no claim to represent Q or the group of researchers who follow his posts. I'm merely providing a survey of the topics I've found to be the most helpful and the most compelling. That is a reflection of my own personal tastes. Others will undoubtedly disagree, and perhaps that will inspire them to write their own books. I hope that many others share their thoughts about Q with the world.

CHAPTER 1

Tumbling Down the Rabbit Hole

UNLIKE MOST PEOPLE WHO READ Q's posts, I'm not what you would call a "truther." The term *truther* was popularized after the September 11th attacks in New York. It describes people who don't believe the official narrative of how and why the attacks happened. Some truthers question the official explanations of the mass shootings in Las Vegas, Sandy Hook, or the Pulse Night Club in Orlando, Florida. Some truthers question the official narrative regarding past Presidential assassinations. Truthers are often labeled "conspiracy theorists." I'm an oddball among those who follow Q. I've never been interested in alternative explanations of historical events. I've always accepted official accounts. I was drawn to Q through an interesting set of circumstances that I'd like to briefly explain.

Like a talent scout, my wife, Denise, has discovered most of the people I now follow on social media. She has a knack for finding good content providers. She'll be listening to a broadcast by someone she recently found when a pearl of wisdom will drop into a quiet room. I'll wander over and ask, "Who's that?" One day, she was listening to a YouTube broadcaster as they read a post from Q:

What is a key?
What is a key used for?

What is a guard?
What is a guard used for?
Who unlocked the door of all doors?
Was it pre-planned?
Do you believe in coincidences?
What is information?
Who controls the release of information?
WHO HAS ALL OF THE INFORMATION?
Who disseminates information?
What is the MSM?
Who controls the MSM?
Who really controls the MSM?
Why are we made to believe the MSM are the only credible news sources?

A couple of times a week, Denise would listen to a decode of the latest Q post. I tried to ignore them. I had books to write, and Q seemed like a waste of time. What was the point of these coded messages anyway? And the cryptic questions? What purpose did they serve?

Nearly 20 years ago, after living most of my life as an atheist, I surrendered my life to the will of God. I've done my best to follow His lead since then, and He often leads me through dreams at night. Let me provide a couple of examples. In 2008, I had a dream where God instructed me to pray for my patients to be healed. I reluctantly obeyed and since then, I have seen thousands of people healed. Dreams seem like foolishness to many people, but I take mine seriously. Several weeks before we moved to Arizona in 2011, my wife and I had the same dream on the same night. In our dreams, we sat in the office of a title company signing documents to close on a home loan. Months later, we had a harrowing experience with a lender as we tried to purchase the home where we now live. Were it not for the dreams we both had—which confirmed that we were doing the right thing—we may have backed out of the home purchase due to all the obstacles we encountered along the way.

On August 22nd, 2016, I had a dream that may have foreshadowed Q's operation. In the dream, Donald Trump released vast amounts of sensitive documents over the internet to anyone who wanted it. The information came from sources that would not normally divulge such secrets and pertained mostly to finance and politics. These secrets enabled the political and economic ruling class to remain in power. If word ever got out about what they were doing behind closed doors, their house of cards would come crashing down. In the dream, Trump made all this information available to the public. I picked up much of what he released and shared it with people in my sphere of influence.

One night in December of 2017, I had a dream where I met a man. As we sat on a couch and talked, he informed me that my understanding of historical events was wrong. One by one, he recalled events from history and corrected my false perceptions of them. Then we got up and walked into a large, open room. As we walked, he asked questions. He mentioned a couple of famous people. Then he mentioned a news headline and said, "Do you remember these people? Do you remember the event? How are they connected?" He brought up another event and a couple more people. "Do you know who they are? How were they involved?" The questions went on. In the dream, I realized that this was exactly the way Q asked questions. Suddenly, the man stopped and turned to look me in the eye. "Do you understand that this is primarily about the children?" With that, the dream ended.

Because of a dream God had given me, I had done some research in 2016 regarding public corruption and child trafficking and stumbled upon some disturbing things. I knew what the man in the dream meant when he said this was primarily about the children. I spent the next week reviewing videos that decoded Q posts. Then I spent about a month researching Q's posts for myself. (There were only a few hundred at the time, so it was fairly easy to do.) It wasn't long before I was creating broadcasts explaining what I had discovered about Q.

CHAPTER 2

4chan, 8chan, 8kun, and Q

PART OF Q'S MISSION INVOLVES the exposure of global corruption. Naturally, those who commit criminal acts would not want their deeds exposed. That makes Q an enemy of the rich and powerful, and a target for retaliation. As a potential target of powerful people, if he were wise, he would want to avoid being identified. One way to conceal your identity from corrupt people would be to post anonymously on the internet. People have been doing that for years on the internet message boards called 4chan and 8chan (sometimes called the *chans*).

Q originally posted on the 4chan board named *politically incorrect* (sometimes called /pol/). That board was chosen for some specific reasons. 4chan users can remain anonymous, which is why government employees sometimes use it to drop information about public corruption. The board is frequented by computer geeks who are adept at bringing together data from articles, videos, public records, and other sources. By day, anonymous users (also called anons or autists) work as systems analysts, coders, and game designers. By night, they research the clues people drop, without the knowledge of their employers, and without knowing who authored the posts they're investigating. (The term *autist*, as used on message boards like 4chan, does not infer that a person has autism. Instead, it's a slang term that describes people with the ability to be hyperfocused as they process large amounts of information).

The presence of thousands of skilled researchers was another reason Q's operation was launched on 4chan. The anons have proven to be excellent internet researchers.

Anons have researched posts from intelligence community insiders (both real and fake) for years. People regularly show up on the chans claiming to be an agent from the CIA or another intelligence agency. They'll claim to have insider information on an investigation or predict the arrest of a famous person, and usually, they're never heard from again. Their predictions seldom come true because most people claiming to be intelligence insiders are frauds. Dealing with phonies has made the anons a jaded lot. They'll expect a mountain of proof before they'll buy your "intelligence insider" story. On the chans, a phony is also called a LARP (or Live Action Role Player). LARP indicates that the perpetrator of the fraud is merely acting out a role.

Q knew the anons were hardened skeptics. It's one of the reasons he chose to post on 4chan. His messages needed to be vetted for legitimacy. He knew anons would intensely scrutinize his posts, and if they could be verified, Q would gain the trust of some of the most skeptical people on the planet. Gaining the trust of skeptics was vital to the operation. Q claims to have access to the President of the United States. Such a claim could only be verified through careful and exhaustive analysis. Once verified by anons, it would permit Q to provide vetted information about the real stories behind world events and the facts of history that have been hidden from us.

Q has managed to convince anons of his legitimacy, but mainstream media outlets haven't bothered to explain this to their readers. In the many articles they've written trying to discredit Q, reporters tend to portray anons as violent and gullible extremists. (This has not been my experience; I've found them to be highly intelligent and analytical. Although they can be passionate about their beliefs, the anons who follow Q don't endorse violence.) After a slew of negative articles had been published about Q and the anons near the end of July 2018, one of the anons posted the following message:

Anonymous • Jul 30 2018
ARTICLES ABOUT Q
WHY DO THEY NEVER ASK THE ANONS WHY THEY ARE HERE?
REAL ANON'S are here as we follow the EVIDENCE (documented verifiable evidence), we are building the TRUTH of our HISTORY so we can expose and dismantle the corruption that has PLAGUED our world for millennia.
I invite any publication to print this as a statement of fact from an

ACTUAL ANON.
WE do not tell YOU what to think or how to FEEL about a topic. WE
simply dig for TRUTH and then PRESENT what we find so it can be
scrutinized by our PEERS and further corroborated.
The CHOICE to KNOW what we have found, verified and presented is
entirely up to YOU.
Presenting OUR work in a way to imply WE are some sort of cult, shows
the WORLD how corrupt the MAINSTREAM MEDIA has become.
WE are NOT about violence, subversion or control. WE are simply
providing FACT based information FREE of charge to the WORLD.
WWG1WGA
Feel FREE to SHARE
End

Q responded to the anon:

Excellent!
You cannot fool a massive group of dedicated gold star researchers.
At what point does it become mathematically impossible?
Comms structure designed for a very specific reason.
Q

National security laws restrict the information government officials can provide to the public. Classified information is off-limits, but there is a wealth of
valuable information that is open source. In fact, open source information is so
important that in 2005, the Office of the Director of National Intelligence (ODNI)
created the Director of National Intelligence Open Source Center (OSC). The
OSC is tasked with improving the availability of open sources to intelligence
officers and other government officials. In the same way that the OSC provides
non-classified information to its clients, Q provides his readers with information
that is freely available to the public and which, if brought together and correctly
interpreted, paints a picture of what would otherwise require *classified* information to understand.

Q Can Be Difficult to Understand

Many people find Q's posts perplexing. There are a number of reasons for that.
The first reason is that Q uses a method of instruction that is rarely used today.
In the second half of the 5th century BC, sophists were lecturers who used

philosophy and rhetoric to entertain, impress, or persuade their audience to accept a point of view. The Greek philosopher Socrates used a different approach to teaching. The Socratic method is a form of cooperative argumentative dialogue between individuals. The alternating asking and answering of questions is used to force critical thinking, the analysis of ideas, and the examination of underlying presuppositions. The Socratic method leads to hypothesis elimination; better hypotheses emerge by steadily identifying and eliminating weak ones or ones that lead to contradictions. Typically, a series of questions are introduced that are intended as tests of logic and fact. These questions help a person discover their underlying beliefs about some topic and identify beliefs that should be discarded.

We live in a culture today where reporters write articles and record interviews conveying *their* understanding of a given subject to us. It's more like a monologue; there is no debate involved. There is no examination of underlying beliefs. There is no testing of logic or investigation of the factual basis of statements. We're expected to accept the facts as they are given to us by the presenter without questioning them. The presenter doesn't merely tell us "the facts." They also assign meaning to the facts. Whoever assigns meaning to information determines the public narrative on that subject. The media tend to interpret information in a way that supports an ideological belief system. If you accept a person's presentation of facts, you're more likely to accept their ideological beliefs.

In contrast to the model of the mainstream media, Q uses the Socratic method. Using questions, he'll examine our current beliefs on a given subject. He'll ask if our belief is logical, then drop hints about facts we may not have uncovered, and suggest an alternative hypothesis. He may provide a link to a news story and encourage us to do more research. The information we need is publicly available. We're free to conduct our research in whatever way we want. We're also free to interpret the information however we want. We must come to our own conclusions because Q keeps his interpretations to a minimum. For many people, researching for themselves, thinking for themselves, and trusting their own conclusions can make following Q difficult. When you're accustomed to someone telling you what to think, thinking for yourself can be a painful adjustment.

Oct 6 2018
UNPLUG FROM FAKE NEWS [FALSE REALITY]
[PROPAGANDA ARM OF D PARTY]
THINK for yourself.

RESEARCH for yourself.
TRUST yourself.
FIND THE TRUTH.
DON'T BE A PAWN IN THEIR SICK GAME.
Q

Although Q has an ideological framework that is centered on freedom and justice, he provides information in a way that can be interpreted however one chooses. Indeed, a common criticism of Q is that his messages don't impart any real meaning because they can be interpreted in virtually any way imaginable. The fact that we're free to interpret Q's information however we choose doesn't mean there are no right or wrong answers. Q set up a system of communication where researchers can ask for clues or post the findings of their research and have theories verified. Many people have received confirmation or help from Q simply by posting their work on Twitter. Q may confirm our theory as was the case in this series of posts from December 22nd and 23rd, 2017.

Dec 22 2017
How did NK suddenly have miniaturized nukes upon POTUS taking office?
What was stated during Hussein's term by agencies?
How did NK suddenly obtain missle guidance cap?
What is leverage?
Define hostage.
Their last hope!
Q

An anon asked why the letter "i" was missing from the word "missile" in the above post.

Anonymous • Dec 23 2017
Q posts missing letter "i" are markers?

Q responded with a clue:

What rocket fired today?
[i]
Message sent.
Q

An anon responded, noting that SpaceX had recently launched its Falcon 9 rocket to deploy an array of satellites for Iridium Communications.

Anonymous
Iridium?

Q confirmed the missing letter "i" in his posts was a signal about the Iridium satellites and said future news would unlock more information.

Future news will unlock more of the message.
Missing [i] confirmed.
Q

Investigating the clues provided by Q is time consuming work, but I've found that doing my own research, connecting the dots, and coming to my own conclusions helps me understand historical and current events in a more complete way.

Learning the Lingo of the Chans

Conversations on 4chan, 8chan, and 8kun are hosted on various subdomains called *boards*. Each board hosts discussions on a particular topic. The boards are run by volunteers (board volunteers or BVs) who create and moderate conversations (threads). Board volunteers are sometimes called *bakers*. The threads are called *breads*. When a baker creates a new thread, they're said to be "baking a bread." A single comment in a thread is called a *crumb*. Helpful information on a topic is called *sauce*. The term sauce is derived from the word "source." If a point is made that isn't common knowledge, others will naturally ask for the source (sauce) of the information.

Q first began posting on the 4chan board, politically incorrect (/pol/), on October 28th, 2017. One problem with /pol/ is the high amount of traffic it receives. Some users are interested in participating in open discussions and research but many users are *trolls* and *shills*. Trolls and shills aren't interested in fruitful discussions. They derail conversations with pointless objections and oppose whatever idea is being discussed. Some people are paid to do this. Q's posts on 4chan were swarmed by trolls and shills which made it difficult for serious discussions to take place. One month after Q began posting, his threads had drawn enough opposition that the decision was made to move to 8chan which receives less traffic. 8chan was used by people around the globe to communicate on whatever subjects they want. Some users live in countries where freedom of speech is severely restricted. Many people are shocked to see nudity when they first visit these message boards. Jim Watkins, the owner of 8chan and 8kun, is a free speech advocate. If content isn't explicitly illegal according to U.S. law, he allows it to be posted.

Most people use social media platforms where nudity or profanity isn't allowed. Such restrictions are a form of censorship. One may argue that a small amount of censorship makes for a better platform, but it's still censorship. Many social media platforms have begun removing accounts for expressing dissenting political views, and deleting posts *they* deem to be factually inaccurate. The question is: who is the gatekeeper of truth? Q's posts are controversial enough that they would eventually be removed from such platforms. Freedom of information without censorship is one reason why he chose to post on the chans.

May 15 2018
Autists - we thank you.
Patriots - we thank you.
We came here for a reason.
Freedom of information.
No filters.
History books.
Be proud.
TOGETHER.
WWG1WGA!
Q

Opposition to Q

Q's mission involves the exposure of public corruption and the distortion by the media of the true way in which certain historical events have happened. That makes him a threat to people who would rather not have the truth known. Since he began posting, actions aimed at silencing Q have increased. After a week of intense attacks by the mainstream media, in February of 2019, Q wrote this:

Feb 11 2019
You attack those you fear the most.
The sheer volume of attacks by the largest media corporations in the world, should, using common sense and logic, indicate there is something more to the story.
Q

Attempts to silence Q come in many forms. Two mobile apps that provide Q posts—that were once available in the Apple store—were removed because of false claims that Q promotes violence related to white supremacy. 8chan was accused of allowing violent extremists to post on their website and there were public demands that the platform be shut down. In August of 2019, due to pressure on 8chan's tech providers, the website went offline, permanently. Jim Watkins, the site's owner, testified before Congress and explained the steps he has taken to restrict the use of his website by people who endorse violence. Watkins has stated that he doesn't endorse violence and his website complies with all federal regulations and information requests by law enforcement. Watkins created a new website, 8kun, to replace 8chan. The new website came online in November of 2019.

It's ironic that 8chan was accused of allowing violent extremists to spread hate. Violent extremists of all types are radicalized on popular social media platforms. Mass murderers often post manifestos on those platforms and mass shootings and suicides have been livestreamed on Facebook. Many children have been lured into sexual encounters through predators posting on Instagram and Facebook. Nevertheless, a media narrative was created that somehow 8chan was solely responsible for the spread of violence and extremism. That narrative led to the website being shut down. It seems more likely that the accusations and attacks were aimed at silencing Q.

Social media platforms like YouTube have restricted videos about Q. More than a dozen threads about Q were hosted on Reddit until the decision was made to delete them. All Q-related threads have been permanently banned from the platform. Q seems to have kicked the proverbial hornet's nest and the hornets are doing everything in their power to silence him.

The Boards

After Q moved from 4chan to 8chan, due to problems with previous board owners and moderators concerning the authenticity (AUTH) of his identity (IDEN), he asked one of the technicians, Codemonkey (CM), if it would be possible to set up a read-only board in addition to a discussion board.

Jan 6 2018
♦♦♦
CM – thank you for IDEN verification.
CM – how can a secure 'read only' board be set up whereby the message can be safely delivered?

If a board was created, you verified IDEN, and control was w/ you/us,
that would eliminate confusion as to IDEN/AUTH correct?
No mod management – only info dumps.
Fact-finding, archiving, discussion, etc. can then be done on a
designated 'follow up' board.
Message is all that matters.
THE GREAT AWAKENING.
Time is severely limited.
Q

Q's request was granted and a second (read-only) board was setup. Under the current system, Q communicates some messages on a board that he controls. Posts on that board can be viewed, but readers cannot leave comments there. The posts on this board are messages of general interest that don't require responses. Posts that are intended for discussion are posted on a separate research board where anyone can comment. As Q has moved through different phases of his mission, the names of his boards have changed. Currently, Q is posting on /projectdcomms/ and /qresearch/. Prior to that, Q posted on /patriotsfight/. There were also boards named /greatawakening/ and /calmbeforethestorm/.

Tripcodes

Q first began posting on 4chan as one of the anons but was distinguished from everyone else by his signature—the single letter Q. After a while, he began using a tripcode (or simply, *trip*) which is a string of characters that give a user a unique identity. A tripcode also provides *confirmation* of a user's identity since it is secured with a password. Although Q uses a tripcode, he is still anonymous in the sense that no one knows his name and he cannot be tracked to his device since he uses multiple devices linked in a series to conceal his IP address.

Q said his messages are of vital importance to the President. He has suggested that his communications are done under the watchful eye of government agencies like the Secret Service, Homeland Security and the NSA.

Dec 19 2017
Board owner, mods, and other patriots:
Sincere thanks for all that you do.
You are true heroes.
Long overdue - my apologies.
There will be a day (within the next few months) that a scary but safe

personalized message finds its way to you on multiple platforms recognizing your contributions.
We thank you for your service.
Godspeed,
Q

One of the board volunteers replied after a mistake regarding Q's tripcode:

Anonymous
Thank you Sir...
Sorry for the Trip mess up earlier...

Q responded:

Safety first.
We have the USSS, NSA, and DHS, also protecting this message.
No random IP needed (though we can implement at a moments notice)
Godspeed,
Q

Reading Q's Posts

The infrastructure of the chans are somewhat tricky for newbies who are accustomed to corporate-branded sites like Facebook or Twitter. A friend and fellow researcher described it this way:

> *"Think of all the friendliness of a Unix command-line, translated into a web page—that's kinda what it's like. And it's done deliberately to be some-what hostile to the newcomer, and to discourage those who are not willing to invest a certain amount of effort to learn the paradigm. It comes across as very raw, badly formatted, and hard to navigate. And that's deliberate."*
> —Martin Geddes

Lots of open source data collection and analysis happens on the chans, but there's also crude humor, distasteful posts, and an element of pranksterism. So, if you're bewildered, or offended, you've encountered an apparatus that was designed to keep you out.

I recommend avoiding 8kun. You can easily find Q's posts on other websites. If you do visit 8kun, consider using a Virtual Private Network (VPN) to conceal your IP address and don't post using your email or any identifying information.

Most people read Q's messages on websites that aggregate posts and display them for the general public.

At the time of this book publishing, there are mobile apps available for Android devices that will alert you to new Q posts and display them. iOS apps have been removed from the App Store. Access to Q-related resources will likely change due to political and economic pressure that is being applied to software and web developers to prevent access to such products.

CHAPTER 3

Saudi Arabia

THE DAUNTING PART OF DECIPHERING Q's posts is determining where to begin. With thousands of messages covering hundreds of subjects, making sense of them may seem like an insurmountable task. A mountain is climbed one step at a time. Q's posts are best analyzed one message and one subject at a time.

When I compose a thread on Twitter explaining Q's posts, I don't post them in chronological order. To the greatest degree possible, I group them by topic. This allows me to focus on one topic at a time and it allows me to explore each subject as fully as possible, before moving on to a different one. Many times, I'll repost older but related messages to give additional context to newer ones. This approach necessarily involves repeatedly examining previous posts. If we hope to become familiar with all the subjects discussed in a single post, we must examine it repeatedly, bearing in mind a particular subject of interest each time we look at it.

These books will explore Q's posts in a topic-by-topic fashion. One of the major subjects in the first two months of Q's mission was Saudi Arabia. We'll look at the Kingdom of Saudi Arabia as it has been described and interpreted in parts of a select number of posts by Q.

Let's begin by examining an assertion by Q that world leaders are secretly controlled by a few powerful people.

Oct 31 2017

There are more good people than bad. The wizards and warlocks (inside term) will not allow another Satanic Evil POS control our country. Realize Soros, Clintons, Obama, Putin, etc. are all controlled by 3 families (the 4th was removed post Trump's victory).

11.3 - Podesta indicted

11.6 - Huma indicted

Manafort was placed into Trump's camp (as well as others). The corruption that will come out is so serious that deals must be cut for people to walk away otherwise 70% of elected politicians would be in jail (you are seeing it already begin). A deep cleaning is occurring and the prevention and defense of pure evil is occurring on a daily basis. They never thought they were going to lose control of the Presidency (not just D's) and thought they had control since making past mistakes (JFK, Reagan).

Good speed, Patriots.

PS, Soros is targeted.

Q assured his readers that there are more good people than bad in government. He said a team of people called the "wizards and warlocks" (which will be explained in a different chapter) would not allow another evil person to control our country, and that select politicians are controlled by three families (a fourth had been removed from power). Q also claimed that Podesta and Huma would be indicted the first week of November. (That claim will be examined later in this chapter.)

Now let's look at a post from November 2nd, 2017. This is one that you may want to read carefully:

Nov 2 2017

How did SA welcome POTUS during his trip?

Why was this historic and not covered by MSM?

How did SA welcome BO during his trip?

How did SA welcome HRC during her trip?

Why is this relevant?

Not suggesting SA is clean by any means but they play a role in this global game of RISK.

Combine all posts and analyze.

The questions provide answers.

Remember, information is everything, the flow of information is no longer controlled by the MSM but by you/others.

Hence, why we are dedicating 'critical' time to distribute crumbs which can be followed in greater detail to paint the entire picture once more information is released.

Why has POTUS dedicated so much time into labeling the MSM as fake news?

Why is this relevant?

We are fully prepared that all social media will be shut down to prevent the spread of this information (i.e. POTUS' Twitter etc. and/or mass censoring).

Sealed Federal orders pre-submitted as prevention and masked as 'in general' (though that does not account for rogue agents/programmers within).

Dates (impending actions) are deliberately provided for authenticity.

Alice & Wonderland.

Note that there are five abbreviations used in the above post, three of which have a standard meaning and two of which do not. POTUS is a widely recognized abbreviation for President of the United States. HRC is a common abbreviation for former First Lady Hillary Rodham Clinton. MSM is a common abbreviation for mainstream media.

Let's look at the context of the first five lines. Q asked how three people were received when they visited a certain place he referred to as SA. We know two of the people in question are Hillary Clinton (HRC) and POTUS. At the time of the post, Donald Trump was President. We might infer that the third person, BO, is Barack Obama.

Now let's consider the places that Donald Trump visited during his first 10 months in office. One place we know he visited is Saudi Arabia, which conveniently fits the abbreviation SA. Barack Obama and Hillary Clinton have also visited there. We can form a tentative hypothesis that this post is referring to those people and that nation, but we'll hold the theory loosely. Additional information in other posts will either confirm or refute our theory.

There are key points in the above message that should not be overlooked, including the assertion that "information is everything" and the idea that the mainstream media no longer controls the flow of it. Q said it is controlled by average people like us. His mission is to disseminate information that helps us see a bigger picture. Our task is to share it with the world. Q indicated that more information would be provided and he encouraged readers to combine all his posts and analyze them. He also asked why President Trump had spent so much time trying to make people understand that the mainstream media is "fake news." Each of these subjects will be explored in other chapters.

Next, let's examine the last part of another Q post. This one was from the following day, November 3rd, 2017:

Nov 3 2017

♦♦♦

Why did JK travel to SA recently?

What is SA known for?

Where do the biggest donations originate from?

Why is this relevant?

What else is relevant w/ SA?

Safe harbor?

Port of transfer?

Why was there a recent smear campaign against JK and POTUS?

Why is the timing important?

Who released the article?

The council of Wizards & Warlocks cannot be defeated.

Nice view up here.

Q

Once again, we see a reference to SA, which we believe may represent Saudi Arabia. But now, Q asked why a person with the initials JK recently made an unannounced trip there. To answer this question, we would need to research news stories for someone prominent who made such a trip, and we'd confine the search terms to the time period immediately prior to November 3rd, 2017.

My research showed that between October 29th and 30th of 2017, news outlets published a number of stories about an unannounced trip made by President Trump's son-in-law, Jared Kushner, to Saudi Arabia. It was reported that he returned home from this trip on Saturday, October 28th. (Oddly, this was the same day Q first posted.) Apparently, this was Kushner's third trip to the country in 2017.

These news reports solve the riddle, giving us Jared Kushner as the decode for JK taking the unannounced trip. It also confirms our theory that SA (at least in this post) refers to Saudi Arabia. We can then go on to consider the rest of Q's questions:

What is Saudi Arabia known for?

Where do the biggest donations originate from?

Safe harbor? (For whom?) Port of transfer? (For what?)

Then, there are the other questions found in the original post:

◆◆◆

Why was there a recent smear campaign against JK and POTUS?
Why is the timing important?
Who released the article?

◆◆◆

To answer these questions, we would need to search for relevant news stories. I performed a search using the terms Jared Kushner and Donald Trump and limited the search results to eight weeks prior to November 5th.

My research brought up more than one story published on September 24th, 2017, regarding the use of a private email account by Jared Kushner. Many of the articles implied that Donald Trump was a hypocrite for criticizing Hillary Clinton's use of a private email server, although some reports gave a more balanced view when comparing Kushner's email account to Hillary's private server. *The Washington Post* noted that *Politico* first reported the story of Kushner's trip.

The timing was important because the FBI's investigation of Hillary's use of a private server, and their decision not to prosecute her, was a topic of much discussion at that time. An issue in Trump's White House over the same topic regarding one of his relatives could impact public opinion toward them.

Q asked, "What is Saudi Arabia known for." It's known for many things. The Kingdom of Saudi Arabia is a monarchy ruled by the Saud family, and it's the home of Mecca and Medina—the two holy cities of Islam. A strict form of Islam, called Wahhabism, is practiced in the country.

Saudi Arabia is also known for being a significant exporter of oil, which brought a flood of extravagant financial wealth and spurred the country's rapid growth and modernization.

Saudi Arabia has been under critique for many years. There have been plenty of articles written about its funding of terrorist groups. The country has also been criticized sharply for its unjust treatment of women and girls. In 2017, Saudi women were still not allowed to drive cars. Forced marriages are common there, and since there is no minimum legal age for marriage, girls as young as one year old have been married to much, much older men. When we research the topic of child brides, there is ample discussion about the practice of marrying off minor girls for a substantial price.

If we build on the theory that Q is drawing our attention to the problem of marriage and sex with children (pedophilia) in Saudi Arabia, then the next questions might be answered.

Safe harbor? (For whom?)

Port of transfer? (For what?)

Q may be hinting that Saudi Arabia was a safe harbor for pedophiles and a port of transfer for its victims. He also suggested that Saudi Arabia is a source of funding for politicians. Further research may determine if those two matters are related, and we'll look at that issue again, shortly. That concludes our brief examination of the subjects mentioned in this particular post.

This is the method I use to make sense of Q's posts. I take what information I know to be true and combine it with new information I find through research. Bear in mind that these conclusions are merely guesses. They could be wrong, but thankfully, Q has provided a system that allows for confirmation of our theories. It's vitally important to check to see which theories have been confirmed and which have been disproven. (Confirmation will be covered in another chapter.) As disturbing as it might be to consider the horrors suffered by child brides in Saudi Arabia, the next section may give you hope.

The messages we just studied about Saudi Arabia and Jared Kushner were posted by Q on November 3rd, 2017. The following day, November 4th, headlines around the globe carried news of a massive crackdown of corruption in Saudi Arabia. Q reposted part of the previous day's message that contained questions about Saudi Arabia and asked these new questions:

Nov 4 2017

[Repost]

Why did JK travel to SA recently?

◆◆◆

Martial law declared in SA.

Why is this relevant? How much money was donated to CF by SA?

How much money was donated to John M Institute by SA?

How much money was donated to Pelosi Foundation?

How much money was donated to CS by SA?

What other bad actors have been paid by SA (bribed)(Not just D's)?

Why did the Bush family recently come out against POTUS?

Who is good?

What are the laws in SA v. US (charged criminals)?

What information might be gained by these detainees?

Why is this important?

SA ---> US

What force is actively deployed in SA?

NG?

Have faith.
These, the crumbs, in time, will equate to the biggest drops ever
disclosed in our history.
Remember, disinformation is real.
God bless.
Alice & Wonderland.
The Great Awakening.
Q

An anon responded to Q:

Anonymous • Nov 4 2017
WAIT
WAIT
WAIT
GO BACK TO THE POST ABOUT THE FAMILES THAT RUN
EVERYTHING AND TRUMP TAKING ONE OUT
WAS ONE OF THEM THIS SAUDI FAMILY
SERIOUSLY
BECAUSE THAT MAKES THIS A HAPPENING
I Remember the phrasing not making sense, I was like "oh does he
mean that dt took out the Clintons?" But the Clintons were on the list as
remaining so I didn't know who was taken out

The anon was referencing this Q post—found earlier in this chapter:

Oct 31 2017
There are more good people than bad. The wizards and warlocks
(inside term) will not allow another Satanic Evil POS control our country.
Realize Soros, Clintons, Obama, Putin, etc. are all controlled by
3 families (the 4th was removed post Trump's victory).
♦♦♦

The anon realized Q must have known something was about to happen in Saudi
Arabia to make these posts just before the arrest of members of the Saudi royal
family. Q responded to the anon:

Very smart, Anon.
Disinformation is real.

Distractions are necessary.
SA is the primary, US is secondary, (Asia/EU)...
Alice & Wonderland.
Q

Two days prior to the arrests in Saudi Arabia, Q asked why someone traveled there *in person* to have a face-to-face (f2f) meeting instead of making a phone call.

Nov 2 2017
♦♦♦
Who took an undisclosed trip to SA?
What was the purpose of a f2f v phone call?
Alice & Wonderland.

Four months later, on March 21st, 2018, *The Intercept* published a story telling of the trip in October where Kushner visited Riyadh and was said to have spoken with Mohammad bin Salman in person. The story suggested Kushner may have been helping the crown prince develop a strategy against his opponents inside the royal family.

On November 4th, a week after Kushner returned to the United States, bin Salman launched his anti-corruption crackdown. In his post from that day (which we previously looked at) Q asked a number of questions including how much money Saudi Arabia had donated to the Clinton Foundation (CF) the McCain Institute, the Pelosi Foundation and Chuck Schumer (CS). He also asked why the Bush family had recently criticized President Trump. Q asked about the law regarding political detainees in Saudi Arabia, what information might be obtained from them, and what force might be deployed there to assist in the operation. The answers to Q's questions can be found by searching the internet. The McCain Institute, for example, received a $1 million dollar donation from The Royal Embassy of Saudi Arabia in 2014.

Q uses diagrams like this: SA ---> US to indicate the order of operations. We would infer then, that a crackdown on corrupt leaders in Saudi Arabia would be followed by a crackdown on corrupt leaders in the United States.

Q posted a message containing clues about people like Pakistani IT expert, Imran Awan, who was hired by dozens of members of Congress. He asked about organizations like the Muslim Brotherhood (MB) and the Clinton Foundation (CF).

Nov 4 2017
Follow HUMA.

Who connects HRC/CF to SA?

Why is this relevant?

Who is the Muslim Brotherhood?

Who has ties to the MB?

Who is Awan?

What is the Awan Group?

Where do they have offices?

Why is this relevant?

Define cash laundering.

What is the relationship between SA & Pakistan?

Why is this relevant?

Why would SA provide tens of millions of dollars to US senior gov't officials?

What does SA obtain in exchange for payment?

Why is access important?

What happened when HRC lost the election of 2016?

How much money was provided to the CF by SA during 15/16?

HRC lost.

Loss of access/power/control.

Does repayment of funds to SA occur?

If so, how?

Why did BO send billions in cash to Iran?

Why wasn't Congress notified?

Why was this classified under 'State Secrets'?

Who has access to 'State Secrets'?

Where did the planes carrying the cash depart from and land?

Did the planes all land in the same location?

How many planes carried the cash?

Why is this relevant?

What does this have to do w/ NK?

What does this have to do w/ SA/CF cash donations?

What does this have to do w/ ISIS?

What does this have to do w/ slush funds?

Why is SA so vitally important?

Follow the money.

Who has the money?

What is happening in SA today?

Why is this relevant?

Who was Abdullah bin Abdulaziz?

What events transpired directly thereafter?
How was POTUS greeted compared to other former US President's when in SA?
Why is this relevant?
What is the meaning of this tradition?
What coincidentally was the last Tweet sent out by POTUS?
Why is this relevant?
Was that an instruction of some kind?
To who?
Why is this relevant?
Where was POTUS when that Tweet was sent?
Why is that relevant?
What attack took place in SA as operations were undertaken?
Flying objects.
What US operators are currently in SA?
Why is this relevant?
Questions provide answers.
Alice & Wonderland.

There are many clues in the above post and you should consider each of them carefully. For now, I'd like to focus on a couple of the clues. Q asked about President Trump's last tweet before the arrests in Saudi Arabia.

◆◆◆
What coincidentally was the last Tweet sent out by POTUS?
Why is this relevant?
Was that an instruction of some kind?
To who?
Why is this relevant?
Where was POTUS when that Tweet was sent?
◆◆◆

In the early morning hours of November 4th, the President tweeted the following message as he visited U.S. military forces in Japan:

Donald J. Trump (from his Twitter account):
Would very much appreciate Saudi Arabia doing their IPO of Aramco with the New York Stock Exchange. Important to the United States!
5:49 AM - 4 Nov 2017

Was the tweet a signal to someone, and if so, who? Q asked what American operators were currently working in Saudi Arabia.

◆◆◆

What US operators are currently in SA?

◆◆◆

Weeks later, on November 22nd, 2017, *Daily Mail.com* published a story explaining that the American private security company Blackwater had been recruited to assist in the detention and questioning of the Saudi princes and businessmen. The day after the article was published, Q responded to it:

Nov 23 2017
What news broke?
American contractors where?
Hanging from feet?
Re-read dumps.
Why is this relevant?
News unlocks map.
Expand your thinking.
Q

Q seems to have known about several things before any of them were reported in the news. He anticipated the arrests in Saudi Arabia before they happened. He foretold what the media would report about Jared Kushner's face-to-face meeting with Mohammad bin Salman months before the story broke. He knew contractors from Blackwater were assisting in the detention of the Saudi princes weeks before it was reported in the news, and he seemed to know that President's Trump's tweet that morning was a signal to launch their operation. A rational person must ask how Q could have guessed at even one of these events, much less all of them. He appears to have access to information the rest of us do not. This level of access suggests that Q is closely connected to the President. And it's why so many people are following him today.

What is Q's relationship to the President? Consider these two posts from October 29th, the second day of Q's mission.

Oct 29 2017
Key:
Military Intelligence v FBI CIA NSA

No approval or congressional oversight
State Secrets upheld under SC
Who is the Commander and Chief of the military?
Under what article can the President impose MI take over investigations
for the 3 letter agencies?
What conditions must present itself? Why is this so VERY important?
Who surrounds POTUS?
They lost this very important power _ the one area of the govt not
corrupt and directly serves POTUS.

Oct 29 2017
Military Intelligence ref above is the absolute biggest inside drop this
board will ever receive.
Now think about why Antifa plays right into the plan?
Always ahead. Good guys are winning.

How does Q know the details of events before they are reported by the press?
Q has suggested that he's involved in a military intelligence (MI) operation
under the direction of the President. Because the press isn't trusted by Donald
Trump and his allies, they've chosen to communicate through channels outside
of the mainstream media. We know President Trump uses Twitter to speak
directly to the public, but it appears he also uses Q. Many people believe the
President is conducting an operation involving the prosecution of corrupt people
and organizations around the world. Q is aware of all phases of the operation
and he helps us uncover what we need to know about it. Is Q a backchannel of
communication for the Commander in Chief? An anon made the observation
that it must be hard for Q to empathize with average people when Q has access
to information we don't.

Anonymous • Mar 4 2019
Q,
sometimes I think it is hard for yall to empathize with us. yall on
operating from a position of knowledge. We are in the dark. We are
desperate for truth and justice.

Q responded:

Define 'backchannel'.
Q

Some of the information Q provides is operational in nature but much of it is educational. Some is intended as disinformation for enemies who follow his posts and act on that information. (The use of disinformation will be covered in another chapter.)

In the first week of his operation, Q often discussed the pending arrests of U.S. political figures Hillary Clinton, John Podesta and Huma Abedin. As indicated in the following post, that information was a distraction to keep the focus in the U.S. while the arrest of corrupt political figures was being planned in Saudi Arabia.

Nov 5 2017
♦♦♦
SA --> US --> Asia --> EU
Disinformation is real.
Distractions are necessary.
Focus was US today while real happening in SA under same context (military control, martial law, missile strike (rogue) etc).
Necessary.
POTUS' Twitter attack (see above).
♦♦♦
Q

In the above post, Q indicated an order of operation for the takedown of corruption with a diagram: SA --> US --> Asia --> EU. Corruption was first addressed in the Saudi royal family because it's one of the three wealthiest blocks of power in the world. Q has suggested that Saudi money has funded terrorism, nuclear proliferation, war, drug trafficking, human trafficking and it's kept corrupt politicians in power. By removing this source of funding, these activities have been significantly curtailed and the politicians who were funded by the Saudis were left scrambling for cover.

Nov 5 2017
Nothing is a coincidence.
We are at war.
SA cut the strings.
They are scrambling for cover and using any means necessary out of their remaining power/control.
God bless.
Q

Having a grasp of the next post is critical if we are to understand who controls power on a global scale.

Dec 7 2017
Rothschilds (cult leaders)(church)(P)
Banks / Financial Institutions
WW Gov Control
Gov Controls People
SA
Oil Tech Sex/Children
SA Controls (assigned) US / UK Politicians / Tech Co's (primary)
Soros
Controls organizations of people (create division / brainwash) +
management / operator of slush funds (personal net worth never
reduces think DOJ settlements Consumer Iran Enviro pacts etc etc)
/_\ - Rock (past)(auth over followers)
_\ (present)
(Future)
Order is critical.
Strings cut to US/UK.
Expand your thinking.
Swamp drain.
1 - sexual harassment exit + future
....
[R] - No.
Bomb away.
Q

Q illustrated the wealth, power and worldwide (WW) influence of a small group of people with a triangle. One side of Q's triangle represents the Saudi royal family; one side represents the Rothschild banking family; and the third side, George Soros. According to Q, each plays a part in the control of the geopolitical landscape—the Rothschilds primarily control banks and financial institutions and through them, national governments as well as the church. By controlling governments and the church, they control large numbers of people. (I do not claim to know the extent to which any particular church denomination is controlled by the Rothschilds, or if any are in fact controlled by them.) Q has hinted that Saudi Arabia maintains economic control via its oil reserves, and exerts control over some U.S. and U.K. politicians though pedophilia and blackmail.

Saudi princes like Alwaleed bin Talal have been major investors in the tech sector and the media, including social media platforms. Elitist investor George Soros funds left-leaning political activists and progressive organizations. Q has suggested that slush funds (like the Department of Justice Settlements fund) have been set up by politicians to take taxpayer money and re-route it to fund Soros organizations which provide propaganda to keep people unaware of all this.

Q indicated that the triangular shaped diagram—which illustrates the power structure of the Saudi royal family, George Soros and the Rothschilds—has changed. With the change of leadership in Saudi Arabia and the ascension of moderate Mohammad bin Salman, one side of the triangle of power has been removed. Its removal cut the strings of control the Saudis had over many U.S. and U.K. politicians. Could this explain why some Congressmen and Senators did not run for re-election in 2018?

Nov 1 2017
Any person making statements they will not be seeking re-election was put in submission. For the betterment of the country not all will be prosecuted and all will do as told. You will see more of this occur (not normal yet disregarded) and even on the D side.

An anon asked Q about Hillary Clinton:

Anonymous • Nov 5 2017
Is HRC just a puppet and the goal is to take down her minders and the real kingpins?

Q responded:

Correction:
HRC was a puppet but her strings were recently cut.
She's now on her own and fighting for her life.
Q

I'll close this chapter by decoding one of Q's *signatures*. A signature is a statement made at the end of a Q post that contains a coded message. There are two signatures in the post below: Snow White and Godfather III.

Nov 5 2017
My signatures all reference upcoming events about to drop if this hasn't

been caught on.
Snow White
Godfather III
Q

Most signatures are titles of films or books. Q said his signatures reference future news stories. I've also noticed that each signature represents a particular topic or theme. Sometimes Q ends a post with one signature and sometimes there are two or three. The signatures correspond with different subjects discussed in that post. The signature "Alice & Wonderland" is used to close a number of posts in this chapter.

Q said the anons needed to develop a more organized approach to understanding his messages.

Nov 4 2017
We need to get organized.
Things need to be solved to understand what is about to happen.
Let's start w/ Alice & Wonderland.
Hillary Clinton in Wonderland by Lewis Carroll.
Saudi Arabia - the Bloody Wonderland.
Snow White.
Wizards & Warlocks.
Q

Q suggested they start by decoding the signature "Alice & Wonderland" and he provided two clues. The first clue was the title of a book: *Hillary Clinton in Wonderland* by Lewis Carroll. The second clue was Saudi Arabia - the Bloody Wonderland.

An internet search using the terms "Saudi Arabia" and "the Bloody Wonderland" returned an article written by Jean Perier, published by *New Eastern Outlook* titled, *Saudi Arabia – The Bloody Wonderland*. The story describes the violent punishments and beheadings going on in Saudi Arabia, citing reports from *Amnesty International* for 2013, 2015, and 2016 (the year the article was written). In the opening sentence, the author drew a comparison between Saudi Arabia's routine beheading of people and "living in Lewis Caroll's, surreal 'Wonderland.'" Q elaborated on this signature in the following post:

Nov 4 2017
Simplified.

Alice & Wonderland.
Hillary & Saudi Arabia.
References:
Hillary Clinton in Wonderland by Lewis Carroll.
Saudi Arabia - the Bloody Wonderland.
Q

An anon posted a link to the book, *Hillary Clinton in Wonderland,* and Q verified the information by reposting it with this reply:

Finally.
Correct reference.
Saudi Arabia - The Bloody Wonderland.
=Alice & Wonderland signatures
Study.
Important.
Q

The signature, Alice & Wonderland, ties together Q's posts that discuss a common topic: the relationship between Saudi Arabia and Hillary Clinton. In a similar way, Q's other signatures tie together posts about different subjects. Once you correctly decode a signature, it provides insights into the meaning of the posts where it appears. Throughout this series, I'll provide decodes of Q's signatures.

CHAPTER 4

What Storm, Mr. President?

THREE TERMS HAVE BEEN USED to describe critical aspects of Q's operation. "The Great Awakening" describes a mass public awareness (an awakening) to the existence of a two-tiered system of justice that has allowed powerful people to commit crimes and go unpunished. A major thrust of Q's operation is informing the public of the existence of this corruption. "The Storm" refers to a coming time when those who are guilty of corruption in every segment of society will be prosecuted as the two-tiered system of justice is replaced with one that allows equal justice for all. A third term used by Q is "The Calm Before the Storm." In 2017, an October 6th article written by Mark Landler was published in *The New York Times*. The story gives an account of the evening when President Trump referred to "the calm before the storm."

Many of us remember the video of President Trump and the First Lady standing together with senior military commanders and their wives after a dinner held on October 5th, 2017. The large group was gathered around the President for photos. Then the President said, "You guys know what this represents? Maybe it's the calm before the storm." Reporters were perplexed and asked what he meant. They speculated. Was he was referring to Iran or ISIS? But the President did not confirm any of their guesses. He merely smiled and said, "You'll find out."

Nearly a month later, on November 2nd, 2017, Q posted this message that hinted at his identity.

Nov 2 2017
What is Q Clearance?
What hint does that explicitly refer to?
DOE?
Who would have the goods on U1?
Does stating 'Q' refer that person works in DOE?
No.
Does it refer that someone dropping such information has the highest level of security within all departments?
Why is this relevant?

(May 2010) BO "Russia should be viewed as a friendly partner under Section 123 the Atomic Energy Act of 1954" after agreeing to a new nuclear weapons reduction deal and helping US w/ Iran.
Who is the enemy?
What is being continually stated by all D's?
Russia is what?
What did the Russia reset really provide?
Clearance/pathway to complete the U1 deal?
Why is the Canadian PM so important?
They never thought they were going to lose.
The calm before the storm.

If we keep in mind the subjects mentioned in this post, we'll get an idea of the meaning of the signature "the calm before the storm." It hints at the truth regarding one of the most controversial measures ever approved by the U.S. government—the sale of North American Uranium to Russia. The statement, "They never thought they were going to lose" is a suggestion that if Hillary Clinton had won the 2016 Presidential election, she may have continued to hide certain details of the sale of Uranium One from the public. Q has suggested that because Donald Trump won, those hidden details may be exposed. *The storm* speaks about the coming prosecution of corrupt people. *The calm before the storm* would then be the time interval between Trump's election and the prosecution of corruption.

On November 2nd, 2017, Q wrote the following message drawing attention to the deployment of U.S. Naval aircraft carriers in the Pacific Ocean, suggesting there was a strategic reason for the deployment that most people would not appreciate.

Nov 2 2017
Four carriers & escorts in the pacific?
Why is that relevant?
To prevent other state actors from attempting to harm us during this transition? Russia / China?
Or conversely all for NK? Or all three.
Think logically about the timing of everything happening.
Note increased military movement.
Note NG deployments starting tomorrow.
Note false flags.
Follow Huma.
Prepare messages of reassurance based on what was dropped here to spread on different platforms.

The calm before the storm.

The hint here was that rogue powers in China, Russia, or North Korea might attempt to interfere with the peaceful transition of power between the election of Donald Trump and his inauguration. Because the post referred to the time interval between Trump's election and the prosecution of corruption, the post ends with the signature "the calm before the storm."

Near the end of November 2017, Q was experiencing heavy opposition to his posts. On November 24th, he made one of his last posts on 4chan in response to a post by an anon who connected Department of Education Secretary, Betsy DeVos; her brother and founder of Blackwater, Erik Prince; and President Trump. The observations made by the anon were based on an article in *The Intercept*, which suggested that Erik Prince was secretly advising President Trump (POTUS) from the shadows. Here is the anon's post:

Anonymous • Nov 24 2017
Betsy DeVos > Erik Prince > POTUS

Q reposted the anon's post and replied:

Who knows where the bodies are buried?
The map is in front of you.

Re-read.
Expand your thinking.
Purpose for time being spent here.
Q

An anon responded

Anonymous
>Who knows where the bodies are buried?
The ones who put the bodies there.

Blackwater was used in a shitton of shady ops by the US government
back when it was under Cabal control and, as a proper PMC, they've got
it all kept on the books.

Books which the POTUS just got access to.

The anon figured Erik Prince, as the founder and former CEO of the private
military contractor (PMC) Blackwater, would have information on corrupt
people, and that the President had access to it. Q responded, confirming the
anon's research and encouraged him to make more connections. The "map" is
a graphic containing all of Q's posts, which the anons had been updating regularly.

Expand further.
Make the connection.
Map currently has 43 confirmed connections.
Important to understand.
When this breaks many won't swallow.
MSM not trusted.
You are the voice.
We are here to help guide.
Future proves past.
You are the calm before and during the storm.
Q

The post above is self-explanatory. Q is a guide to help us. We are to act as
a calming influence to the world before and during the storm.

After running a series of tests on November 24th and 25th, Q determined that
the board on 4chan had been infiltrated and he moved to a new board on 8chan.

Nov 25 2017
Test
Test
4Chan infiltrated.
Future posts will be relayed here.
Q

The first 8chan board on which Q posted after he left 4chan was called Calm Before the Storm (sometimes abbreviated CBTS).

Part of the exposure of global corruption involves the President's decision in September of 2018 to declassify certain documents related to the investigation into Russian interference in the 2016 Presidential election. Those documents, Q says, will expose illegal activities that occurred when Obama's FBI obtained FISA warrants to spy on members of Donald Trump's campaign. In December of 2018, an anon asked if the plan was still moving forward.

Anonymous • Dec 3 2018
Okay. Is the plot moving forward? I think we all understand the characters and conflict at this point. Time for the plot twist? Declas, FINALLY?

Q reminded anons that the plan to expose corruption was set in motion the night the President uttered the words "Maybe it's the calm before the storm."

The President of the United States initiated and confirmed the order when he stated "The Calm Before the Storm."
When was the statement made?
When did "Q" go active?
Watch the News.
Watch the FBI.
Watch the DOJ.
Q

The statement by the President was made on October 5th, 2017. Q's first post was on October 28th, 2017. (Isn't it interesting that U.S. Attorney John Durham, who is investigating potential crimes committed during the 2016 Presidential election, was appointed by Jeff Sessions on the same date, October 28th, 2017?) The prosecution of corruption isn't happening the way anyone imagined it would. We envision federal agents quickly rounding up corrupt people and then, if we're lucky, watching their public trials. What would the process look like if senior federal investigators at the FBI and attorneys at the Department of Justice were the ones who needed to be arrested and put on trial? If those corrupt people weren't first removed from the justice system, how could we expect fair outcomes from the trials?

Many people have given up their hope of seeing true justice—feeling like past practices continue, and powerful, corrupt people aren't prosecuted. I don't think that's the case. Q asked us to consider the ongoing cleanout at the FBI and Department of Justice and the rapid appointment by President Trump of new Federal Judges.

Apr 27 2018
Who makes arrests?
FBI & DOJ?
Can you make arrests w/ a crooked FBI sr team?
See prev post re: FBI.
Not easy for anyone.
We are in this together.
Much appreciation.
It's what you don't know and can't see (ongoing) that will validate your efforts.
Trust the plan.
Step back.
Remove arrests.
What do you see?
Stage being set?
Godspeed, Patriot.
Q

The entire justice system must be reformed if corrupt people are going to be prosecuted successfully. And there is abundant evidence that this is precisely what is happening. Since Donald Trump was elected, dozens of top-level career officials in the FBI and Department of Justice have been fired. Many have been cooperating with investigations into corruption, and at the time of this printing, it looks like some are about to be indicted on felony charges. Once they've been removed and replaced, the justice phase of the operation can begin.

On November 13th, 2017, Assistant Attorney General Stephen Boyd wrote a letter to members of Congress informing them that Jeff Sessions had appointed senior Justice Department attorneys to investigate matters that had been brought to their attention, including the Department's handling of its investigation of the Clinton Foundation; Hillary Clinton's involvement in the sale of Uranium One; and allegations of corruption in the FBI. Members of Congress had requested the appointment of a second Special Counsel to look into these matters. Sessions informed them that their concerns would be investigated outside of the Washington D.C. area by senior DOJ attorneys.

Q posted the following day.

Nov 14 2017
How do you capture a very dangerous animal?
Do you attack it from the front?
Do you walk through the front door?
Do you signal ahead of time you will be attacking?
How do you distinguish between good and bad?
Who do you trust to keep secrets?
How do you prevent leaks?
Who do you trust to complete the mission?
♦♦♦
Nothing is as it appears.
What was the DC vote breakdown between Trump & Clinton?
What is the nickname for DC?
Why would sealed indictments be outside of DC jurisdiction?
What purpose would this serve?
Why are judicial appointments being rapidly completed?
Who can you trust?
Have faith, Patriots.
Q

Q asked why sealed indictments might be made outside of Washington D.C. The suggestion was that the corrupt people who need to be investigated would escape prosecution if the investigation took place in the nation's capital. Appointing a special prosecutor in Washington D.C., where the electorate voted overwhelmingly for Hillary Clinton in the 2016 election, would not be the best approach since grand juries would need to be empaneled and it could be difficult to find objective jurors in the D.C. area.

Q also pointed out that the corrupt people in question are sly and dangerous therefore any investigation of them would need to be done in a way that would not be detected by them, lest they interfere in the process. Ideally, it would need to be done in a way that would suggest there was no investigation at all. Although mainstream media outlets like to deny the possibility that there are corrupt people in the highest levels of government (much less admit they might be under investigation), there are signs that justice is indeed coming. Q posted a link on December 6th, 2018, to a newly published piece by John Solomon in *The Hill,* about federal officials receiving information from whistleblowers in 2017 about alleged crimes by the Clinton Foundation.

Dec 6 2018
https://thehill.com/opinion/white-house/420131-feds-received-whistleblower-evidence-in-2017-alleging-clinton-foundation
Read carefully.
Why is "The Clinton Foundation" back in the news?
Q

Q responded to his above post:

When did POTUS make the statement "Calm Before the Storm?"
When was HUBER activated by SESSIONS?
Who was/is assigned to HUBER?
ACTING AG PRIMARY PURPOSE?
◆◆◆
HUBER to testify re: Clinton Foundation?
HUBER to reveal 'active' probe actively underway into organization?
OIG to release report #2 [overview indicating many 'potentially criminal referrals' made]?
"We do not discuss active/ongoing DOJ / FBI investigations."
MIL INTEL
FISA
THE WORLD IS WATCHING.
Q

CHAPTER 5

Disinformation Is Real

WHEN A MESSENGER ADDRESSES AN audience that has a singular interest, the message can be delivered in a straight-forward fashion. I assume those who read my books are interested in learning about a particular topic, so I present the information without any objective other than to plainly reveal what I believe to be true and helpful to the reader. What you see is what you get.

Q was aware from the beginning of his operation that there were people reading his posts with different interests, different loyalties, and different agendas. Not everyone hoped to learn from him, and not everyone wanted him to succeed. Some came to oppose him and President Trump. What do you do when you know there is an opponent in the audience?

Dealing with an opponent requires an assessment of their ability to impact you. Are they in a position where they can take harmful action against you or someone you care about? If not, they're relatively powerless. The safest and easiest way to deal with a powerless opponent is to ignore them.

But what do you do when an opponent holds a position of power where they're able to take action that could have negative consequence on you or someone you care about? In that case, ignoring them is not the safest move. If you know there is a good likelihood they'll take action based on what you say, a better strategy is to mislead them. Give them information that will cause them to take the wrong action. Welcome to the world of *disinformation*. Disinformation is false information that is known to be false by the one who releases it, and is spread for the purpose of deception. It's been used successfully by political regimes, the military, and intelligence agencies for centuries.

Knowing there were hostile readers in the audience, Q's first posts were designed to open a disinformation campaign. Before giving any valid information to followers with honest motives, he laid a trap for his enemies. The ideal opening move containing disinformation is one that if it were believed by his enemies, would cause them to make the wrong move and expend resources prematurely. At the same time, if the information were believed by his true followers, it would do them no harm. Did Q know there was a *specific* enemy following his posts on 4chan?

Although technically, you can post anonymously on 4chan, with the right technology, users can be identified by their IP address. Agencies like the NSA can access user information that the average person can't. It's possible that if someone hostile to Q were checking in on 4chan, the NSA would know about it. And if they knew about it, did Donald Trump and Q also know about it?

Q's first post on October 28, 2017 was a response to this anonymous post on the 4chan board /pol/:

Anonymous
Why are all the Fox anchors smiling. CNN MSNBC NBC are freaking out like election night.

Q responded:

Oct 28 2017
Hillary Clinton will be arrested between 7:45 AM - 8:30 AM EST on Monday - the morning on Oct 30, 2017.

This post has been misunderstood by just about everyone who has read it including me. But that *is* the nature of disinformation. As people scrutinized the post, they criticized Q for wrongly predicting Hillary's arrest. Their mistake was assuming that Q *only* intended to predict future events accurately. If that were the case, we would have to conclude that Q made a lot of wrong predictions, especially early on. But part of Q's operation involves disinformation:

Nov 4 2017
♦♦♦

Disinformation is real.
Distractions are necessary.

Q

At the time it was posted, no one outside of Donald Trump's inner circle would have known if the prediction of Hillary's arrest were true. The proof would not arrive for two more days. Q didn't stop there. He posted again about an hour later:

Oct 28 2017
HRC extradition already in motion effective yesterday with several countries in case of cross border run. Passport approved to be flagged effective 10/30 @ 12:01am. Expect massive riots organized in defiance and others fleeing the US to occur. US M's will conduct the operation while NG activated. Proof check: Locate a NG member and ask if activated for duty 10/30 across most major cities.

Q doubled down on his prediction of Hillary's impending arrest adding that because of anticipated riots, the U.S. military (M's) would be in control and that the National Guard (NG) had been activated. (Again, remember that at the time, no one knew if these claims were true.) A few days later Q posted this:

Oct 31 2017
There are more good people than bad. The wizards and warlocks (inside term) will not allow another Satanic Evil POS control our country. Realize Soros, Clintons, Obama, Putin, etc. are all controlled by 3 families (the 4th was removed post Trump's victory).

11.3 - Podesta indicted
11.6 - Huma indicted
♦♦♦

It appears as though Q predicted that Hillary Clinton's personal assistant Huma Abedin and one of the Podesta brothers would be indicted the first week of November. We don't know with certainty whether the "Podesta" referred to in the above post, was the lobbyist, Tony Podesta, or Hillary Clinton's campaign manager, John Podesta. I'm not saying any of these people are guilty of a crime. But for the sake of argument, ask yourself if: a) you were one of these people; and b) if you had been involved in any kind of illegal activity; and c) if you saw this post, what action might you consider taking? What would you do if you had a tip that your arrest or indictment were imminent and you wanted to avoid prosecution? You might book a flight to a non-extradition country. And if you were receiving financial support from a wealthy Saudi prince, you might alert him and have him assist you in making long-term plans.

Disinformation isn't purely false. It can be a mixture of true and false information. In the above post, it's likely the information *not* related to Abedin and Podesta was true. Good people in a place of power *were not* going to allow another corrupt person to be elected President. 70 percent of elected politicians could probably be arrested for their crimes. Q asserted that the people who call the shots made mistakes in the past. They allowed John F. Kennedy and Ronald Reagan to be elected. Kennedy and Reagan were unwilling to cooperate with the plans of the puppet masters. They believed they had fixed the problems that allowed these two men into the White House, but the election of Donald Trump was another miscalculation on their part.

Q continued posting on various subjects over the next few days. On November 3rd, the day a "Podesta" was supposed to be indicted, Q posted this message which we looked at previously.

Nov 3 2017

◆◆◆

Why did JK travel to SA recently?

What is SA known for?

Where do the biggest donations originate from?

Why is this relevant?

What else is relevant w/ SA?

◆◆◆

Q

Was it a coincidence that Q predicted the arrest of powerful politicians and the implementation of martial law in the U.S. the first week of November and it actually happened in Saudi Arabia? Or was that information provided to cause powerful people to make plans to secure the safety of certain U.S. politicians when they should have been making plans to secure the safety of the Saudi royal family?

I believe, rather than getting it wrong, Q intentionally set up U.S. politicians and their associates in Saudi Arabia with false information about arrests to get them to focus on the wrong people and the wrong place. They were anticipating and preparing for arrests in the U.S. while the plan was to arrest the

Saudi princes who funded them. As Q indicated in the post below, the arrest of corrupt politicians in other nations is coming.

Nov 5 2017
What happened in SA will happen here, Asia, and EU.
Keep digging and keep organizing the info into graphics (critical).
God bless.
Hillary & Saudi Arabia
Snow White
Godfather III
Q

I'd like to provide a caution regarding disinformation:

Some people have developed a habit of reading Q's posts and when the information provided doesn't support their current view, they say "Remember, disinformation is real." Although disinformation *is* real, it is also provided for a specific purpose: to keep the enemies of the President off guard. Q doesn't provide disinformation to intentionally mislead his readers. He employs the strategic use of disinformation to make corrupt people nervous or to cause them to make wrong moves. (This will be covered more thoroughly in the chapter on game theory.) Q's mission with respect to his followers is to provide truth that counters mainstream propaganda.

CHAPTER 6

Learn to Read the Map

Q PROVIDES INFORMATION IN A somewhat chaotic fashion. The way in which he posts has confused many people—but the chaos has a purpose. It conceals the truth from those who aren't interested in finding it, but makes it available to those who sincerely want to understand it. If we want to understand the truth hidden in Q's posts, we must sift through and organize them so they make sense. On October 31st, 2017, after 21 messages had been posted, Q said enough information had been provided that anons could begin making sense of his posts.

Oct 31 2017
I've dumped some crumbs like this over the weekend which started the intense shilling. At this point we are far enough along you can paint the picture without risk of jeopardizing the operation.

Q told anons to gather all his posts into one graphic and analyze them.

Nov 2 2017
◆◆◆
Combine all posts and analyze.

The questions provide answers.

Remember, information is everything, the flow of information is no longer controlled by the MSM but by you/others.

Hence, why we are dedicating 'critical' time to distribute crumbs which can be followed in greater detail to paint the entire picture once more information is released.

◆◆◆

Q

Note that Q said, "The questions provide answers." Many times, you can assume the correct answer to a "yes" or "no" question by applying logic. In March of 2019, near the end of Robert Mueller's investigation into Russian interference in the 2016 Presidential election, Donald Trump appointed a new Attorney General, William Barr. Unlike his predecessor, Jeff Sessions, Barr was not recused from the Russia investigation. He assumed oversight over Mueller's investigation, which had previously been the responsibility of Rod Rosenstein [RR]. It's customary for a new Attorney General to pick his own Deputy Attorney General, so it was anticipated that Rosenstein would soon be leaving his position. Q posted a link to an article claiming the new Attorney General permitted Mueller to indict the President's adult children—Ivanka, Eric, and Don Jr., as well as Jared Kushner. Q asked if Mueller had sealed the indictments in the jurisdiction of Washington D.C. prior to Rosenstein's departure. Q then asked if President Trump had appointed his new Attorney General, only to have his own children indicted on false pretenses. The obvious answer to this question is "no," but Q asked another question to drive the point home: Do unicorns exist?

Mar 12 2019

◆◆◆

>>[MUELLER] sealed indictments installed [DC] prior to [RR] loss of
>>power?

◆◆◆

Did POTUS just install a rogue AG who allows for the indictment of his children based on false pretenses?

◆◆◆

Do UNICORNS exist?

Q

The Socratic method used by Q may infer the correct answer even when no direct, corroborating evidence is provided. If open source information can be found, we might attempt to confirm our suspicion. If no direct evidence is available in the public domain, there may be circumstantial evidence that corroborates the answer.

Sometimes Q provides the actual answer to a question either before or after it. In May of 2018, Q asked who was missing from a meeting, and then provided the answer—U.S. Deputy Attorney General Rod Rosenstein [RR].

May 22 2018

♦♦♦

Who is missing from the scheduled meeting?

[RR]

♦♦♦

Now let's look at another post.

Oct 31 2017

♦♦♦

Why did Adm R (NSA) meet Trump privately w/o auth?

Does POTUS know where the bodies are buried?

Does POTUS have the goods on most bad actors?

Was TRUMP asked to run for President?

Why?

By Who?

Was HRC next in line?

Was the election suppose to be rigged?

Did good people prevent the rigging?

♦♦♦

The implied answers are that Trump *does* have incriminating evidence on bad actors (he knows where the proverbial bodies are buried). Q asked why then-NSA Director Admiral Rogers (Adm R) gave Trump information in a private meeting without authorization. News reports confirmed that Admiral Rogers took an undisclosed trip to Trump Tower nine days after the election to meet with the president-elect. (This meeting will be discussed in more detail in the chapter on Admiral Rogers.)

Q implied that Trump was asked to run for President by members of the military. We learned on October 1st, 2019, at the retirement ceremony of General Joseph Dunford that in 2015, at a Marine ceremony where Trump received an award, General Dunford asked Trump to consider running for President.

Q hinted that Hillary Clinton (HRC) was slated to be next in line for President, and that the military helped prevent the rigging of the election, giving Trump a legitimate chance to win.

On November 4th, an anon posted a graphic showing 56 messages that were posted between October 31st and November 4th, 2017. Q responded by reposting the image. He indicated that the graphic was correct and asked the anon to add a few more crumbs that he had posted since the graphic had been created.

Nov 4 2017
1509840715226.png
Graphic is right.
Add above points to graphic.
Stay organized.
Q

The graphic began with Q's October 31st post about Military Intelligence and ended with the online exchange he had with an anon on November 4th about the arrests in Saudi Arabia that happened that day. The graphic was the first map to be confirmed by Q. Later that evening, Q let the anons know it was time to solve the Alice & Wonderland signature. The following day, he asked the anons to update the graphic to include the latest posts.

Nov 5 2017
Please add crumbs above in new complete graphic.
Organized and in order.
Critical for understanding and review.
Spider web.
Hillary & Saudi Arabia (Alice & Wonderland)(see above).
This is staged and deliberate.
Snow White
Godfather III
Q

Q noted that the actions of corrupt people are like a spider's web. To avoid confusion, it's important to keep an organized graphic (map) to track the themes, players, signatures, and actions that are taken during the operation. He signed off with the signatures Snow White and Godfather III.

Q often says, "News unlocks map." In the post below, he reminded anons to regularly review the map, especially when a big news story dropped.

Nov 4 2017

When big news drops please re-read entire graphic.

This is so critical and why information is provided in a certain order and why some topics are continually emphasized more than others as those will be the recent happenings.

This is the purpose of this new thread (re-organize).

Snow White

Wizards & Warlocks.

Q

The map was updated three times on November 5th, 2017. This was one of Q's responses:

Nov 5 2017

Graphic is good.

Please update and continue to log.

Important more than you know.

Review each sentence post happenings.

Big picture.

Signatures have necessary meaning.

Snow White.

Godfather III.

Q

On November 10th, an anon posted an updated graphic and asked if anything was missing from it:

Anonymous • Nov 10 2017

Q Graphic.png

Q confirmed

is anything in this image wrong? i added posts from the 5th

Q responded:

Nov 10 2017

Confirmed.

Correct.

Q

Anons have continually updated the map which now contains thousands of posts. Several sources periodically publish an updated map in PDF form. Many websites host graphic images showing all of Q's posts with relevant links and images. I've found it helpful to refer back to past posts particularly after major news stories break.

Nov 1 2017
Not everything can be publicly disclosed because so much ties back to foreign heads of state. Much will be revealed, we want transparency but not at a cost we can't recover from.

President Trump is interested in transparency. Secrets have been hidden by the private sector and government that he intends to make public. He will provide the world with as much information as possible with certain restrictions. He wants transparency, but if revealing certain information causes a risk of war or rioting, that is a risk they cannot take. That same day, Q posted again.

Some things must remain classified to the very end. NK is not being run by Kim, he's an actor in the play. Who is the director? The truth would sound so outrageous most Americans would riot, revolt, reject, etc.
The pedo networks are being dismantled.
The child abductions for satanic rituals (ie Haiti and other 3rd world countries) are paused (not terminated until players in custody).
We pray every single day for God's guidance and direction as we are truly up against pure evil.

Corruption is being addressed even though the media doesn't report it. The same day, Q posted this.

World stalemate.
We all have the goods on everyone else.
That's part of the reason why some things that tie back to foreign heads of state will remain classified (not all).
We are in one of the most critical times of our country. Trump and others are working to balance the we're doing well for America (for the common person to endorse) while at the same time purify our govt and remove the bad actors who are entrenched. There is so much string pulling and blackmail that we need to cut these off to truly gain the power granted to us by the Patriots and hardworking people of this great country.

Q claims to have information about the real powers that are controlling global events. He has also suggested that if the complete truth were known, it would cause irreparable harm. In the post that follows, Q told anons that 80 percent of the information the government had on global corruption would need to remain classified, while 20 percent would be made public so that average citizens would understand the need for justice.

Nov 22 2017
USA vs.
Necessary to cut strings from foreign bad actors.
Necessary to form WW alliances to defeat.
Think Merkel is a coincidence?
They are puppets.
They are weak.
They are scared.
80% dark ops necessary.
20% public for justice.
The stage must be set.
Have faith.
Q

The following day, Q posted this.

Nov 23 2017
The world cannot swallow the truth.
Q

Anons were disappointed that only 20 percent of the government's classified information on global corruption would be made public. Over the next month, there was considerable discussion on the board about declassifying a greater percentage.

Sometimes Q will post a message that contains coded text which he calls a *stringer*. On December 19th, 2017, Q posted a series of stringers. Here is the first one.

Dec 19 2017 23:10:31
SEA_TO_SHINING_SEA
DIRECT: CODE 234 SEC: B1-3
DIRECT: CODE 299 SEC: F19-A

[·C   P   19]
Show the World Our Power.
RED_OCTOBER >
Q

The stringer contained the phrase "sea to shining sea" which would later become a signature. It also contained the signature "Red October." I would draw your attention to the letters "C" and "P" and the number 19 (which happened to be the date of the post). When I examined the posts between December 19th and December 21st, I noticed Q referred to how much information would be made public and how much would remain classified. I wondered if perhaps the letter "C" in the first stringer stood for "classified" and "P" stood for "public." Two minutes after posting the first stringer, Q posted a second one.

Dec 19 2017 23:12:54
SWEET DREAMS.
P_pers: Public (not private).
NATSEC_19384z_A_DT-approve
Q

Note the code "P_pers" in the post above. Q has used this code multiple times. We've learned that this is his way of indicating that a message was sent from the President (P), personally (pers) to the board.

Q said the subject was the ongoing discussion of how much information would be kept private and how much would be made public. The post closes with a stringer about Donald Trump (DT) approving something related to National Security (NATSEC).

Eight minutes later, Q posted another stringer:

Dec 19 2017 23:20:14
21_[f]_SEQ1239
22 _SEQ_FREE_9-ZBA
22 _WH_POTUS_PRESS
Divert-ATT_CAP_H
Q

On December 21st, it was announced that President Trump had signed an executive order authorizing the U.S. Treasury Department to freeze the assets of individuals and organizations found to be involved in corruption, human rights abuse and human trafficking. An anon posted the message below after finding a tweet from *ABC News* about the Executive Order.

Anonymous • Dec 21 2017
FOUND IT!!! HOLY SHIT!
https://twitter.com/ABCPolitics/status/943866651803611136

Q responded, saying that the President's mind had been changed about greater transparency regarding the exposure of corruption. He indicated that the signal of the change had been posted two days earlier on the 19th.

We were inspired by anons here to make our efforts more public.
Find the exchange 2 days ago.
Feel proud!
Q

An anon replied saying he believed the Executive Order had to do with greater public disclosure.

Anonymous
Multiple people were asking Q to make things more public. RE: calling for full disclosure

Q responded, saying the President listened to them and honored their request. He asked anons to find the exchange two days earlier and implied that it had to do with an Executive Order (EO).

Did you find the exchange 2 days ago re: WH EO today?
We listened.
Feel proud.
Q

Q provided a hint about the stringer where the exchange was made.

Dec 21 2017
News unlocks Map.
Future proves past.
Stringers important.

Hint:
12/19
22_WH_POTUS_PRESS
Divert-ATT_CAP_H
(Find Post)
News:
POTUS Tax Bill Speech (learn (22)(2+2_)).
AT&T Diverted Capital Home.
Q

An anon located the stringer from the 19th and Q confirmed.

Dec 21 2017
Correct exchange.
Anon(s) changed our mind re: Private / Public.
We are listening.
Highest priorty.
Have faith.
Q

On January 13th, 2018, Q reminded the anons that their persistence in asking for greater disclosure changed the President's mind. The decision was made to keep 60 percent secret and declassify 40 percent.

Jan 13 2018
[MONDAY]
Next Week - BIGGER.
PUBLIC.
We LISTENED [20/80 />/ 40/60].
Q

CHAPTER 7

Game Theory

A MESSAGE WAS POSTED FROM Q on November 2nd, 2017, letting us know that only a very small number of people had access to the full picture.

> Nov 2 2017
> You can count the people who have the full picture on two hands.
> Of those (less than 10 people) only three are non-military.
> Why is this relevant?
> Game theory.
> Outside of a potential operator who has been dialed-in w/ orders (specific to his/her mission) nobody else has this information.
> Operators never divulge.
> Alice & Wonderland.

In a post two hours prior, Q referred to a "global game of risk." Those who understand how global events are controlled (those who have the full picture) number less than 10. Only three of these people are non-military. Q asked, "Why is this relevant?" Q's mission requires an extremely high level of operational security—the kind that isn't found in civilian operations, but in the military. Thus, nearly all those who are directly involved in the mission are military. The few civilians who are involved have demonstrated that they can be trusted. There are a handful of people who carry out various operations, but their knowledge of the larger operation is confined to only what they need to know to accomplish *their* part of the mission. These operators are sworn to secrecy. Like everything involving national security, information is highly compartmentalized. Access is granted on a "need to know" basis.

What is Game Theory?

In the above post, Q mentioned "Game Theory." When I began my research, I made a mental note of it, but didn't immediately research the subject. Months later, I found myself wishing I had. If you don't understand the principles of game theory, you'll never understand the strategy behind the ways in which Q communicates to us—and his enemies.

Game theory is the science of strategy and decision-making. It attempts to determine the course of action people ought to take if they want to obtain the best possible outcomes in a variety of simulated game situations. The games that are studied in game theory are interdependent. That is to say, the outcome for a particular player depends on the choices (strategies) taken by all players. Different kinds of games result in different types of wins and losses. In a "zero-sum" game, one player's gain always results in another player's loss. Some games have the potential for either mutual gain (positive sum) or mutual harm (negative sum).

A game theory player, like a military general, must consider the choices made by others—both potential opponents and allies. Game theory looks at strategies and the interdependence of players. There are two different types of interdependence—sequential and simultaneous.

In a game of chess, each player moves in sequence, having full knowledge of their opponent's previous moves. A player involved in a sequential-move game must learn to develop strategies based on what they glean from their opponent's moves. A player accumulates information about their opponent's strategy and uses it to form their own strategy, which determines their current best choice.

Simple sequential games like tic-tac-toe that end after a few moves can be solved completely for every possible combination of moves. Each player's best strategy is determined by looking at every possible outcome. Games such as chess that involve millions of possible moves are too complex to solve for all possible outcomes. Players attempt to look a few moves ahead and predict how their opponent will respond to a certain move, a countermove, and so on. Sequential games require linear thinking.

In addition to sequential games, we must consider simultaneous ones. Simultaneous games require a logical circle of reasoning. In simultaneous decision making, players make decisions without knowing what the other players have chosen to do. Although players move at the same time in ignorance of the other's actions, they are aware that other players are making moves at the same time, who are likewise unaware of their opponent's moves. Players must reason: "I think that he thinks that I think..." Players must put themselves in the shoes of their opponent and attempt to calculate their best possible outcome by predicting what their opponent would do given their current situation. The Nobel Prize-winning mathematician John Nash described the optimal outcome that results when players make the best possible choice based on what they believe others will do. Nash illustrated this principle in what has become known as the "prisoner's dilemma."

Imagine two accomplices to a murder—held in separate prison cells—each contemplating the same plea deal that was offered by the prosecuting attorney. If either suspect provides information about the crime, they will receive a more lenient sentence. The suspects are not able to communicate with each other. If both suspects cooperate with the prosecutor, they each face 10 years in jail. If one cooperates while the other refuses, the one who cooperates receives immunity, while the other faces a lifetime in jail. If both suspects refuse to give any information, they both face a minor charge, and only a year in jail.

Because each person must make their choice without knowing what the other has chosen, and because the other person's choice affects their fate, the only way to eliminate the worst possible outcome (life in jail) is to confess to the murder. This is the best response one could make in anticipation of the other's range of choices.

In some situations, a player's best option is the same no matter what other players do. This is called a "dominant strategy." Sometimes, a player may only have bad choices. This is called a "dominated strategy."

If a player uses a rigid approach to decision making, it can be exploited by an opponent. It's helpful to keep your opponent guessing by mixing up your moves. In professional football, a mix of running the ball and passing prevents opponents from developing a dominant strategy. Even better is to incorporate fake pass plays and fake running plays.

Taking it one step further, a player may use threats or promises to alter an opponent's perception or expectations of their own strategy, causing the opponent to take actions that are favorable to them or deter them from taking action that would harm them. Threats and promises may cause an opponent to put themselves in a dominated strategy. For promises and threats to work, they must be perceived as credible. Misdirection, distraction, deception, and disinformation are important components of a successful game theory strategy.

An interesting situation arises when one player has access to information that others do not. When playing stud poker, when a player is dealt a royal flush, this hand can't be beat. But the advantage must be leveraged carefully to maximize its impact. A preferred strategy is pretending (bluffing) to have a terrible hand. Bluffing encourages your opponents to wager more money on their hand, which maximizes your eventual winnings.

"Appear weak when you are strong, and strong when you are weak."
—Sun Tzu, *The Art of War*

Bluffing does provide disinformation to an opponent. But if a player bluffs too frequently, their opponent may see the pattern and develop a strategy to take advantage of it. Therefore, bluffing, like every other strategy, must be mixed in with different strategies.

Why Is This Relevant?

Many people explore interesting theories without ever considering how the subject they're investigating is relevant. Interesting, perhaps, but if it's not relevant, what's the point? Like everything else related to Q, we must answer the question: "Why is this relevant?"

Game decisions are different from decisions that we make in a neutral environment. If you need to change a flat tire on your car, certain decisions must be made. Do you leave the car on the shoulder of the road while you change the tire, or do you attempt to drive it to a parking lot? Do you change it yourself or ask for help? While these decisions may result in slightly different experiences, the decisions of an opponent are not factored in. Compare that to the decisions made by a military general who must develop a strategy to win control of, and occupy a city inhabited by enemy forces. The general may have an initial battle plan in mind, which might involve the use of artillery to weaken enemy forces inside the city, but as soon as the enemy responds to the initial assault, the battlefield changes. The strategy may need to be modified depending on casualties, logistics, weather, terrain, etc.

It is well-known that members of the intelligence community frequent the boards of 4chan, 8chan, and 8kun. Many of them oppose the agenda of President Trump and Q. These agents are opponents in an elaborate game theory environment. But their moves are not part of a parlor game.

Rather than a game theory scenario where neither side knows the moves being made by the other, Q and the President may have the upper hand. Do they have access to all emails, phone calls, text messages, and other communications made by bad actors? Might they be using bluffs, disinformation, and distractions to maneuver them into a no-win situation?

Nov 5 2017
Game Theory.
Define.
Why is this relevant?
Moves and countermoves.
Who is the enemy?
False flags.
Shooter identification.
Shooter history.
Shooter background.
Shooter family.
MS13.
Define hostage.
Define leverage.
MS13.
Shooter.
Family.
Hostage.
Force.
Narrative.
Race.
Background.
Why is this relevant?
Flynn.
What is Flynn's background?
What was his rank?
Was he involved in intel ops?
What access or special priv?
Why is this relevant?
Set up.
Who wins?
Who becomes exposed?
Who knows where the bodies are buried?

Who has access?
What is MI?
Who was part of MI during BO term?
Who was fired during BO term (MI)?
Why is this relevant?
Re-read complete crumb graphic (confirmed good).
Paint the picture.
Disinformation exists and is necessary.
10 days.
Darnkess.
War.
Good v. Evil.
Roadmap of big picture is here.
Review post happenings.
Clarified.
Crumbs not only for /pol/.
The silent ones.
Others monitoring (friends and enemies).
Instructions.
Snow White.
Godfather III.
Q

Retired Lieutenant General Mike Flynn was the Director of the Defense Intelligence Agency (DIA) under Barack Obama until he was fired in 2014 over disagreements he had with Obama's policies. Military Intelligence (MI) was his specialty. As a former Director of the DIA, do you think he is among a handful of people who have personal knowledge of those who committed acts of murder, extortion, blackmail, and other forms of corruption?

Q confirmed that the graphic that had been put together displaying his previous posts was correct. It provided a roadmap of the big picture. The conflict in our country was never really about left versus right, liberal versus conservative. That narrative serves as a distraction to keep us at each other's throats and to prevent us from seeing that it's always been about good versus evil.

Not all of Q's posts are intended for the anons and autists. Some messages are designed to reach others (the silent ones) who monitor the boards, members of the intelligence community (friends and enemies), as well as the global elites—for whom disinformation exists and is necessary. They must make their moves based on the information and disinformation he provides.

Nov 2 2017

To those watching (you know who you are):

You have a choice to make.

You can stand up and do what you know to be right.

Or you can suffer the consequences of your previous actions.

Make no mistake, you are on the losing side.

The choice is yours.

If you decide to take down /pol/ and the net we will be ready.

4920-a 293883 zAj-1 0020192

Alice & Wonderland.

CHAPTER 8

General Flynn

IN THIS CHAPTER, I'LL SHARE more of what Q has said about retired Lieutenant General Michael Flynn. A key post about General Flynn is this one from October 31st, 2017. Q said that President Trump found favor with a group of military leaders who've used military intelligence to keep him ahead of the moves of his enemies. One of those leaders is General Flynn.

Oct 31 2017
SCI[F]
Military Intelligence.
What is 'State Secrets' and how upheld in the SC?
What must be completed to engage MI over other (3) letter agencies?
What must occur to allow for civilian trials?
Why is this relevant?
What was Flynn's background?
Why is this relevant?
Why did Adm R (NSA) meet Trump privately w/o auth?
Does POTUS know where the bodies are buried?
Does POTUS have the goods on most bad actors?
Was TRUMP asked to run for President?

Why?
By Who?
Was HRC next in line?
Was the election suppose to be rigged?
Did good people prevent the rigging?
Why did POTUS form a panel to investigate?
Has POTUS *ever* made a statement that did not become proven as true/fact?
What is POTUS in control of?
What is the one organization left that isn't corrupt?
Why does the military play such a vital role?
Why is POTUS surrounded by highly respected generals?
Who guards former Presidents?
Why is that relevant?
Who guards HRC?
Why is ANTIFA allowed to operate?
Why hasn't the MB been classified as a terrorist org?
What happens if Soros funded operations get violent and engage in domestic terrorism?
What happens if mayors/ police comms/chiefs do not enforce the law?
What authority does POTUS have specifically over the Marines?
Why is this important?
What is Mueller's background? Military?
Was Trump asked to run for President w/ assurances made to prevent tampering?
How is POTUS always 5-steps ahead?
Who is helping POTUS?

Q suggested that Donald Trump was approached by military leaders to run for President with assurances that they would minimize election rigging to give him a fair shot at being elected. Q also suggested that because senior leaders at the 3-letter agencies (FBI, DOJ, CIA, etc.) had been compromised before he came into office, President Trump needed to rely on *military* intelligence to keep him updated about global events and to help ensure matters of national security.

Oct 28 2017
◆◆◆
Why does Potus surround himself w/ generals?
What is military intelligence?

Why go around the 3 letter agencies?
What Supreme Court case allows for the use of MI v Congressional
assembled and approved agencies?
Who has ultimate authority over our branches of military w\o approval
conditions unless 90+ in wartime conditions?
What is the military code?
◆◆◆

General Flynn was investigated by the FBI, and then by Special Counsel Robert
Mueller's team. The General pled guilty to making "materially false statements"
to the FBI. On October 31st, 2017, Q asked why Mueller met with Donald Trump
the day before he was appointed Special Counsel.

Oct 31 2017
Why did Mueller meet POTUS 1-day prior to FBI announcement if
Mueller COULD NOT be offered director due to prev term limits rule?
Why is Pelosi begging for a new special counsel?
◆◆◆

It has been reported that Donald Trump interviewed Robert Mueller for FBI
Director—a job he could not accept due to a 10-year term limit which Mueller had already exceeded. If he was ineligible to be FBI Director, why was he
interviewed? Q has suggested Mueller may have been recruited by Trump to
prosecute the swamp. Q has also portrayed Mueller as a compromised and
corrupt person who was hired to remove Trump from office. Were these con-
flicting narratives created to lull the President's opponents into a false sense of
security? In Robert Mueller's final report—after the conclusion of his lengthy
Special Counsel investigation—Donald Trump was cleared of the charge that
he colluded with Russia to win the election. The Department of Justice found
no evidence of an attempt by him to obstruct justice.

Q has suggested that General Flynn had the upper hand over his enemies
due to his background in military intelligence (MI), his access to that system,
and the knowledge he has of his enemies' crimes.

Nov 5 2017
◆◆◆
Set up.
Who wins?
Who becomes exposed?

Who knows where the bodies are buried?
Who has access?
♦♦♦
What is MI?
Who was part of MI during BO term?
Who was fired during BO term (MI)?
Why is this relevant?
Re-read complete crumb graphic (confirmed good).
Paint the picture.
Disinformation exists and is necessary.
♦♦♦

On November 1st, 2017, Q asked us to consider how many generals with military intelligence backgrounds had visited the White House. He suggested that General Flynn had a vital role in the Trump administration, albeit a behind-the-scenes one.

Nov 1 2017
♦♦♦
Focus on Flynn.
Background and potential role.
What is the common denominator in terms of military backgrounds close to POTUS?
♦♦♦

Q said that contrary to what was being said on social media and in the news, General Flynn was safe.

Dec 5 2017
Who knows where the bodies are buried?
FLYNN is safe.
We protect our Patriots.
Q

Despite Q's assurances that General Flynn was in no real danger, many people were still concerned. An anon demanded General Flynn be set free.

Anonymous • Mar 27 2018
Free Flynn

Q responded, saying things would change within 30 days.

Done in 30.
House cleaning.
WH secured.
Final stage.
Q

Thirty days later, Q posted a link to a *Fox News* article by Judson Berger about the House Intelligence Committee's report on its investigation, which concluded that Donald Trump had not colluded with Russia during the 2016 election. It also cleared General Flynn.

It's been noted that FBI agents said they did not believe General Flynn lied to them despite his guilty plea in the Mueller investigation. Q suggested that Flynn's time with Mueller served a different purpose than what was being reported.

Apr 27 2018
"Done in 30."
[30]
◆◆◆
Why would Flynn plead guilty to something untrue?
Define testimony.
Define 'on record'.
Who knows where the bodies are buried?
Flynn is safe.
Expand your thinking.
Q

What purpose would be served by General Flynn testifying to Mueller's team? Did he testify about corruption that he knew existed in the FBI & DOJ? Or malfeasance he witnessed in the Obama administration as Director of the Defense Intelligence Agency? Or fraud in other parts of the world? Define "witness." Define "on the record."

In a criminal prosecution, a suspect may be given a plea bargain when they become a cooperating witness. They're charged with a minor offense (like lying to investigators) in exchange for telling everything they know about the crimes in question. What if General Flynn is a cooperating witness with U.S. Attorneys who are investigating alleged corruption in the FBI & DOJ, the Clinton Foundation, and the Uranium One deal? To hammer home the point, Q posted a link to an article about General Flynn's plea agreement. Why would he plead guilty to a crime the FBI said he didn't commit? It doesn't add up.

Apr 27 2018
If the FBI found NO evidence of lying why was Flynn charged?
Expand your thinking.
1 & 1 don't equal 2.
EYES OPEN?
COMMS GOOD?
Q

Around the same time the House Intelligence Committee's Russia investigation final report clearing General Flynn was released, some of the texts by FBI agent Peter Strzok and FBI attorney Lisa Page were also released. (Strzok was one of the agents who interviewed General Flynn during the "Crossfire Hurricane" investigation.)

Apr 27 2018
Expand.
Who interviewed Flynn?
What redacted texts were released yesterday?
Coincidence?
Why did Flynn take the bullet?
Rubber bullet?
Lawmakers make public?
Lawmakers learned gmail draft comms yesterday?
Lawmakers go hunting?
What is the purpose of a laser pointer?
You have more than you know.
Comms understood?
Q

Q suggested the timing of the release of FBI texts, and the House Intelligence report was not a coincidence. The individual who authorized their release seemed to have a specific goal in mind. Members of Congress like Devin Nunes and Mark Meadows learned that officials in the Obama administration and high-ranking members of the intelligence community had been using Gmail drafts (perhaps as a way to avoid detection by the NSA). They also learned from the newly released texts that there seemed to be a plot to remove President Trump from office. Like a laser pointer, the new information helped members of Congress acquire new targets to investigate.

Apr 25 2018
We knew this day would come.
We knew people would need a guide.
We all have a part to play.
We knew FLYNN would be challenged.
Part of the plan?
Flynn JR recent "did not lie to VP."
Timing.
Plan.
SIG sent [WH position]?
Moves & countermoves.
Role outside of WH?
"Lost house."
"Funds for legal."
"Beat up."
You are watching a .....
What is right?
What is wrong?
Up is down.
Left is right.
Left is LEFT.
WH position [rapid] changes.
Why?
Planned?
Visibility in one helps another?
Connected?
C_A to SEC of STATE NK IRAN RUSSIA CHINA MX .....
Why is this relevant?
Think pushback.
Open source.
Why?
They are watching.
Proofs provided to retain.
Future proves past.
History books.
Q

Q noted that Mike Pompeo was rapidly moved from CIA Director to Secretary of State, to establish President Trump's foreign policy with nations like North Korea, Iran, Russia, China, and Mexico. Q's statement "they are watching" suggests there are enemies of General Flynn and the President who are observing Q's posts. Is the narrative about General Flynn part of a disinformation campaign? That possibility creates uncertainty for people like myself who use Q's posts in an attempt to paint an accurate picture of these events.

In May of 2018, Q asked about the firing of U.S. Attorney Preet Bharara, the removal of Attorney General Schneiderman in New York, and the addition of Rudy Giuliani to President Trump's legal team. He also asked about cleaning out the Justice Department and how it is critical to prosecuting corruption.

May 15 2018
Why was Preet Bharara fired?
Why was the NY AG just removed?
Why did Rudy recently join POTUS' legal team after being 'quiet' for so long?
What must be cleaned first?
Who investigates?
Who prosecutes?
WHAT CAN FINALLY BE DONE?
WHO HAS THE ULTIMATE AUTHORITY?
DOES IT FALL UNDER THE RUSSIA RECUSAL?
DOES FLYNN KNOW?
Define "On the Record."
You have more than you know.
ENJOY THE SHOW.
Q

In October of 2016, the FBI obtained a FISA warrant to surveil Carter Page, a volunteer staffer with Donald Trump's 2016 Presidential campaign. The surveillance of Page was part of the FBI's "Crossfire Hurricane" investigation that sought to determine if the Trump campaign colluded with Russia. (I'll provide a detailed discussion of Page's surveillance in the chapter on Admiral Rogers and the NSA.)

On December 9th, 2019, the Department of Justice Inspector General released a report on the FBI's abuse of FISA against Carter Page.

At this point, I'd like to take a brief diversion to highlight an intriguing set of circumstances related to the release of the Inspector General's report.

Timestamps

One way in which Q provides evidence to support the claim that he is connected to the President is by posting in synchronicity with the President's tweets. During the duration of his mission, Q has managed to post more than 20 times within a minute of the President. In these situations, Q posts first, and the President tweets immediately afterward. Due to the use of multiple devices and lag time in the system, the results are unpredictable, but the timing of their posts suggests collaboration.

On November 2nd, 2019, (exactly one week before the release of the Department of Justice Inspector General's report), Q posted for the first time on a new platform called 8kun using the same tripcode he had used previously on 8chan. Although tripcodes are secured with a password, followers wanted more verification that this user was actually Q. A timestamp comparison would be used to help verify that this user was, in fact, Q.

After a new read-only board, /projectdcomms/, had been set up on 8kun, Q posted on it using a new tripcode. The message indicated this was for the purpose of tripcode configuration.

Q !!Hs1Jq13jV6   Dec 2 2019   12:55:59
/trip_config/
Q

Less than a minute later, President Trump tweeted.

Donald J. Trump (from his Twitter account):
The Republican Party has NEVER been so united! This Impeachment Scam is just a continuation of the 3 year Witch Hunt, but it is only bringing us even closer together!
12:56:48 PM - Dec 2, 2019

Eleven minutes later, Q posted again. This message signified confirmation of his tripcode.

Q !!Hs1Jq13jV6   Dec 2 2019   13:07:32
♦♦♦
/trip_confirmed/
/relay_1-99/
Q

Q's post was a graphic showing his previous post alongside the tweet by POTUS. The timestamps showed a 49-second interval (delta) between them. Posting less than one minute before the President is very hard to do without coordination. Anons are aware of the relevance of timestamps and monitor them regularly. That was the first part of Q's identity re-confirmation. Q's next post was a second confirmation.

Dec 2 2019
IDENconf.PNG
/trip_confirmed2/
/relay_1-99/
Q

The above post included a photograph of a pen and a wristwatch. The hands on the watch showed the time of 1:29. The date on the watch was the 2nd. At the time of the post, anons did not know the relevance of the time or date indicated on the watch, but Q has posted many similar images that turned out to be evidence of foreknowledge of future events. The pen shown in the image appears to be identical to the ones posted in the past. (It's worth noting that when an internet search is done for these images, no search results are returned, suggesting these are original photos not posted before on the internet.)

Exactly one week later, Inspector General Horowitz's report on the FBI's operation "Crossfire Hurricane" was made public through a link posted on the Department of Justice Inspector General Twitter account. The timestamp of the tweet was 1:29 eastern time, the same time on the watch image posted by Q.

Justice OIG (from their Twitter account):
DOJ OIG releases Review of Four FISA Applications and Other Aspects of the FBI's Crossfire Hurricane Investigation.
View on website here: https://www.justice.gov/storage/120919-examination.pdf
View on https://www.oversight.gov/report/doj/review-four-fisa-applications-and-other-aspects-fbi%E2%80%99s-crossfire-hurricane-investigation
1:29 pm - 9 Dec 2019

Attorney General William Barr disagreed with some of the findings of the report. His response was posted on the DOJ Twitter account at 1:29, again, the same time on the watch image posted by Q, a week earlier.

Justice Department (from their Twitter account):
Statement by Attorney General William P. Barr on the Inspector
General's Report of the Review of Four FISA Applications and Other
Aspects of the FBI's Crossfire Hurricane Investigation
https://www.justice.gov/opa/pr/statement-attorney-general-william-p-
barr-inspector-generals-report-review-four-fisa
1:29 pm - 9 Dec 2019

U.S. Attorney John Durham likewise disagreed with some of the findings of
the report. His response was posted on the Connecticut U.S. Attorney's Twitter
account at 1:29. Once again, the timestamp was the same time as the hands on
the watch image posted by Q.

U.S. Attorney CT (from their Twitter account):
Statement of U.S. Attorney John H. Durham
https://go.usa.gov/xpVkk
1:29 pm - 9 Dec 2019

What do you suppose the odds are that all these events would happen at the
same time, on the same day—*and* that the exact time would be predicted by
Q a week in advance?

Back to General Flynn. It was reported by CNN in January of 2017, that Flynn
was under FISA surveillance during 2016. (The details have not yet been made
public as to how and why he was surveilled, but there is enough open source
information available to paint a picture of what likely happened.)

Flynn was entered into Robert Mueller's Trump-Russia investigation and—
as part of a plea deal—admitted to making materially false statements. After
repeated sentencing delays, Flynn hired a new legal team headed by Sidney
Powell, who took a different approach in the handling of his case. Powell filed
a motion to receive documents that she believed would exonerate the General.
On December 16th, 2019, her request was denied by Judge Emmet Sullivan.
The judge felt the requested documents had no bearing on Flynn's admission
to making materially false statements. The day the decision was made public,
Q posted this:

Dec 16 2019 16:37
Same evidence to FREE FLYNN currently being used to INDICT others
[GJ]?
[302]_mod [1] count.

Who listened in [2] count [FISA?]

....

[6] counts.
FBI agent [1][P] - FLYNN interview........
If FISA warrant was ILLEGAL..........
If FISA warrant predicated on ILLEGAL/UNCORROBORATED........
If FISA 'actors' purposely withheld exculpatory evidence from the
court.............
[Watch] what happens next.
Q

Q implied that the evidence Powell requested was being presented to a grand jury (GJ). If that were true, it could not be released without potentially compromising the jurors.

Flynn was questioned on January 24th, 2017, by FBI agents Peter Strzok and Joe Pientka. Strzok asked the questions. Pientka wrote the report. Does the letter [P] in the above post refer to Pientka? Although the interview with Flynn was conducted on January 24th, the FBI 302 was officially submitted on February 15th. Publicly released text messages between Peter Strzok and Lisa Page reveal ongoing deliberations as to how the narrative of the final FBI 302 was to be framed. One text message between Page and Strzok on February 14th (the day before the final report was submitted) asked if Andy (Deputy FBI Director Andrew McCabe) was okay with the 302. On May 17th, Robert Mueller was appointed Special Counsel to investigate allegations of Trump-Russia collusion. On May 31st, the FBI 302 was again changed, and it became part of the evidentiary basis for the prosecution of General Flynn. After obtaining a FISA warrant on Flynn, all his communications would have been monitored.

On December 17th, 2019, Q posted a link to a court order from Rosemary Collyer, the presiding judge of the FISA Court, who ordered the FBI to provide assurances that it would comply with all regulations in the future. Included in Q's post was a quote from Judge Collyer's 4-page document.

Dec 17 2019
https://www.fisc.uscourts.gov/sites/default/files/Misc%2019%20
02%20191217.pdf
"The frequency with which representations made by FBI personnel
turned out to be unsupported or contradicted by information in their
possession, and with which they withheld information detrimental to
their case, calls into question whether information contained in other

FBI applications is reliable."
Think FLYNN_FISA [ILLEGAL?]
Q

Q suggested that just as the FBI illegally obtained Carter Page's FISA warrant, it illegally obtained one against General Flynn. Later that day, Q made another post.

Dec 17 2019
First indictment [unseal] will trigger mass pop awakening.
First arrest will verify action and confirm future direction.
They will fight but you are ready.
Marker [9].
Q

I would draw your attention to the first and last lines: "The first indictment [unseal]" and "Marker [9]." The previous post from December 16th mentioned indictments and had three numbers in brackets [1], [2], and [6] along with the word "count." Q hinted that indictments had already been returned against people who illegally obtained a FISA warrant to spy on General Flynn. It seems one count in the indictment (which has yet to be made public) is for illegally modifying the FBI report of Flynn's interview (the FBI 302). Two additional counts in the indictment are related to illegally listening to Flynn's phone calls, and six more counts are related to other crimes not listed by Q. That brings the total number of counts to 9. I believe "Marker [9]" is a prediction that we will soon learn of a 9-count indictment against those who illegally spied on General Flynn. These indictments may be the first related to the effort to illegally spy on the Trump campaign, and they could trigger a mass public awakening to the severity of corruption in government.

As of this writing, General Flynn's final disposition—concerning his guilty plea—is still unknown. I suspect he will be cleared of wrongdoing in the future. History books will show him to be a great patriot and, perhaps, the star witness in the prosecution of corruption.

CHAPTER 9

The Deep State

MANY PEOPLE CONCEPTUALIZE THE U.S. federal government as being run by elected officials. The total number of elected officials in Washington D.C. is 537, which includes the President, the Vice President, 435 members of the House of Representatives, and 100 Senators.

By comparison, the Department of Defense is the nation's largest employer, with over 1.4 million active-duty personnel and 1.1 million reservists. It also employs 861,000 civilians. Some 23,000 military and civilian employees and another 3,000 non-defense support personnel work in the Pentagon.

The State Department is estimated to have 13,000 Foreign Service employees, 11,000 Civil Service employees, and 45,000 local employees. The Department of Justice employs 113,543 people among its more than 30 agencies. Of that number, 35,000 are employed by the FBI.

Intelligence agencies in the Department of Defense include the National Security Agency, which employs around 21,000 people. More than 16,000 men and women work for the Defense Intelligence Agency. A 1996 bipartisan commission report described the National Reconnaissance Office as having by far the largest budget of any intelligence agency, and "virtually no federal workforce," accomplishing most of its work through "tens of thousands" of defense contractor personnel.

According to *Wikipedia* and *The Washington Post,* about 21,000 people worked for the Central Intelligence Agency in 2013. *The New York Times* estimated the number of foreign spies recruited to work for CIA at around 4,000.

Unlike *elected* officials who can be voted out of office after a few years, most *unelected* government employees can make a career out of working for the federal government. How much power do unelected officials have? Are they at the mercy of the President and Congress, or are they the ones silently steering the ship?

Some believe it is the unelected officials in government who plot the course of a nation. Their decades-long tenure allows them to develop long-term objectives and employ tactics that tend to neutralize the effects of short-term elected politicians. These commentators believe career employees have created a system that allows them to thwart the will of elected leaders and exert more significant influence than the public realizes.

Evidence of such an arrangement surfaced on September 5th, 2018, when *The New York Times* published an anonymous editorial under the following headline: *I Am Part of the Resistance Inside the Trump Administration.* The anonymous author claimed to be a top White House advisor who was working against the President's agenda. The writer warned, "...many Trump appointees have vowed to do what we can to preserve our democratic institutions while thwarting Mr. Trump's more misguided impulses until he is out of office."

The term *deep state* is used by some to describe a system of government where unelected officials in the intelligence community, the military, the State Department, the National Security Council, and other agencies control much of the decision making at the federal level.

Does the Deep State Really Exist?

In April of 2018, while on a book signing tour, former FBI Director Comey addressed a crowd at a Barnes & Noble in New York's Union Square.

"There is a deep state in this sense. There is a collection of people, CIA, NSA, FBI in the United States military services who care passionately about getting it right, who care passionately about the values we try to talk about."
—James Comey, former FBI Director

Comey was instrumental in launching an investigation that sought to remove President Trump from office. After the President was inaugurated, he had several meetings with Comey, who memorialized the interactions in a series of memos. Comey said he had provided one of his memos to *The New York Times* through a trusted friend for the specific purpose of having a special counsel appointed. Comey was then fired, and soon afterward, Robert Mueller was appointed special counsel.

Robert Mueller testified before Congress on July 24th, 2019, about his investigation, which found no wrongdoing by the President. The following day, July 25th, President Trump had a phone call with Ukrainian President Volodymyr Zelensky. During their conversation, Trump urged Zelensky to do everything possible to combat corruption.

Trump told Zelensky he wanted to have Attorney General William Barr call "him or his people" and "get to the bottom" of possible criminal activities. He mentioned the tech company Crowdstrike and later, former Vice-President Joe Biden and his son Hunter.

"There's a lot of talk about Biden's son, that Biden stopped the prosecution and a lot of people want to find out about that so whatever you can do with the Attorney General would be great. Biden went around bragging that he stopped the prosecution so if you can look into it... It sounds horrible to me."
—President Donald J. Trump

The Ukrainian President replied:

"...the next prosecutor general will be "100% my person, my candidate, who will be approved, by the parliament and will start as a new prosecutor in September. He or she will look into the situation, specifically to the company that you mentioned in this issue. The issue of the investigation of the case is actually the issue of making sure to restore the honesty so we will take care of that and will work on the investigation of the case."
—Ukrainian President Volodymyr Zelensky

It happened at this time that military aid to Ukraine had been temporarily paused, while routine checks were done by the White House Office of Management and Budget (OMB). In a memo, Mark Paoletta explained:

"Often, in managing appropriations, OMB must briefly pause an agency's legal ability to spend those funds for a number of reasons, including to ensure that the funds are being spent efficiently, that they are being spent in accordance with statutory directives, or to assess how or whether funds should be used for a particular activity."
—Mark Paoletta, Office of Management and Budget General Counsel

The aid to Ukraine was released before the promised deadline. Zelensky took no action to have the aid released and said he was not pressured in any way by President Trump.

Despite these facts, Democrats in the House of Representatives opened an impeachment inquiry against the President based on a whistleblower complaint about Trump's phone call with Zelensky. The complaint expressed concern that Trump may have engaged in illegal activity by withholding aid in exchange for a promise from Zelensky to investigate Hunter Biden.

The whistleblower had no firsthand experience upon which to base a complaint. They had not heard the phone call, but had heard details about it from someone else. On the whistleblower submission form, instructions state that secondhand information is not acceptable. Nevertheless, the whistleblower submitted a complaint. When questioned about an apparent violation of whistleblower protocol prohibiting complaints based on secondhand information, the Intelligence Community Inspector General, Michael Atkinson, said he had not rejected secondhand complaints in the past.

During their hearings, Democrats in Congress called 18 witnesses from the National Security Council, the State Department, and other agencies to testify against the President. (Only 17 have been reported by the press.) Most had no firsthand information to report. Only two had personally heard the phone call, and only one, U.S. Ambassador to the EU Gordon Sondland, had spoken with the President personally. Sondland reported that when he asked Trump what he wanted from Ukraine, Trump said, "I want nothing. I want no quid pro quo. I want Zelensky to do the right thing... to do what he ran on."

On September 24th, 2019, President Trump took an unprecedented step and announced he would make the transcript of the phone call available to the public, which he did the following day. That same day, before having a chance to read the transcript of the call, House Speaker Nancy Pelosi announced that she was initiating an impeachment inquiry. Adam Schiff played a major role in the House investigation of the President.

On February 11th, 2019, Adam Schiff tweeted a list of complaints he had against the President regarding his goal of building on wall on the border.

Adam Schiff (from his Twitter account):
Step One: Hype an invented threat of an invasion of terrorists, murderers, and rapists.
Step Two: Send troops to border to address the imaginary threat.
Step Three: Justify the WALL as necessary to protect troops sent to meet the nonexistent threat.

Step Four: Executive Time!
1:05 PM - 11 Feb 2019

Q responded to Schiff's tweet:

Feb 11 2019
https://twitter.com/RepAdamSchiff/status/1095051195658522625
Let's actually use 'FACTS':
Step One: Hype an invented threat of POTUS working w/ the RUSSIANS
(disinformation campaign).
Step Two: Send FBI/DOJ/CONGRESS/SENATE/C_A/NSA/INTEL/
FVEY/etc... to address and investigate the IMAGINARY THREAT.
Step Three: Justify the 'SPECIAL COUNSEL' and MILLIONS OF
TAXPAYER DOLLARS SPENT as necessary to protect the public and our
election process against an imaginary, made-up, non-existent threat
(which really is) designed to protect the illegal activities of many elected
officials.
Step Four: Open 'new' Fake & False investigations as CHAIRMAN of
the House Intel Comm to retain disinformation campaign designed
to keep liberal/D Americans onboard to regain POWER & PREVENT
prosecution - Executive Time!
Q

President Trump is an outsider who poses a threat to the reigning political establishment. The plan to remove him from office began long ago. On January 30th, 2017, just ten days after he was sworn in, President Trump fired acting Attorney General Sally Yates for insubordination when she refused to allow the Department of Justice to enforce immigration laws. In response, Mark Zaid (who would later become the whistleblower's attorney) tweeted:

Mark S. Zaid (from his Twitter account):
#coup has started. First of many steps. #rebellion. #impeachment will
follow ultimately. #lawyers
7:54 PM - 30 Jan 2017

On the day of the President's inauguration, *The Washington Post* published an article with the headline: *The campaign to impeach President Trump has begun.* Eleven days earlier, they ran another story with the headline: *How to remove Trump from office.*

Prior to being inaugurated, Trump had resisted some of the briefings the intelligence community wanted to give him regarding Russia. Senator Chuck Schumer famously warned him: "Let me tell you: You take on the intelligence community—they have six ways from Sunday at getting back at you."

If there is any doubt that there are people in government whose goal is to thwart the plans of a duly elected President, this should put those doubts to rest. Whether you call them "government resisters," the "administrative state," the "permanent state," or the "deep state" isn't the point. Call them whatever you want. There is a faction inside the government that strives to subvert the policies and agenda of the President.

Nov 7 2017
The graphic is your key.
Let's pause and say hello to the rogue intelligence agencies currently monitoring these threads.
Was the money worth it?
Titanic.
Q

CHAPTER 10

Who Is Q?

IN THE INTRODUCTION TO THIS book, I said I don't know if Q is a male or female, an individual or a group. I've chosen to refer to Q as "him" or "he," but this is strictly for ease of writing.

I've heard many theories about the identity of Qanon. A popular theory among skeptics is that Q is an artificial intelligence program—or "internet bot"—that posts and responds to people according to a computer program. One aspect of Q's posts would seem to discredit this idea. Q sometimes makes typographical errors.

In April of 2018, Q posted about the Supreme Court and former Attorney General Loretta Lynch. He normally uses the abbreviation SC for Supreme Court and LL for Loretta Lynch. In this post, Q accidentally wrote SS instead of SC for Supreme Court:

Apr 15 2018
Side by side graphic.
SS/LL deal drop(s) w/ orig timestamp(s).
POTUS' Tweet.
Important going forward.
Q

An anon responded:

Anonymous
SS/LL deal drop(s) w/ orig timestamp(s).
Q is "SS" correct or a typo? please clarify

Q responded:

Typo.
SC = Supreme Court.
Q

If Q were an artificial intelligence program, it seems unlikely this mistake would have been made since computers only do what they're programmed to do. Secondly, we might ask whether such a computer program would have the capacity to recognize and confirm its own typographical error.

In May of 2018, Q's tripcode was either hacked or intentionally exposed (or both). At the time, Q !4pRcUA0lBE was Q's tripcode. Whenever Q was logged in under his credentials, this code was displayed on the top line at the far left of his posts. Below is an example:

Q !4pRcUAOlBE   May 12 2018   22:24
If America falls, the World falls.
God bless our brave fighting men & women.
They deserve our deepest gratitude.
Through their strength, and the millions of united Patriots around the World, we will succeed in this fight.
Peace through strength.
Now comes the pain.
Q

In the post below, (written a few days later) note in the top line at the left, there is a tripcode containing a message:

NowC@mesTHEP@in—-23!!!   May 19 2018   15:03
They thought it was coming yesterday.
They were wrong.
Follow the pen.
Q

While Q was posting the above message, his password was exposed which allowed an enemy to get it and post as Q. Below was the next post by the individual who obtained Q's password four minutes later:

Q !4pRcUAOIBE   May 19 2018   15:07
Reeeee

Q responded:

Password exposed?

Q responded again:

Mistake or on purpose?
Q

An anon responded to Q:

Anonymous
You knew when you set that trip, that the PAIN would be delivered
"—-23!!!"
More evidence of foreknowledge.

Q responded, notifying the board he was about to change his tripcode.

Q !4pRcUAOIBE   May 19 2018   17:06
TRIP CHANGE
Q

Q responded again after changing his tripcode (Note the tripcode below is different from the one above):

Q !CbboFOtcZs   May 19 2018   17:07
Updated.
Q

For about a week, Q had been posting about "pain," which was a reference to the arrest of corrupt people. The stolen tripcode "NowC@mesTHEP@in—-23!!!" was a direct message to them. Does it seem likely that an artificial intelligence program would employ these types of tactics to intimidate and harass corrupt people, or does it look more like something a human would do?

Q has provided hints about his identity in certain posts like this one from the first week of November, 2017:

Nov 1 2017
Q Clearance Patriot
My fellow Americans, over the course of the next several days you will undoubtedly realize that we are taking back our great country (the land of the free) from the evil tyrants that wish to do us harm and destroy the last remaining refuge of shining light. On POTUS' order, we have initiated certain fail-safes that shall safeguard the public from the primary fallout which is slated to occur 11.3 upon the arrest announcement of Mr. Podesta (actionable 11.4). Confirmation (to the public) of what is occurring will then be revealed and will not be openly accepted. Public riots are being organized in serious numbers in an effort to prevent the arrest and capture of more senior public officials. On POTUS' order, a state of temporary military control will be actioned and special ops carried out. False leaks have been made to retain several within the confines of the United States to prevent extradition and special operator necessity. Rest assured, the safety and well-being of every man, woman, and child of this country is being exhausted in full. However, the atmosphere within the country will unfortunately be divided as so many have fallen for the corrupt and evil narrative that has long been broadcast. We will be initiating the Emergency Broadcast System (EMS) during this time in an effort to provide a direct message (avoiding the fake news) to all citizens. Organizations and/or people that wish to do us harm during this time will be met with swift fury – certain laws have been pre-lifted to provide our great military the necessary authority to handle and conduct these operations (at home and abroad).

Researchers learned that Q clearance is the highest level of security clearance issued by the U.S. Department of Energy. That caused some to conclude that Q worked for (or was somehow associated with) the Department of Energy. The next day, Q posted a message clarifying what he meant.

Nov 2 2017
What is Q Clearance?

What hint does that explicitly refer to?
DOE?
Who would have the goods on U1?
Does stating 'Q' refer that person works in DOE?
No.
Does it refer that someone dropping such information has the highest level of security within all departments?
Why is this relevant?

♦♦♦

Q did not intend to suggest he was a Department of Energy employee but rather, that he held a security clearance which allowed him the highest level of access to information across multiple government departments. That access would enable him to provide information on the controversial sale of the North American company Uranium One (U1) to the Russian energy company Rosatom.

Let's examine this statement by Q: "someone dropping such information has the highest level of security within all departments." Information retained by the U.S. government is highly compartmentalized. There are hundreds of different government agencies and departments. Each department or agency retains information that is not shared with other agencies unless the individual has a legitimate "need to know." If the information is "classified" for security purposes, the requesting person also needs to have the proper security clearance to view it. The Secretary of Energy, for example, would have access to all information retained by the Department of Energy, but he would only be permitted to access information stored by the Department of Defense if he had a legitimate need to know and the proper security clearance.

Q implied that he has access to information at the highest level across multiple governmental departments. There are very few people who would have both the need to know and the security clearance for that kind of access. The U.S. Office of the Director of National Intelligence (ODNI) is one example. The ODNI receives information from all U.S. intelligence agencies and brings it together into reports and briefings for its customers who include the Congress, the Chairman of the Joint Chiefs of Staff, the National Security Council, and the President. By virtue of that responsibility, the ODNI would have access to information across multiple agencies and departments. But the previous post suggests Q has access to information across *all* departments. That narrows the field of possible candidates even further. Only someone in a high-level position like the President would have unlimited access to information across all departments.

At the time of these posts, the President (POTUS) was preparing to leave on a trip to Asia. The same day he posted the "Q Clearance Patriot" message, Q also posted this:

Nov 1 2017
POTUS will be well insulated/protected on AF1 and abroad (specific locations classified) while these operations are conducted due to the nature of the entrenchment. It is time to take back our country and make America great again. Let us salute and pray for the brave men and women in uniform who will undertake this assignment to bring forth peace, unity, and return power to the people.

It is our hope that this message reaches enough people to make a meaningful impact. We cannot yet telegraph this message through normal methods for reasons I'm sure everyone here can understand. Follow the questions from the previous thread(s) and remain calm, the primary targets are within DC and remain at the top (on both sides). The spill over in the streets will be quickly shut down. Look for more false flags – stay alert, be vigilant, and above all, please pray.

"For God so loved the world that he gave his one and only Son, that whoever believes in him shall not perish but have eternal life. Love is patient, love is kind."
God bless my fellow Americans.
4,10,20

A clue can be found in the last line of this post. Note the curious signature which contains the numbers: 4,10,20. The anons weren't certain what it meant so they asked for a clue. Q responded with a hint that was intended to help them solve the riddle:

Nov 2 2017
4,10,20 A,b,c,d,e……

Now, let's decode the signature. If you assign a number to each letter of the alphabet, the corresponding decode for "4,10,20" is DJT—the initials of Donald J. Trump.

Q suggested this message came directly from the President. If, as Q claims, the President is directly involved in the operation, then these posts would be coming from someone who has the highest security clearance across all government departments. I must emphasize that, as of this writing, President Trump has not directly confirmed his connection to Q's operation.

Individual or Group?

Some posts, like this one, suggest that Q is an individual and not part of a team:

Oct 31 2017
I've dumped some crumbs like this over the weekend which started the intense shilling. At this point we are far enough along you can paint the picture without risk of jeopardizing the operation.

In the post below, Q does not refer to himself as an individual, but rather, he uses the term "we":

Jan 19 2018
Why are we here?
Why are we providing crumbs?
◆◆◆
Q

Q has used the term "Wizards & Warlocks" to refer to a group of which he is apparently a member.

Nov 12 2017
◆◆◆
Who are the Wizards & Warloc[k]s?
What council do the Wizards & Warlocks control?
Think Snowden (inside terms dropped).
◆◆◆

Is Q pointing us to the NSA, whose surveillance programs were leaked by Edward Snowden? In another drop, Q said the Wizards and Warlocks have a view no one else has:

Nov 3 2017
◆◆◆
The council of Wizards & Warlocks cannot be defeated.

Nice view up here.
Q

In December of 2018, Q hosted a question and answer session. An anon asked about the identity of the Wizards and Warlocks:

Anonymous • Dec 12 2018
Q, please tell us who or what the Wizards and Warlocks are.

Q responded:

'Guardians' of intelligence.
Q

Q seemed to confirm that his operation is closely connected to the NSA whose job is to gather intelligence and "guard" it or keep it safe.

Many people have claimed to know Q's identity. Some claim to have spoken with Q personally. Others have claimed they received messages from Q via social media or email. Some have posted as Q on different social media platforms. Q reminded followers that he does not communicate outside the boards of 4chan, 8chan, and 8kun:

Jan 5 2018
One post today.
No other platforms used.
No comms privately w/ anyone.
Don't get lost.
Q

Jan 8 2018
IMPORTANT:
NO private comms past/present/future.
NO comms made outside of this platform.
Any claims that contradict the above should be considered FAKE NEWS and disregarded immediately.
WHERE WE GO ONE, WE GO ALL.
PATRIOTS.
Q

In the following post, Q said he serves at the pleasure of the President.

Nov 2 2017
We serve at the pleasure of the President. DJT

After Q had moved from one board to another, he was asked a question by an anon who had followed him since he was on the board /calmbeforethestorm/ (CBTS).

Anonymous • Mar 28
I am terrified to go to bed but I have to, I have work tomorrow... What if I wake up and everyone has moved to a new board, how will I know? I've been on this train since CBTS. I can't lose communication now!

Q responded:

You are safe.
THEY are terrified.
Sleep well, Patriot.
You elected us to keep you safe.
We will not fail.
/GA/ will change.
Notification will be made.
Where we go one, we go all.
Q

At the time, Q was posting on a board called Great Awakening (/GA/). He made an odd remark: "You elected us to keep you safe." That statement is pregnant with implications. It suggests that elected members of government are on the team. There are only certain people we elect; among them are the President and Vice-President.

CHAPTER 11

Admiral Rogers and No Such Agency

ADMIRAL MICHAEL ROGERS HAS SERVED in the U.S. Navy since his graduation from the Naval Officers Reserve Training Corps in 1981. He was appointed head of the National Security Agency (NSA) and U.S. Cyber Command in 2014 and served in that capacity until his retirement in 2018.

On January 13th, 2018, Q posted the following message.

Jan 13 2018

◆◆◆

>ADM R

◆◆◆

The MAP is the KEY.

PLANNED for [3] years.

CORRUPTION and EVIL DEEP WITHIN.

EVERYWHERE.

PATIENCE.

THERE IS NO ESCAPE.

THERE ARE NO DEALS.

TREASON AT HIGHEST LEVELS.

FOREIGN AGENTS WITHIN OUR GOV'T.
HIGHEST LEVELS.
THE PUPPET MASTERS HAVE BEEN REMOVED.
ALL VEHICLES OF DELIVERY REMOVED.
STRINGS CUT.
7TH FLOOR IS NO MORE>FBI/SD
WE SEE ALL.
WE HEAR ALL.
THE HUNT CONTINUES.
PRISON.
DEATH.
[CLAS_GITMO_ J z9-A][89]
RED_RED_
IRON EAGLE.
Q

Q informed us that the highest levels of the U.S. government had been infiltrated not just with corrupt people, but with foreign agents. Agencies infiltrated include the State Department (SD), the Department of Justice (DOJ), the Federal Bureau of Investigation (FBI), and the Central Intelligence Agency (CIA). Corruption had reached a point where its continued spread would plunge the nation (and the world) into darkness and war. Because they weren't willing to suffer that fate without a battle, a group of patriots in the military developed a plan three years earlier to take back control.

Oct 29 2017
Key:
Military Intelligence v FBI CIA NSA
No approval or congressional oversight
State Secrets upheld under SC
Who is the Commander and Chief of the military?
Under what article can the President impose MI take over investigations for the 3 letter agencies? What conditions must present itself? Why is this so VERY important? Who surrounds POTUS? They lost this very important power _ the one area of the govt not corrupt and directly serves POTUS.

Some U.S. intelligence agencies are under civilian control. Some are part of the military. Civilian intelligence agencies like the CIA are subject to oversight by

Congress, but that is not true of military intelligence. The National Security Agency (NSA) is part of the Defense Department. It was an unacknowledged entity for decades, and for that reason, it was often referred to as "No Such Agency." Since civilian intelligence agencies had become corrupt, parallel investigations of corruption were begun by military intelligence (MI) agencies.

The next post is long; it contains important information about the NSA, the CIA, and Edward Snowden. A summary of relevant takeaways will follow the post.

Jan 6th 2019

When will the public discover that Ted Cruz was also illegally SURV (pre_POTUS_R nomination)?

C_A 'illegal' SURV > members of Congress?

C_A 'illegal' SURV > members of the Press?

C_A 'illegal' SURV > SENATE INTEL COMM?

https://www.theguardian.com/us-news/2016/sep/10/cia-senate-investigation-constitutional-crisis-daniel-jones

https://www.nytimes.com/2014/08/01/world/senate-intelligence-commitee-cia-interrogation-report.html

Who ordered the SURV?

What justification was provided to AUTH SURV of ELECTED OFFICIALS?

SURV fall under scope of FISA warrant or internal to Dept or outsourced to FVEY?

Reality check - friend or foe, we all spy on each other?

Should we be spying on ourselves?

Should we be tasking others to spy on ourselves in order to avoid U.S. law?

Was FVEY established designed by the INTEL COMM as a backchannel SURV apparatus to avoid domestic laws triggers and Congressional/Senate oversight?

What keylogs exist to monitor FVEY intel collection?

What ability do former GOV officials have re: ability to access C_LEVEL FVEY offshore data?

How did HRC gain access to highest CLAS SAPs (closed system access) and able to transfer to remote/home server?

(Q above should scare every single American)

How did CHINA locate primary C_A assets within CHINA [187]?

Money buys POWER.

No punishment [Brennan] by HUSSEIN ADMIN re: SURV of Senate etc?

Logical thinking, why?

https://www.mcclatchydc.com/news/nation-world/national/national-security/article24770296.html

Justice Dept declines to pursue?

Fake News media limits exposure to public?

When did @Snowden breach NSA PUBLICLY RELEASE (CRIPPLE) INTEL GATHERING ABILITY (NSA)?

NSA targeted?

Where did @Snowden work prior to NSA contractor ACCEPT?

What SENIOR LEVEL GOV/C_A OFFICIAL rec @Snowden for NSA contractor OFF/TAR position?

Post public release of CLAS NSA PRO > U1?

Where is @Snowden today?

What country was involved in U1?

If real target country was VENEZUELA or ECUADOR - why didn't @Snowden take a direct flight from Hong Kong to those locations?

How many direct flights run daily from HK to VE?

If @Snowden was C_A/NSA would he not understand (simple logic) going public

PRIOR TO END DESTINATION SAFETY would 'LIMIT' ACTIVE PASSPORT TRAVEL ABILITY due to block_DEREG?

WHY WOULDN'T @Snowden PUBLICLY RELEASE INFO AFTER HE ALREADY WAS SAFELY AT FINAL DESTINATION?

Why then would @Snowden route through RUSSIA?

Was RUSSIA final destination?

Was RUSSIA true destination?

Could @Snowden be seen releasing CLAS programs/intel FROM INSIDE OF RUSSIA?

What role did BRENNAN PLAY in the @Snowden leaks re: NSA?

What was BRENNAN's background re: SAUDI ARABIA?

Does the C_A hold blackmail on political leaders?

Does the C_A protect those who protect them?

Why are ex C_A contractors running for office?

How many ex C_A contractors are currently in office?

Hello, [AS].

Once an agent, always an agent.

Q

Q said that in addition to Donald Trump, the Ted Cruz campaign was spied on by the Obama administration in 2016. Q asked about the illegal spying the CIA did on members of Congress, the press, and the Senate Intelligence Committee. Q then mentioned the so-called *five eyes* agreement (FVEY) in which Canada, the United Kingdom, Australia, New Zealand, and the United States conduct joint surveillance of member nations. Domestic surveillance laws prevent these nations from spying on their own citizens. The five eyes agreement is a backchannel by which governments circumvent surveillance laws and permit other countries to spy on their own citizens and pass the information along.

Q implied that Hillary Clinton's security clearance gave her access to highly classified intelligence (Special Access Programs) that she kept on an unsecured server. Special Access Programs (SAPs) are some of the most highly classified government secrets. They contain information on matters such as the deployment of submarines and special forces. Q suggested that Hillary sold access to SAPs to China, which enabled their government to locate and kill or imprison more than a dozen CIA agents during her tenure as Secretary of State.

Edward Snowden is considered by many to be a hero for leaking to *The Guardian* information about the NSA's surveillance programs. Q highlighted things about Snowden that are not reported by the mainstream media. Before becoming an NSA contractor, Snowden worked for the CIA. The NSA uses a number of programs to collect and analyze information shared on the internet and in private communications. Two of those programs are PRISM and XKeyscore. After he had gained access to the PRISM and XKeyscore programs, Snowden flew to Hong Kong, where he illegally leaked classified information about them to reporters.

Jan 27, 2019
HK allowed his passport to clear customs WITH THE CLOWNS IN AMERICA AND DEPT OF DEFENSE PUTTING A NAT SEC HOLD WW?
How does he clear customs?
How does he end up in Russia?
Coincidence?
Who was the 1st agency he worked for?
Who taught him the game?
Who assigned him w/ foreign ops?
Why is this relevant?
Future unlocks past.
Watch the news.
Spider web.
Stop taking the sleeping pill.
Q

With an international security hold placed on Snowden's passport, he somehow managed to fly to Russia. Q has suggested the CIA facilitated his travel. It has been reported that Snowden intended to fly to Venezuela or Ecuador but became stranded in Russia. Q has suggested his original destination was Russia. Of course, it would look terrible if he leaked the information from Russia, so he first visited Hong Kong to leak the information there, creating the appearance that his motives were altruistic. The end game for the CIA appears to be the destruction of public trust in the NSA. If the public distrusted the NSA, it would move the CIA one step closer to a time when they might usurp the NSA's domestic surveillance authority. (The CIA's charter at present only permits surveillance outside the United States.) Q closed the message by asking why so many former CIA agents were trying to be elected to Congress and hinted that Congressman Adam Schiff [AS] was once a CIA asset and is still under their control.

In November of 2018, Q asked about the NSA Q group.

Nov 12, 2017
◆◆◆
What is No Such Agency - Q group?
Who has clearance to full picture?
Important.
SIS is good.
+++Adm R+++
What agency is at war w/ Clowns In America?
◆◆◆

The National Security Agency has employees who specialize in different areas. The agency is organized into sub-groups called "directorates." The directorates are given letter designations. The "E" directorate corresponds to the agency's Education Division. The "D" directorate corresponds to the agency's Director. The Q directorate corresponds to the Security and Counterintelligence Division, which is their police force. Among other duties, they investigate leaks and security breaches within the NSA. After Edward Snowden illegally leaked files from the NSA, the Q directorate was responsible for finding him and bringing him to justice.

In a world where most communication is done via computers, phones, and tablets, electronic signals carry the bulk of information that is shared around the globe. Signals Intelligence (sometimes abbreviated SIGINT) is the science of gathering, storing, and decoding these communications. It's what the NSA does. If you were able to gather and categorize the discussions of the world's most powerful and wealthy people, it would tell you what's happening behind closed doors on the geopolitical scene. It would give you what Q calls the 40,000-foot view. People like Admiral Rogers and the NSA's Q directorate have access to the full picture.

During the last 70 years, our governments have created an intelligence apparatus capable of accessing and storing all our private information. What purpose does it serve?

Imagine that the NSA picked up the transmission of an email where people discussed a plan to detonate a bomb in a public building. The FBI could obtain a warrant to access that information. If the NSA deemed the threat credible, they might alert the appropriate law enforcement agencies. The NSA's collection of our data is intended to keep us safe, but when corrupt people gain access to it, we can expect it to be used for nefarious purposes.

Snowden's leak of information has made the public aware that our intelligence agencies have been abused. But Snowden's story, as told by the press, presents a skewed perspective of the problem and hides the most dangerous types of abuse. If we're going to end the current misuse of intelligence gathering, we must understand how it happened so we can demand that reasonable safeguards be put in place to prevent it from happening again. When I began my investigation of Q, I was relatively ignorant about government surveillance. My research uncovered details that have been ignored by the mainstream media. I'll explain in layman's terms the relevant laws that define the use of surveillance, how our intelligence agencies were misused, and the role Admiral Rogers played in uncovering the abuse.

Electronic Surveillance

The National Security Agency maintains a database that is used by intelligence and law enforcement agencies to obtain information on the targets of their investigations. The 4th amendment protects citizens from unreasonable search and seizure. This protection extends to electronic surveillance. Non-citizens are not granted the same protection as citizens, and our surveillance laws reflect these differences.

In the United States, two laws authorize two different types of electronic surveillance. Title III of The Omnibus Crime Control and Safe Streets Act of 1968 applies to U.S. citizens. The Foreign Intelligence Surveillance Act (FISA) of 1978 applies to non-citizens.

Title III surveillance, because it applies to U.S. citizens, provides tighter restrictions. It requires a court warrant for intercepting electronic communications. It regulates the use and disclosure of information obtained through surveillance, and conditions must be met before authorization for surveillance is granted.

Probable cause is defined as the reasonable belief that a crime was committed and that the suspect in question committed it. To obtain a warrant for Title III surveillance, there must be probable cause to believe the target has committed, is committing, or is about to commit a crime. There must be probable cause to believe that communications related to the crime will be obtained by surveillance. Furthermore, there must be probable cause to believe that facilities to be surveilled are being used in connection with the offense. Additionally, normal investigative techniques must have been tried and failed—or are believed unlikely to succeed if tried.

Because FISA surveillance generally deals with non-citizens, it is less restrictive than Title III and is easier to use for corrupt purposes. There are a couple of types of FISA surveillance we need to discuss. FISA Title I pertains to the electronic surveillance of persons inside the United States. FISA Title VII involves electronic monitoring outside the United States. Title VII is divided into several subsections. Section 702 of Title VII pertains to the surveillance of non-citizens outside the United States, and it is the type of surveillance we will discuss throughout the rest of the chapter.

There are different ways to search for information on an individual (commonly referred to as a "target") in the NSA database. You can search for messages sent "to" or received "from" a targeted person. Generally, a name, email, or phone number is used (selected) as the search term. Because the target must be either the sender or receiver, this type of query returns a small data set.

The database can also be searched using the "about" option. In this case, all communications about the target (from virtually anyone) will be returned when the search term is found somewhere in a message. An "about" search returns a much larger data set. Targeting procedures are designed to ensure that only foreign persons located outside the U.S. are targeted for foreign intelligence collection under Section 702.

When searching for information on a non-citizen, data on U.S. citizens is inadvertently collected. These occurrences must be handled in a way that is consistent with 4th amendment protections. Minimization is the practice of maintaining the necessary privacy of information that is incidentally collected on U.S. citizens. Minimization procedures are intended to restrict the ability of analysts to search "raw" intelligence (data that has not been minimized) using an identifier, such as a name, email, or telephone number of a U.S. person. When a U.S. citizen is found in a search, their identifying information is anonymized. They will be called "U.S. person #1" or something similar.

Oversight of foreign intelligence surveillance is conducted by the Foreign Intelligence Surveillance Court (FISC), which reviews the government's certifications, targeting, and minimization procedures, and compliance with applicable laws.

Oversight of the intelligence agencies that access the NSA database is the responsibility of the Department of Justice National Security Division (NSD). The NSD conducts joint reviews with the Office of Director of National Intelligence (ODNI). Both agencies are required to report incidents of non-compliance to the Foreign Intelligence Surveillance Court.

Unlike Title I and Title III FISA surveillance, section 702 surveillance (because it pertains strictly to non-citizens) does not require court approval. Section 702 collection happens in an ongoing fashion. The ODNI and Department of Justice provide annual certifications to the FISA court regarding section 702 compliance.

Surveillance of the Trump Campaign

Carter Page, a volunteer with Donald Trump's 2016 Presidential campaign, was targeted by the FBI for surveillance using FISA Title I—which, by law, requires probable cause to believe he was an agent of a foreign power. Why was Page targeted for surveillance?

A person under FISA surveillance has all of their electronic communications monitored. Every email, phone call, and text message they send is collected and analyzed. In addition, every person in their circle of contacts has their electronic communications monitored. This first circle of contacts is referred to as the first hop because electronic monitoring leapfrogs (or "hops") from an individual to larger and larger circles of contacts. Under FISA surveillance, every contact of anyone in the first circle also has all their electronic communications monitored. This second circle of contacts is called a second hop. Each person in the second hop, likewise, has all of their contacts under electronic surveillance. FISA surveillance allows the collection and analysis of communications three "hops" away from the target, meaning potentially more than a million people could be under surveillance through a single FISA warrant.

The goal of obtaining a FISA warrant on Carter Page was not to spy on him but on his contacts—specifically, his contacts in the Trump campaign.

The FBI's investigation of Donald Trump's campaign was officially opened on July 31st of 2016 after the bureau received information that a staffer,

George Papadopoulos, may have colluded with someone who was said to be a Russian asset. A timeline of events suggests the FBI was scrutinizing people related to the Trump campaign much earlier.

On February 26th, 2016, *Reuters* reported that Lt. General Michael Flynn was advising the Trump campaign.

On February 29th, Paul Manafort made his first contact with the Trump campaign. (CNN later reported that he was under surveillance at that time.)

Carter Page said the FBI first considered spying on him on March 2nd of 2016. (His comments were made in a December 2019 interview with Maria Bartiromo.) At the time, Mr. Page was helping the FBI with a case involving a Russian national by the name of Evgeny Buryakov. In a meeting on March 2nd, 2016, he informed the FBI that he was joining the Trump campaign. Soon thereafter, according to him, the bureau began looking for a way to surveil him.

In early March of 2016, George Papadopoulos interviewed for a position on the Trump campaign.

On March 9th, 2016, during a minimization review, the Department of Justice learned that the FBI had disclosed to "an agency largely staffed by private contractors" raw FISA information, "including but not limited to Section 702-acquired information."

The discovery was disclosed in a 99-page ruling by presiding FISA court judge, Rosemary Collyer. Footnotes on pages 86 and 87 of the ruling lead one to believe the contractors may have worked for the CIA. An "interagency memorandum of understanding" is mentioned in the footnotes, and there is discussion about whether disclosures made to the contractors were made to private individuals or to a government agency.

The disclosures of 702 information weren't accidental. A footnote on page 87 of the ruling said the improper access "seems to have been the result of deliberate decision making." In noting the "FBI's apparent disregard of minimization rules," Collyer wondered "whether the FBI may be engaging in similar disclosures of raw Section 702 information that have not been reported."

On the same day, FBI attorney Lisa Page (no relation to Carter Page) sent a text to FBI agent Peter Strzok: "Need to try to fix a HUGE who f-up." Ms. Page then corrected her typo by texting "Wfo"—an abbreviation for the FBI's Washington field office. Apparently, contractors in the FBI's Washington field office were caught conducting illegal 702 searches. Later that day, Ms. Page sent another text to agent Strzok: "Need to go meet with andy again now." (Andy was then-Deputy FBI Director Andrew McCabe.) Following the discovery, Admiral Rogers ordered a 702 compliance review. On April 18th, he halted access to 702 searches to outside contractors.

On March 11th, 2016 (two days after the discovery of illegal 702 searches) Evgeny Buryakov pled guilty to criminal conspiracy and failing to register as a foreign agent. He and his accomplices tried to gather economic intelligence on behalf of Russia and recruit New York residents as intelligence sources. One of the people they tried to recruit was Carter Page. Page assisted the government's investigation by meeting with Buryakov and his accomplices—giving them binders full of information. Listening devices had been concealed inside the binders. Carter Page played a key role in helping the U.S. government expose and prosecute a Russian espionage operation.

After Buryakov's case was closed, the FBI applied for a FISA warrant to surveil Carter Page. To do so, they had to convince a FISA judge that he was acting as an agent of Russia. The DOJ Inspector General's report on the FBI's handling of Mr. Page's FISA application revealed an astounding level of deception by the bureau. An attorney for the FBI emailed the CIA to asked if Carter Page was one of their sources. The response confirmed that Mr. Page *was* a CIA source, but the FBI Office of General Counsel (OGC) attorney who received the reply added text to the email, making it appear as if he was *not* a CIA source. A second application to the FISA court included this falsified report and salacious and unverified information from a dossier created by former British spy Christopher Steele, who admitted he would do anything to keep Donald Trump from being elected. (A *dossier* is a loose collection of information of things such as notes, copies of emails, receipts, travel itineraries, etc. Although such information may be used in a formal intelligence report, a dossier differs in that it is not structured and often contains information that has not been verified.) The media lauded the information found in Steele's dossier, but the Inspector General report on the handling of Page's FISA application said the dossier was pure fiction.

On March 14th, George Papadopoulos traveled to Rome and met with Joseph Mifsud.

On March 16th, FBI agent Peter Strzok texted Lisa Page: "Our guy is talking."

On March 17th, Papadopoulos returned to London.

On March 21st, both Papadopoulos and Carter Page joined the Trump campaign.

On March 28th, Paul Manafort joined the Trump campaign as their convention manager.

On May 10th, 2016, George Papadopoulos met with Australian Commissioner Alexander Downer in a London pub. Papadopoulos allegedly discussed the idea that Russia may have had compromising information on Hillary Clinton. Conversations were abuzz at the time with rumors and speculation on that subject since the FBI's investigation of Hillary's email scandal was in full swing, and it was the subject of daily news reports. Papadopoulos noted that Downer recorded their conversation. When comparing publicly released emails and texts between FBI personnel, it appears that the FBI's head of counterintelligence, Bill Priestap was in London at the same time. Priestap would later formally open a counterintelligence investigation of the Trump campaign based on allegations made by Downer about Papadopoulos.

Kushner, Manafort, and Don Jr.

Nine months earlier, in October of 2015, Natalya Veselnitskaya, a Russian attorney and lobbyist, applied for a visa to represent a Cyprus-based company that was being sued by the U.S. government. Her visa request was denied. The Department of Justice (headed by Loretta Lynch) then took a highly unusual step. Lynch permitted her to come to the U.S. under "immigration parole," which allowed Veselnitskaya to travel here for court proceedings from October of 2015 through January 7th of 2016. In January, Veselnitskaya returned to Russia. In March of 2016, U.S. Attorney Preet Bharara denied a second request for a visa, saying that she and her client were not required to appear in court personally. In June of 2016, she was allowed back into the U.S., this time by the State Department (headed by John Kerry). That move was questioned since, according to the DOJ, Veselnitskaya had no legitimate reason to return to the United States.

On June 3rd, 2016, Rob Goldstone emailed Donald Trump Jr., saying Russian pop star Emin Agalarov asked him to arrange a meeting to provide the Trump campaign with opposition research that would incriminate Hillary Clinton. Don Jr. didn't know at the time who he would be meeting or what information would be provided. On June 7th, he confirmed a meeting at Trump Tower with himself, Paul Manafort, and Jared Kushner for June 9th.

The meeting on June 9th was with a group of people that included Natalya Veselnitskaya. Trump's people were offered no information on Hillary Clinton. Instead, Veselnitskaya made a case for changes to the Magnitsky Act, a cause for which Vladimir Putin had given her virtually unlimited resources as a lobbyist. It appears as if she was sent to Trump Tower to create the appearance that Trump's people were conspiring with an agent of Vladimir Putin in an attempt to influence the election.

The Guardian reported that in the lead up to the 2016 election, the FBI requested FISA warrants on Lt. General Michael Flynn, George Papadopoulos, Carter Page, and Paul Manafort.

Q agreed with *The Guardian* story and also said these men were entered into Robert Mueller's investigation, and threatened with prosecution to keep them quiet about the illegal surveillance that was used against them. As this book goes to print, only Carter Page's FISA has been confirmed to the public.

Aug 31 2018
Special Approval
P729173009391_Z
[SETUP EX 1]
http://thehill.com/homenews/administration/342118-homeland-security-confirms-special-entry-for-russian-lawyer
[LL]>paper trail>special entry
[Natalia Veselnitskaya]>Manafort
FISA warrant issued / approved>Manafort
Mueller>>Manafort
FISA warrant issued / approved>Papadopoulos
Mueller>>Papadopoulos
FISA warrant issued / approved>Page
Mueller>>Page
FISA warrant issued / approved>FLYNN
Mueller>>FLYNN
YOU MUST TARGET, REMOVE, AND SILENCE ALL THOSE ILLEGALLY TARGETED FOR FISA SURV + UK ASSIST.
UK ASSIST + FISA SURV INCLUDED ALL UPSTREAM COLLECTION + TANGENT CONTACTS [UMBRELLA SURV].
FOREIGN TARGET DESIGNATOR(S) CREATE LEAPFROG (HOPS) TO ISOLATED 'REAL' TARGET(S) NON F_COMMS.
[SEC 702]

♦♦♦

Q suggested there was a paper trail that might incriminate Loretta Lynch for approving Veselnitskaya's admission to the United States.

Carter Page was the only member of the Trump campaign under surveillance who was not prosecuted. The risk of prosecuting him was too high, given what the public might learn about the FBI's questionable motives and unlawful methods.

May 23, 2019
Important to remember.
Page is public.

Remainder are still classified.
+Cruz
Q

A Race Against Time

The DOJ National Security Division is required to file an annual Section 702 compliance certification. In September of 2016, the 702 compliance review Admiral Rogers ordered in April was not yet finalized, but the DOJ was well aware of the non-compliance problems. On September 26th, 2017, John P. Carlin, head of the National Security Division, filed the annual certification but omitted the compliance problems found by Rogers. Carlin announced his resignation the following day, effective October 15th. The timing of his resignation makes one wonder if he was worried about the consequences of an untruthful compliance report. The FBI's application for surveillance of Carter Page had not yet been approved, and those who submitted the request were in a race against time. They wanted surveillance approval before Rogers received news about the compliance audit, which would expose their misuse of the 702 process.

On October 15th, Carlin officially left the DOJ. Five days later, on October 20th, Admiral Rogers was briefed by the NSA's compliance officer about the findings of the compliance audit. The audit uncovered numerous "about" query violations. The following day, October 21st, Rogers halted all "about" searches and reported his findings to the DOJ. On the same day, the FBI's request for surveillance of Carter Page was approved. Three days later, on October 24th, 2016, Rogers verbally reported to the FISA court his findings, and two days later, he appeared formally before the court to brief them.

One might argue that the request to surveil Carter Page would have been denied had Rogers gotten his report to the court sooner, but that probably isn't true. Section 702 non-compliance wasn't a new problem. The NSA and the FISA court had been down this road dozens of times in the previous 15 years. This was only the most recent transgression.

Media outlets have attempted to create a firewall to contain the public's suspicion of criminality regarding surveillance of the Trump campaign. Before the IG report on Carter Page's FISA was made public, *The Washington Post* published a series of articles claiming only low-level FBI employees are implicated. But Q suggested the criminality goes all the way to the oval office.

Aug 29th 2018
What if a paper-trail exists...

PDB via No Such Agency?
HUSSEIN made aware w/ no action?
Why did POTUS refuse 'select' PDBs during transition?
Who knew?
Threat assessment.
Adm Rogers?
FLYNN?
♦♦♦
Q

Q implied that the information obtained by FISA surveillance was placed in the Presidential Daily Brief (PDB) and that a paper trail exists which would incriminate anyone who knowingly participated. That would include people like then-DNI James Clapper, former CIA Director John Brennan, and President Obama. Q hinted that the reason President-elect Trump refused certain briefings before he was inaugurated was to reduce his exposure to criminal liability.

There is a legitimate use for the intelligence gathering capability of the NSA, but there is tremendous potential for abuse. Powerful people have abused our intelligence apparatus in the past, but Donald Trump, Admiral Rogers, and other military leaders are striving to bring that abuse to an end. A system of checks and balances will be put in place to assure that it never happens again, as Q pointed out in the following post.

Feb 12 2019
POTUS: "This can never be allowed to happen again (in our Country or to another President)."
How do you deter & prevent this from happening again?
Simply by terminating employment of those responsible?
Simply by conducting a few 'non-threatening' investigations?
Or by:
Prosecuting those responsible to the fullest extent of the law?
Setting up new checks & balances and oversight designed to increase transparency?
Provide OIG office(s) w/ funding inc (size) ++ authority?
Provide select committees w/ access and in-house viewing of non NAT SEC CLAS material?
Provide a check on Directors/Dep Directors/Asst Directors of all such ABC agencies?
Establish 'financial checks/reviews' of those in senior (critical) positions

(audits) + direct family (close proximity)?

Transparency and Prosecution is the only way forward to save our Republic and safeguard such criminal and treasonous acts from occurring again.

While some want to quietly remove those responsible and go about our business (save face on the World Stage), those in control, understand, this band-aid will simply not work.

Nobody should be above the law (no matter how massive the spider-web is (entangled)).

This will never happen again.

TRUTH WORKS.

FACTS MATTER.

Q

The U.S. President is elected in November and inaugurated the following January. During the two months between the election and inauguration, the President-elect meets with a team of people who help them plan out their transition into the oval office. After the 2016 election, President-elect Trump was meeting with his transition team at Trump Tower in New York. Nine days after he was elected, Admiral Rogers made an unapproved visit to Trump Tower to give his team an intelligence briefing.

Mar 26 2019

Think Rogers T-Tower meeting (right after SCIF set up in Tower).

Think POTUS campaign leaving T-Tower (base of operations) THE VERY NEXT DAY.

1+1=2

Q

Q mentioned that Admiral Rogers set up a SCIF in Trump Tower. A Sensitive Compartmented Information Facility (SCIF) is a secure room where classified briefings are given. A SCIF is intended to be impervious to electronic eavesdropping. (Since electronic surveillance is most easily done by monitoring a phone, electronic devices like tablets and phones are not usually allowed inside a SCIF.) We don't know the subject matter of the briefing, but it has been theorized that, among other things, Rogers informed Trump's team that the Obama intelligence community had them under surveillance. The fact that the transition team moved its operation to Trump's golf course in Bedminster, New Jersey, the following day, makes one suspect that Trump Tower itself was under surveillance. Rogers made his trip to Trump Tower without approval from his supervisors in the Obama administration. Ash Carter was Admiral Rogers' supervisor at the Pentagon. Then-Director of National Intelligence James Clapper was his civilian supervisor. On November 19th, 2016, *The Washington Post* reported that sometime in October of 2016, Carter and Clapper had advised Barack Obama to replace Admiral Rogers as head of the NSA. That time frame coincided with Rogers' attempts to remedy Section 702 abuse. Obama likely knew that replacing Rogers would only draw more attention to their activities. The unapproved meeting with Trump's transition team led to another call by Carter and Clapper to replace Rogers.

Admiral Rogers retired on May 4th, 2018, after a long and distinguished career with the Navy, the NSA, and Cybercommand.

In 2019, William Barr became President Trump's attorney general. It was then announced that U.S. Attorney John Durham would be investigating crimes related to the surveillance of the Trump campaign. But in fact, Durham had been investigating these matters far longer. Thanks to a declassified Congressional interview between Congressman Jim Jordan and former FBI Chief Counsel James Baker, we know that Durham was investigating Baker for illegally leaking information to the press at least as far back as October 3rd of 2018.

On July 9th, 2019, Q hinted that Admiral Rogers' retirement served a strategic purpose and that he had been meeting with Attorney General Barr (AG) and Durham to assist in their investigation.

July 9, 2019
AG Rogers meeting?
Durham Rogers meeting(s)?
Why did Rogers retire?
Why did Rogers visit POTUS @ TT w/o authorization shortly after a SCIF was installed?
Why did select former ABC directors call for the removal of Rogers?
Why did POTUS move his transition command center (base of ops) from TT the VERY NEXT DAY?
Q

On December 20th, 2019, *The Intercept* published an exclusive report confirming that Admiral Rogers was cooperating with Barr and Durham in their investigation of corruption. It's my belief that history books will one day report how Admiral Rogers played a crucial role in the removal of global corruption and the restoration of trust in government.

CHAPTER 12

Barack [Hussein] Obama

MY FIRST POLITICAL SCIENCE CLASS taught me that many politicians run for office with the expectation of becoming rich at the expense of taxpayers. I've never trusted politicians. Whether liberal, conservative, or somewhere in the middle, I never expected one to keep a campaign promise. My distrust of them may be the reason I adopted the practice of keeping my expectations low. If you don't have high expectations, you won't be disappointed. Generally, politicians make whatever promises are necessary to get elected. Once in office, they work for those who fund their campaigns.

Barack Obama was elected President of the United States in 2008. I didn't care for his policies, but I didn't despise him personally. The political pendulum swings predictably to the left and then to the right. After twelve years under Republican Presidents Ronald Reagan and George Herbert Walker Bush, the pendulum swung to the left, and Americans elected Bill Clinton, who served two terms. George W. Bush served two terms, and then Barack Obama served two terms. Not long after he was elected, rumors began circulating that Obama, although professing to be a Christian, was secretly planted in our government by Islamists who intended to subvert our national sovereignty.

Not being interested in conspiracy theories, I ignored these rumors. God instructs us to pray for our leaders, so for the eight years that Barack Obama was in office, I did my best to pray for him. I used my social media accounts to lead others to do the same. With that backdrop in place, we turn to the 44th President of the United States, Barack Hussein Obama, who is referred to by Q in various ways including by the initials "BO" and his middle name "Hussein." In the post below, Q asked about Barack Obama's Secret Service (USSS) code name.

Dec 9 2017
What was the USSS codename for Hussein?
[R]
Define.
They knew all along.
Expand your thinking.
Q

An anon responded to Q's question:

Anonymous
Renegade

Q replied:

A person who deserts and betrays an organization, country, or set of principles.
They always knew.
Q

When the text messages between FBI agent Peter Strzok and FBI attorney Lisa Page were made public, the world learned that Barack Obama was referred to by them simply by the letter "R." Q clarified so there wouldn't be confusion between the initials used for Obama (R) and those used for former Deputy Attorney General Rod Rosenstein (RR). The single letter R pertains only to Obama when he is being referred to in text messages between Strzok and Page.

Apr 26 2018
Important to note [texts only].
[R] = Renegade
Not RR.
Q

On July 1st, 2015, at a news conference, Saudi Prince Alwaleed bin Talal announced that he intended to give away his entire fortune in the coming years. Alwaleed told reporters, "With this pledge, I am honoring my life-long commitment to what matters most—helping to build a more peaceful, equitable, and sustainable world for generations to come."

Alwaleed's statement was well received by the press. How do you criticize someone who promises to give away tens of billions of dollars to charitable causes? Perhaps the question we ought to ask is: How do you reconcile the claim to wanting peace when you're the member of a royal family in a country where practicing Christianity sometimes results in death?

One way in which Alwaleed demonstrated his philanthropy was by establishing centers for Islamic study at prestigious universities. Georgetown University received a $20 million grant to establish the Prince Alwaleed bin Talal Center for Muslim-Christian Understanding. Harvard University received $20 million to create an Islamic study center, as did Cambridge and Edinburgh Universities in the UK and the American Universities in Beirut and Cairo.

Aug 28 2018

◆◆◆

Who paid HUSSEIN to attend HARVARD LAW SCHOOL?
Who is Prince Alwaleed bin Talal?
Why would Prince Alwaleed bin Talal (Saudi Royal) pay HUSSEIN to attend HARVARD LAW SCHOOL?
Was HUSSEIN a prominent political figure or a person of influence at the time?
No.
Who is Valerie Jarrett?
Where was she born?
When did Valerie Jarrett hire Michelle Robinson?
1991
Timeline.

◆◆◆

Q has suggested that Saudi Arabia has maintained control over U.S. politicians in several ways, including helping to finance their educations. When it comes to Saudi funding of higher education in the U.S., no one has been more influential than Prince Alwaleed bin Talal. Several news outlets have reported that Saudi Arabia may have helped finance the Harvard education of Barack Obama. A September 23rd, 2008, *NewsMax* article reported that Percy Sutton said a former business partner approached him in 1988 to help Obama get into Harvard Law School. (The Obama camp has denied Sutton's claim.) Sutton also said he first heard of Obama twenty years earlier from Khalid al-Mansour. Sutton described al-Mansour as an advisor to Saudi Prince Alwaleed bin Talal.

Chicago Tribune columnist Vernon Jarrett wrote in a 1979 column that al-Mansour said wealthy Arabs had planned to spend $20 million a year for ten years to aid minority students and to encourage them to support Arab causes. Vernon Jarrett was the father-in-law of Obama's senior advisor Valerie Jarrett, who was born in Iran.

Valerie Jarrett was Chicago Mayor Daley's Chief of Staff when she hired Michelle Robinson in 1991. Michelle married Barack Obama the following year.

In 2016, during the race for the White House, Hillary Clinton's use of a private email server while serving as Secretary of State came under the scrutiny of the Federal Bureau of Investigation. The bureau's director, James Comey, took the highly unusual step of publicly announcing his decision not to recommend prosecution. (Normally, the FBI would investigate the allegation and leave the prosecution determination to the Department of Justice.)

Oct 29 2017
Why wasn't HRC prosecuted for the emails? Put simply, Obama ultimately OK'd by using the non govt email addy to communicate w/ Clinton. Obama also had an alias along with each of his cabinet members. Therefore indicting HRC would lead to indicting Obama & his cabinet etc which could never happen. Remember he lied about knowing but that ultimately came out in the dump. Poof!

According to Q, Hillary wasn't prosecuted because Barack Obama—by using his own private email address to communicate with her—gave tacit approval of her use of an unsecured server. If she were prosecuted, he and his cabinet members—who also used private emails—could be prosecuted as well. Although Obama denied using a private email address for government business, it was proven that he did in emails published by *WikiLeaks*.

In the next post, Q discussed Barack Obama and North Korea.

Nov 2 2017
Would it blow your mind if I told you BO has been to NK and perhaps there now?
Why did his administration do little to slow their nuclear and missle

capabilities?

Who feeds NK w/ strategic intel? Iran?

What deal was done with Iran under BO?

Why was the deal sealed under a top secret classification?

Why wasn't Congress notified?

Why after BO left office all of a sudden NK has nukes and the tech to miniaturize for payload delivery within the US?

What about NSA CIA DI etc all confirming tech won't be in place for 5+ years (statements made in 2016).

Why is all of this relevant and what does it tell you?

Big picture is rare.

In 2016, U.S. intelligence agencies assured us that North Korea was at least five years away from having the capability of producing a nuclear bomb, but suddenly, after Donald Trump was inaugurated, North Korea was believed to have that capability. Q suggested that North Korea obtained intelligence from Iran and that the Obama administration (covertly) assisted with the development of Iranian and North Korean nuclear weapons programs while denying they had the capability.

Thirty-three minutes after posting the previous message, Q posted this:

Nov 2 2017

What a coincidence the mountain that housed NK's nuclear weapons and testing collapsed. Unbelievable timing. I wonder if critically important materials as well as scientists aka the bomb makers were inside when it happened. Shocking no global news agency suspects we had nothing to do with it. Enjoy the crumbs.

Did Donald Trump use a classified technology to destroy North Korea's weapons facility? More importantly, why didn't previous Presidents do more to impede North Korea's development of nuclear weapons?

In the following post, Q suggested that Barack Obama met with certain leaders for a specific reason before and after President Trump met with them.

29 Nov 2017

◆◆◆

Why does Hussein travel ahead of POTUS?

Why did Hussein travel behind POTUS?

Think Asia.
Think NK.
What was told re: NK during the past 8 years?
What dramatic shift occurred re: NK post election of POTUS?
Reconcile.
Define hostage.
The Sum of all Fears.
♦♦♦

Q asked what shift occurred regarding North Korea after Donald Trump was elected President. Previous administrations had little communication with leaders of North Korea, but Trump quickly engaged in discussions with Kim Jong-un.

Two months after the above post, *Fox News* published a report about Obama's former Secretary of State John Kerry meeting with Palestinian leaders and advising them not to negotiate with President Trump. Q posted a link to the article and highlighted Kerry's claim that Trump would soon be out of office.

Jan 25 2018
CONFIRMED.
http://www.foxnews.com/politics/2018/01/25/john-kerry-reportedly-coaches-palestinians-not-to-yield-to-trump-in-peace-talks-spurring-backlash.html
Why did HUSSEIN travel ahead of POTUS?
"Trump would not be in office for long, suggesting he could be out in a year."
Re-read crumbs.
Future unlocks past.
Q

Were Obama and Kerry undermining Trump negotiations by assuring world leaders that Robert Mueller's investigation would remove him from office?

In the following post, Q suggested that the sale of the North American company Uranium One (U1) to the Russian company Rosatom was not for the purpose that we were told.

Nov 22 2017
U1 - CA - EU - ASIA - IRAN/NK
Where did it end up?

What was the purpose?

Who was suppose to win the election of 2016?

Why was the Iran deal kept from Congress and placed at the highest level of classification?

Meaning, a United States Senator could NOT review the deal but other foreign powers could.

How much money was hand delivered by plane(s)?

Why in cash?

Where did the plane(s) actually land?

What was the cover?

Who paid for BO to attend Harvard?

Why would this occur pre-political days?

Who was the biggest contributor to the CF?

The graphic is the key.

Why does the MSM push conspiracy w/o investigation?

Who controls the MSM?

What does the word 'conspiracy' mean to you?

Has the word 'conspiracy' been branded to mean something shameful in today's society?

The world cannot handle the truth.

This pill cannot be swallowed by most.

Risk in painting this picture.

THE SUM OF ALL FEARS.

Q

Q provided a flowchart indicating that the uranium went from Canada to Europe, then Asia, and then to Iran and North Korea. There is a suggestion that the money supposedly sent to Iran didn't actually go to Iran. Since the planes were not tracked, it's hard to know where they went. Q suggested the hostage exchange connected to the Iran deal was a cover story, and that the full picture would sound so outrageous it would be rejected by most people as a conspiracy.

Sum of All Fears

The last line in this post, "THE SUM OF ALL FEARS" refers to the Tom Clancy novel about the U.S. and Russia being on the brink of nuclear war. Therefore, this post relates to a similar, real-life scenario. In the following post, there is a hint that one goal of the sale of Uranium One was to help rogue nations like Iran and North Korea obtain uranium through covert means.

Apr 30 2018
Define the terms of the Iran nuclear deal.
Does the agreement define & confine cease & desist 'PRO' to the republic of Iran?
What if Iran created a classified 'satellite' Nuclear facility in Northern Syria?
What if the program never ceased?
What other bad actors are possibly involved?
Did the U.S. know?
Where did the cash payments go?
How many planes delivered?
Did all planes land in same location?
Where did the U1 material end up?
Is this material traceable?
Yes.
Define cover.
What if U1 material ended up in Syria?
What would be the primary purpose?
SUM OF ALL FEARS.
In the movie, where did the material come from?
What country?
What would happen if Russia or another foreign state supplied Uranium to Iran/Syria?
WAR.
What does U1 provide?
Define cover.
Why did we strike Syria?
Why did we really strike Syria?
Define cover.
Patriots in control.
Q

Q suggested that part of the uranium from the Uranium One sale was secretly shipped to Iran and then Syria to assist them in developing their covert nuclear weapons program. The post coincided with the public announcement by Benjamin Netanyahu that Israeli intelligence had obtained evidence that Iran was operating a secret nuclear weapons facility in Syria. Because the Uranium One deal transferred uranium holdings to Russia, if it were discovered that Iran had obtained uranium, it would be traced back to Russia (not the U.S.), and they would be blamed for it. That would lead to heightened international tensions and possibly war, which Q suggested was part of the plan. Q also hinted that Trump's missile strike on Syria was an effort to obtain evidence of this plan under cover of a military operation.

The Iran Deal

A frequent topic mentioned by Q is the Joint Comprehensive Plan of Action (JCPOA), more commonly known as the "Iran deal." I'll provide a brief history of Iran's nuclear program and the negotiations that led to the Iran deal. Historical accounts can be tedious to read, but they are important. The intriguing details of corruption are often missing from mainstream media reports.

In April of 2006, Iran's President announced that they had enriched uranium for the first time. (The uranium was enriched to about 3.5 percent and was produced at the pilot enrichment plant in Natanz.)

On June 6th, 2006, China, France, Germany, Russia, the United Kingdom, and the United States (known as the P5+1, which refers to the five permanent members of the UN Security Council plus Germany) offered Iran incentives for halting its uranium enrichment program. Iran rejected the proposal.

On July 31st, 2006, the UN Security Council passed Resolution 1696, which demanded that Iran halt uranium enrichment.

On December 23rd, 2006, the UN Security Council unanimously adopted Resolution 1737, which imposed sanctions on Iran for refusing to suspend its uranium enrichment. The sanctions prohibited countries from transferring sensitive nuclear and missile-related technology to Iran, and required that all nations freeze the assets of ten Iranian organizations and twelve individuals for their involvement in Iran's nuclear and missile programs.

During his campaign for president in 2008, Barack Obama lamented the failures of his predecessor, George W. Bush, in dealing with middle east nations. Rather than military intervention, Obama said diplomacy would be more effective. Apparently, Iran's leaders wanted to know if he was serious about that statement.

In his book, *Alter Egos,* White House correspondent Mark Landler revealed how backchannel communications between Iran and the U.S. led to the negotiation of the Iran nuclear deal.

According to Landler, in May 2009, just four months after Obama took office, Dennis Ross, an advisor to then-Secretary of State Hillary Clinton, met a 51-year-old Omani named Salem ben Nasser al-Ismaily at the State Department. At that meeting, Ismaily offered Americans an opportunity to negotiate with Iran about their nuclear program. Obama had already sent a secret letter to Iran's Ayatollah Ali Khamenei proposing negotiations but had received a less than enthusiastic response. Ismaily assured Ross he could bring the Iranians to the negotiating table and suggested that Oman would be an ideal venue for secret negotiations.

When Iran imprisoned three American hikers in July 2009, Ismaily began secretly negotiating for their release. The first hiker was freed in September of 2010, and the other two were released a year later. Mr. Ismaily also facilitated the return to Tehran from the U.S. and U.K. four Iranians who were highly prized by their government.

John Kerry became acquainted with Ismaily during the hiker negotiations and made several visits to Oman in 2011 and 2012 and also met with him in London, Rome, and Washington. Kerry was still a Senator at the time and was unable to speak officially for the Obama administration. Nevertheless, he suggested that under a nuclear agreement, Iran would be able to continue enriching uranium—a demand by Iran's leaders that had thus far been rejected.

In 2013, Kerry was appointed Secretary of State, and Hassan Rouhani was elected president of Iran, replacing hardliner Mahmoud Ahmadinejad. Kerry met Iran's American-educated foreign minister Javad Zarif at the UN General Assembly in September of 2013. Soon thereafter, Obama and Rouhani spoke by telephone. Their conversation was highest-level official contact between the United States and Iran since 1979.

On November 24th, 2013, Javad Zarif and Catherine Ashton (leader of the P5+1 negotiating team) signed an agreement called the Joint Plan of Action. It outlined a first-phase nuclear agreement and provided a broad framework for further negotiations, which would lead to a final, comprehensive solution.

Almost two years later, on October 18th, 2015, Iran and the P5+1 formally adopted the nuclear deal known as the Joint Comprehensive Plan of Action (JCPOA). The plan would not be implemented until Iran made changes to its enrichment program. These changes would need to be verified by the International Atomic Energy Agency (IAEA). The United States issued waivers on nuclear-related sanctions, which would take effect when the plan was officially implemented. The European Union also passed legislation to lift sanctions upon implementation.

On January 16th, 2016, the IAEA verified that Iran had met its commitments for the implementation of the JCPOA. Based on the IAEA's report, implementation began, and sanctions were lifted.

On the following day, January 17th, the Obama State Department announced it had agreed to pay Iran $1.7 billion to settle a case related to the sale of military equipment prior to the 1979 Iranian revolution.

During the 38-year reign of the shah, Iran was one of the United States' closest allies in the Middle East and purchased billions of dollars' worth of U.S. arms. Weeks before its regime fell in 1979, Iran signed a new military agreement with the Carter administration valued at $400 million. American companies never delivered the weapons because of the Islamic revolution. That $400 million was frozen along with the suspension of diplomatic relations. Iran's claim to recapture the money had been tied up at the Hague Tribunal since 1981. The U.S. said it was returning the principal money invested in the fund along with $1.3 billion in owed interest. In addition to the $1.7 billion repayment (the details of which will be examined shortly), the Obama administration authorized the release of approximately $150 billion in previously frozen assets.

In the following post, Q asked a number of questions about the Iran deal.

Aug 28 2018
◆◆◆
How were the pallets of cash divided?
How many planes were used to transport?
Who operated the planes?
What 'shadow' agency directed operations?
Why wasn't the money [simply] wire transferred?
US had AUTH to open bank-to-bank transfers.
How do you prevent financial T logs?
How were the cash withdrawals in EU categorized/labeled?
Where did the cash originate from?
What time of day did the withdrawals occur?
Who provided SECURITY?
Why wasn't Congress notified?
Why was the U.S. Gov't kept in the DARK?
US law broken?
Did ALL planes land in the same location (airport)?
Why did [1] particular plane land outside of Iran?
Why was a helicopter involved?
[WHO] did the money go to?
HOW DO YOU AUDIT A FOREIGN AID BIG BLOCK TRANSFER?
Did Rouhani keep 'unknown' comms as insurance?
What agency did @Snowden work for orig?
Did he train on THE FARM?
When did @Snowden join No Such Agency?

Define 'Contractor'.
Define the 'PRISM' program.
What year did @Snowden release spec-details of PRISM?
Mid 2013?
IMPACT-LIMIT NSA's ability to utilize/collect?
FAKE NEWS push for Congressional restrictions?
OPEN SOURCE PUSH to create COUNTER-DEF?
PURPOSE?
BLUE SKIES FOR CLOWN OP?
When was the Joint Plan of Action (IRAN DEAL) executed?
Late 2013?
Do you believe in coincidences?
Nothing to See Here.
Q

At the time of the transfer of money to Iran, the Obama administration insisted the payment of cash and the release of previously frozen funds was not related to the implementation of the Iran deal, but later admitted it was an incentive to complete the deal. In January of 2016, no details of the money transfer were publicly available, but on August 3rd, 2016, Jay Solomon of *The Wall Street Journal* broke a story that reported some of the details.

The Obama administration secretly coordinated an airlift of $400 million in cash to Iran. The payment of cash coincided with the release of four Americans (including a journalist with *The Washington Post*) who had been detained in Tehran. In return, the U.S. released seven Iran nationals who were either jailed in the U.S. or facing charges. In addition, the U.S. agreed to drop the names of 14 Iranian nationals it had been seeking from the watch list of Interpol. The Obama administration came under fire when it was reported that the American prisoners in Tehran were not released until Iran had taken possession of the cash payment. Despite the appearance that the money was, in fact, a ransom payment, Obama insisted it was not.

The entire $1.7 billion was wired from the U.S. to the central banks of the Netherlands and Switzerland. The Obama administration said this arrangement was necessary because Iran did not have access to normal banking transactions due to sanctions. News reports have only described the transfer of $400 million in cash to Iran without reporting on what happened to the other $1.3 billion. *The Wall Street Journal* first reported that $400 million in cash was withdrawn in Swiss francs, Euros, and other currencies, and flown from Geneva to Iran on pallets in an unmarked cargo plane.

On August 24th, 2016, an article by *Fox News* provided information about the remaining $1.3 billion. State Department spokeswoman Elizabeth Trudeau said the U.S. government sent the wire transfers as 13 separate payments of $99,999,999.99 each, and a final payment of $10 million. (There was no explanation as to why the individual transactions were kept under $100 million each.) The money came from a little-known fund administered by the Treasury Department for settling litigation claims. The so-called "Judgment Fund" is taxpayer money Congress has permanently approved, which allows the President to bypass Congress to make settlements. On June 7th, 2017, then-Attorney General Jeff Sessions announced changes to the fund. The new policy would ensure that the "settlement funds are only used to compensate victims, redress harm, and punish and deter unlawful conduct."

One Obama official said the $1.3 billion was converted to cash and disbursed to a representative of Iran's central bank. Treasury, Justice, and State Department officials refused to cooperate with a Congressional investigation into the matter. When questioned by *The Washington Free Beacon,* a State Department official admitted they did not know how the $1.3 billion was transferred or to whom it was transferred.

Q suggested the wire transfers and conversion to cash were done *not* because Iran couldn't receive direct payment due to sanctions—as Obama had claimed—but because the details of the transactions had to be concealed since laws had been broken.

Q asked what "shadow" agency directed the operations. An August 3rd, 2016 article by Jay Solomon of *The Wall Street Journal* confirmed that the CIA and FBI were, at a minimum, involved in the prisoner exchange aspect of the deal, having met in Geneva with Iranian intelligence operatives in November and December of 2016.

Q asked if Iranian President Hassan Rouhani kept "unknown comms" as insurance against Obama and asked about Edward Snowden, writing, "Define the PRISM program."

Snowden was hired by the CIA in 2006. "The farm" is a CIA training facility in Virginia. Snowden became a contractor for the NSA in 2013—the same year the Iran deal was finalized. PRISM is an NSA program that allows the agency to collect user data from companies like Microsoft, Google, Apple, Yahoo, and other internet providers. (PRISM comes under the oversight of the Foreign Intelligence Surveillance Court.) Snowden leaked details of the PRISM program to *The Guardian* in June of 2013.

If Iranian President Rouhani had private communications that compromised Obama, the NSA likely had that information as well. There is a suggestion from

Q that the CIA inserted Snowden into the NSA so he could gain access to the NSA's programs, leak them, and cause Congress to demand the NSA's surveillance capabilities be curtailed. All of this was done to decrease the likelihood that Obama's plot would be exposed. It also provided cover for the CIA's operation, which Q alluded to in the post: "BLUE SKIES FOR CLOWN OP?"

The Obama administration cleverly concealed all the details of the money transfer and then, after some time had passed, threw the press a bone by disclosing how $400 million was transferred to Iran. Rather than being sent to Iran, Q said the $1.3 billion was converted to cash and transferred via several aircraft to different locations.

◆◆◆

Did ALL planes land in the same location (airport)?
Why did [1] particular plane land outside of Iran?
Why was a helicopter involved?
[WHO] did the money go to?
HOW DO YOU AUDIT A FOREIGN AID BIG BLOCK TRANSFER?

◆◆◆

On May 8th, 2018, President Trump announced that the U.S. was withdrawing its support for the JCPOA and imposing sanctions on Iran. On May 12th, Q provided more information about the Iran deal, including how many aircraft were used to transport the money and how many routes were taken to deliver it.

May 12 2018
Re_read crumbs re: Iran.
It was never about WW safety & security.
It was never about Nuclear disarmament.
It was about opening a new untapped market.
It was about securing a black site.
The 'Exchange'.
U1.
Risk the welfare of the world.
Why?
Money.
Organized/planned by BC/HRC.
Carried out by Hussein.
[remember HRC ran against Hussein]
U1 [donations to CF].

$1.7b in-cash transfer to Iran [4 routes][5 planes].
Did the total withdrawal actually depart EU?
Why EU?
Define bribe.
Define kickback.
Special Interest Groups (SIG).
What US/EU Co's Immediately closed large deals in Iran post deal?
https://www.nytimes.com/2018/05/09/business/iran-nuclear-trump-
business-europe.html
Cross check Co's against political + foundation payments.
Define bribe.
Define kickback.
Why are people panicking about Iran deal pullout?
THEY NEVER THOUGHT SHE WOULD LOSE.
Truth coming.
Q

On April 24th, 2018, President Trump met with French President Emmanuel Macron. Three days later, Trump met with German Chancellor Angela Merkel. Anons wondered about Macron's intentions.

Anonymous • Apr 24 2018
Q, is Macron a true ally to POTUS?

Q replied.

His sole purpose [WH visit] is to convince POTUS, on behalf of the EU, to remain in the Iran deal.
You decide.
Q

The goal of the meetings was to keep the U.S. in the Iran deal, which wasn't about nuclear disarmament but securing a "black site" for the covert development of nuclear weapons.

According to Q, the money from the Iran deal was never intended to reach Iran. It was wired to European central banks because the recipients were European leaders. The $1.3 billion was converted to cash, then given to them in exchange for their cooperation and silence. Five airplanes delivered the money to four destinations. (In the previous post, Q also said one helicopter was used.)

U.S. and European companies closed lucrative deals with Iranians soon after the Iran deal was announced. The linked article Q posted explained that automakers like Daimler and PSA Peugeot Citroën signed contracts with Iranian companies to sell vehicles. Siemens of Germany signed a deal to deliver locomotives. Total of France began an offshore natural gas exploration project. Some of those companies, according to Q, also made contributions to the Clinton Foundation. The scheme was hatched by Bill and Hillary Clinton (BC/HRC) and executed by Obama.

On April 23rd, 2018, the day before POTUS met with Emanuel Macron, Q posted this.

Apr 23 2018
Reminder.
Iran is next.
Marker.
CLAS - Sec 11A P 2.2.
"Installments."
$250B.
Jan 1.
Jun 1.
No inspection @ GZ NR sites.
No missile tech prevention.
Load carrying.
ICBM.
Think NK.
Who controls the $?
Who really controls the $?
Why does the EU have a vested interest in this deal?
Who receives the money?
When the US sends billions in aid and/or climate and/or etc who or what entity audits / tracks to confirm intended recipient(s) rec?
None.
How does GS fund WW counter-events?
Who funds WW leftist events?
American taxpayer (subsidize).
Define nuclear stand-off.
Who benefits?
How do you 'squeeze' funds out of the US?
Threat to humanity?

Environment push?
Think Paris accord.
Who audits / tracks the funneled money?
Define kickback.
Define slush fund.
EPA.
No oversight re: Hussein.
Why?
How does the C_A fund non sanctioned ops?
Off the books?
Re_ read past drops.
Will become relevant.
Welcome Mr. President.
The U.S. will NOT agree to continue the Iran deal as it currently stands.
Q

Q pointed out that there was no provision in the Iran deal to conduct legitimate inspections of nuclear sites. In what seems to be a related matter, on May 11th, three days after President Trump announced he was withdrawing support for the Iran deal, Tero Varjoranta, the Deputy Director General of the International Atomic Energy Agency unexpectedly quit his job.

An anon commented on the resignation:

Anonymous • May 12 2018
nuke inspector quit

Q replied.

Coincidence days after Iran deal withdrawal?
Corruption everywhere.
Q

Q implied that in addition to cash received at the time of the Iran deal, politicians also expected to receive bi-annual payments of $250 billion. If that is so, it provides a hefty incentive to remain in the deal. He added that many "causes" which are promoted as necessary to save the world, such as the Paris Climate Accord, are, in fact, scams that funnel taxpayer money to politicians and people like George Soros. Q reminded anons that none of these transactions are audited.

In the following post, Q brought up a number of issues. Each will be discussed separately.

Nov 6 2017
Why was the arrest of Alwaleed and others important?
How is Alwaleed and BO tied to HUMA?
Why did Alwaleed finance BO pre-political days?
Why did Alwaleed finance BO pre-political days?
What is HUMA? Define.
What book was BO caught reading?
Why was this immediately disregarded as false?
What is 'Post-American World by Fareed Zakaria'?
Why is this relevant?
Why would the President of the UNITED STATES OF AMERICA be reading this book?
What church did BO attend as pre-POTUS?
Who was BO's mentor?
How is Alwaleed and HRC connected?
Who was HRC's mentor?
How is Alwaleed and Bush Sr./Jr. connected?
What occurred post 9-11?
What war did we enter into?
What was the purpose and disclosures given re: justification?
Who financed 9-11?
Why, recently, are classified 9-11 pages being released?
What just occurred in SA?
What FOIA docs are being publicly released (recently)?
Why is this relevant?
What information is contained within these c-releases?
Why is C Wray important with regards to these releases?
What does money laundering mean?
What is the single biggest event that can generate many nation states to payout billions?
Who audits where the money goes?
$15,000 for a toothbrush?
Reconcile.
Why did we attack Iraq?
Halliburton.
Who are they?

What do they specialize in?
What is oil field service?
Why is this relevant?
What 'senior' level political officials are affiliated w/ Halliburton?
What is the primary goal?
What is the primary mode of influence that drives corruption?
What does money buy?
How is this connected to SA?
How is this connected to Alwaleed?
How is this connected to LV?
Q

Why was the arrest of Alwaleed and other princes important? The Kingdom of Saudi Arabia, Q says, had amassed great wealth and used it to control U.S. and UK politicians, including Barack Obama. If Alwaleed's alleged financial favor to Obama is true, it paid off for the Saudis when he was elected President. Q has proposed that Harvard University Muslim Alumni (HUMA) connects former Harvard grads with their Saudi financiers. Once the wealth of the Saudi princes was removed, the strings of control were cut. Politicians who owed them favors had the option of doing what was right rather than what they were told.

In the following exchange, Q confirmed that Prince Alwaleed's wealth had been confiscated.

Anonymous • Jan 14th 2018
just saw story about alwaleed in prison because he won't pay 6 billion to secure freedom

Q responded.

He doesn't have 6b.
We froze his assets.
Think logically.
When does a BIRD TALK?
Q

Barack Obama was photographed holding the book, *The Post-American World,* by Fareed Zakaria. Obama may have been reading the book to get an understanding of how the global geopolitical landscape was changing (and not in favor of the United States). He attended Trinity United Church of Christ, which was pastored by the Reverend Jeremiah Wright, whose sermons seemed to imply a belief that America deserved the terrorist attack on September 11th, 2001. Hillary Clinton has been accused of harboring racist views but has denied these allegations; she claims to be a champion of civil rights. Oddly, she has said publicly that her political mentor was Senator Robert Byrd, a former Ku Klux Klan member.

Alwaleed bin Talal and the Bush family have a long history involving oil production and wars in the Middle East. The partnership has enriched Saudi Arabia, and has given them greater power over politicians. The September 11th attack led to the war in Afghanistan, which the Bush administration said was an effort to remove Osama bin Laden and the Taliban from power. The U.S. then entered the Iraq war, ostensibly to remove Saddam Hussein from power after he killed hundreds of thousands of Iraqi citizens and was alleged to have harbored weapons of mass destruction.

Halliburton is one of the world's largest oil field service companies with operations in more than 70 countries. Former U.S. Vice President Dick Cheney was chairman and CEO of Halliburton from 1995 to 2000. Cheney retired from the company during the 2000 U.S. Presidential election campaign with a severance package worth $36 million. In the run-up to the Iraq War, Halliburton was awarded a $7 billion contract for which only Halliburton was allowed to bid. (Under U.S. law, the government uses single-bid contracts for a number of reasons including, when in the view of the government, only one organization is capable of fulfilling the requirement.)

What is seldom reported is the effect that war has on people at the very top of the banking industry and the politicians they support. Protracted wars cause nations to borrow billions (in some cases trillions) of dollars, which must be paid back with interest to banks. Would ultra-wealthy bankers share some of that wealth with the politicians who decide which wars will be fought and how long they'll last?

The official narrative of the September 11th attacks was that 19 militants associated with the Islamic extremist group al Qaeda hijacked four airplanes and used them to carry out suicide attacks against targets in the United States. Two of the planes were flown into the twin towers of the World Trade Center in New York City. A third plane hit the Pentagon just outside Washington, D.C., and the fourth plane crashed in a field near Shanksville, Pennsylvania. Almost 3,000 people were killed during the attacks. There was a suggestion from Q that the official story regarding the attacks is not entirely true.

On February 17th, 2016, Donald Trump told the hosts of the *Fox & Friends* show that he believed Saudi Arabia was behind the attacks.

"Who blew up the World Trade Center? It wasn't the Iraqis, it was Saudi — take a look at Saudi Arabia, open the documents... because frankly, if you open the documents, I think you're gonna see that it was Saudi Arabia."
—Donald J. Trump

Q suggested that politicians receive payments for political favors through a complex series of financial transactions. Those transactions require research by forensic financial investigators if they are to be exposed.

Osama bin Laden was a longtime friend of Alwaleed bin Talal. At the time of Q's post, Alwaleed owned the top five floors of the Mandalay Bay Resort and Casino, the location of the Las Vegas (LV) mass shooting.

Deceased Arizona Senator John McCain is the subject of many posts by Q. A future volume will explore what Q has said about him. For now, I'd like to make you aware that McCain is referred to in Q's posts as "we don't say his name." In some posts, he is simply called "no name." When McCain decided not to run for re-election in 2018, Q posted this:

Apr 4 2018
We don't say his name.
Adios.
The protected flow into AZ is no more.
Under the cover of his health, he will not be seeking another term.
Q

"The protected flow" is a reference to human trafficking, weapons trafficking, and drug trafficking across the U.S./Mexico border, which Q suggests is protected by corrupt politicians who benefit from them.

In the post that follows, Q suggested that U.S. politicians receive money through a Chicago-based financial group, Loop Capital, as well as other financial institutions.

Jan 13 2018
LOOP CAPITAL.
CEOs/BODs PAYING TO PLAY.
>Slush Fund
>>Hussein [1] $29,000,000 SINGAPORE
>>We don't say his name [2] $19,000,000 SINGAPORE
(Why don't we say his name?)
>>HRC/BC [3] $15,000,000 Banco de MEXICO

>>NP [4] $8,000,000 Deutsche Bank USA
..........ON......AND.......>ON.......
FOLLOW THE MONEY.
FOCUS on loudest voices in WASH.
Net Worth?
Reconcile?
Q

In this post, "Hussein" is a reference to Barack Obama. "We don't say his name" refers to John McCain, "HRC/BC" refers to Hillary and Bill Clinton and "NP" is Nancy Pelosi. Q alleges that each has received money from the financial institutions he listed as evidenced by their net worth when compared to their salaries.

In January of 2018, Q said 13 members of Barack Obama's cabinet, staff, and members of Congress used private email addresses for government work.

Jan 19 2018
HUSSEIN CABINET / STAFF
Who used private email addresses?
What was the purpose?
LL.
HRC.
JC.
JC.
CS.
AM.
We don't say his name.
RR.
SR.
JB.
HA.
VJ.
Did Hussein use a private email address?
@what?
◆◆◆
Nothing is ever truly erased/deleted.
These people are STUPID.
DECLASS-POTUS_
THE SHOT HEARD AROUND THE WORLD.
Q

When the Department of Justice Inspector General's report on the FBI's handling of the Hillary Clinton email investigation was published six months later, it confirmed that 13 people close to President Obama did *indeed* use private emails. The most logical reason for using a private email address would be to avoid having your emails made public as part of a Freedom of Information Act (FOIA) request. The second most likely reason would be to avoid detection by the NSA. The decodes for the initials in the post are: (LL) Loretta Lynch, (HRC) Hillary Clinton, (JC) James Comey, (JC) James Clapper, (CS) Chuck Schumer, (AM) Andrew McCabe, (We don't say his name) John McCain, (RR) Rod Rosenstein, (SR) Susan Rice, (JB) John Brennan, (HA) Huma Abedin, (VJ) Valerie Jarrett.

There has been considerable controversy over the surveillance of Donald Trump's campaign. Q had this to say about who was ultimately responsible for making that decision.

Mar 4th 2019
Hussein gave the order to start the spy campaign.
It was logged officially 2x.
1x - Domestic.
1x - Foreign.
FISC judge WH meeting?
WH visitor logs are important.
Hussein library CLAS doc move?
Attempt to shelter/protect?
Who has AUTH to obtain?
The More You Know.
Q

Q said the order to surveil the Trump campaign came from President Obama, and there is a paper trail to prove it. Did a FISA Court (FISC) judge meet with Obama at the White House? If so, why? Is Obama trying to hide the evidence in his Presidential library? Will Trump declassify the documents?

The President has the ultimate authority to declassify government documents. Our President could, on his own initiative, release anything he wants. He has instead, authorized Attorney General Barr to declassify records that will help the public understand the corrupt practices of government officials. The Attorney General would not make public anything that might put people (sources) at risk of physical harm, or anything that would compromise investigative methods. He cannot lawfully release information that would be presented to a grand jury. We know that some of the documents to be declassified include Congressional intelligence briefings, and messages between FBI employees involved in the surveillance of the Trump campaign.

As this book goes to print, high-level employees of the Obama administration are under investigation by Attorney General Barr and U.S. Attorney John Durham. Interestingly, as their investigation has turned toward former government officials, the media and politicians are smearing the reputations of these respected investigators.

In January of 2020, the Department of Justice determined that at least two of the three renewals of the warrant to surveil Carter Page were improperly authorized. In his response to the Inspector General report on the FBI's handling of Page's surveillance, Attorney General Barr noted that although the bureau may have had a legitimate reason to *open* an investigation, all the evidence received in the inquiry was exculpatory—that is to say, it proved that the Trump campaign did *not* collude with Russia. Attorney General Barr noted that the FBI should have ended its investigation, but instead, the probe continued. That makes me wonder—will the DOJ, at some point, determine that *all* surveillance of the Trump campaign was improperly authorized?

I'll provide more updates on these matters in future volumes as the news unfolds. More information on Barack Obama is included in the chapter on the Clinton Foundation.

CHAPTER 13

Huma and HUMA

TO BEGIN THIS CHAPTER, I'LL provide a brief overview of a handful of Islamic organizations that have both religious and military interests.

Iranian Militant Organizations

Hezbollah is a Shiite Islamist political party and militant group based in Lebanon. Following Iran's revolution in 1979, and the Israeli invasion of Lebanon in 1982, Lebanese clerics formed Hezbollah with the goal of removing Israel's forces from Lebanon and establishing an Islamic republic there. Since its inception, Hezbollah has played a pivotal role in Lebanon's parliamentary government, but in recent years, they've lost some of their political influence. In the 2018 general elections, Hezbollah did not win control of any major cabinet positions. Its designation as a terrorist organization would have threatened international funding for Lebanon.

Hezbollah's military forces are trained and funded by Iran's Revolutionary Guard Corps (IRGC). Hezbollah, by some estimates, has around 45,000 soldiers. The group played an important role in Syria's civil war, holding off western-backed forces that tried to remove Syria's President Bashar al-Assad. Hezbollah's success stands as an example of how Iran has trained and funded militant groups outside its own borders to advance its religious and political agendas.

Kata'ib Hezbollah is a Shiite militia based in Iraq. Like dozens of other militant groups in the middle east, they receive funding and training from Iran. Kata'ib Hezbollah is part of the Iraqi Popular Mobilization Forces (PMF). They're the largest of Iran's proxy militant groups. Estimates of their troop strength range from 75,000 to 145,000. Until recently, they were led by Abu Mahdi al-Muhandis.

On December 31st, 2019, the Popular Mobilization Forces attacked the United States embassy in Baghdad, Iraq. The attack was repelled by Iraqi security forces and U.S. Marines. On January 3rd, 2020, Iranian general, Qasem Soleimani, and PMF's leader Abu Mahdi al- Muhandis were killed by a U.S. drone strike. Soleimani's death touched off a political firestorm between the United States and Iran. Some Iranians revered Soleimani as a military genius. Others saw him as a bloodthirsty killer. His fame was owed largely to the many proxy militant groups he established, including Hezbollah and Yemen's Houthi rebels.

The Muslim Brotherhood

Hamas, a Palestinian Sunni-Islamic organization, has fought many military conflicts with Israel. In 2007, they became the governing organization of the Gaza strip after a battle with Fatah (formerly the Palestinian National Liberation Movement). The United States, Israel, and the European Union have classified Hamas as a terrorist organization. Hamas was founded in 1987 as an offshoot of the Egypt-based Muslim Brotherhood.

The Muslim Brotherhood was founded in 1928 by Islamic scholar Hassan al-Banna. Although initially concerned with benevolent works like establishing hospitals and assisting business start-ups, the Muslim Brotherhood eventually endorsed political positions and advocated for the establishment of a nation ruled by Sharia law. In 1948, the Egyptian government tried to dissolve the Muslim Brotherhood. The group responded by assassinating then-Prime Minister Mahmud Fahmi al-Nuquarasi. The group's founder Hassan al-Banna was assassinated shortly thereafter. Some suspected his death was retaliation by the government. In 1954, the Muslim Brotherhood attempted to assassinate Egyptian President Gamal Abdel Nasser. Six of the group's leaders were tried and executed for treason, and others were imprisoned. In the 1950s and '60s, the Brotherhood was formally banned by the government, and its operations were carried out covertly. Following the Iranian revolution in 1979, the Muslim Brotherhood experienced a resurgence in Egypt.

In the 2000 Egyptian elections, Muslim Brotherhood-affiliated candidates won 17 seats in parliament. In 2005, they captured 88 seats despite efforts by President Hosni Mubarak to restrict voting in the group's strongholds. In the 2010 elections, Mubarak arrested Muslim Brotherhood members and barred voters in areas where they had strong support. During the Arab Spring of 2011, Hosni Mubarak stepped down. The Muslim Brotherhood took advantage of the opportunity and won several elections that year. In 2012, Mohamed Morsi became the first Muslim Brotherhood candidate to be elected president. In 2013, following widespread demonstrations and civil unrest, Morsi was overthrown by the military and placed under house arrest. The nation was soon thrown into chaos. During the next 12 months, riots and mass shootings claimed thousands of lives. The Egyptian government reinstated the ban on the Muslim Brotherhood and declared it a terrorist organization. In the wake of the killings, mass trials were held for members of the Muslim Brotherhood. At one mass trial in the spring of 2014, 683 death sentences were passed, including sentences for defendants tried in absentia.

The Muslim Brotherhood and its affiliates have benefitted from financial support from the United States. In the 1990s, the U.S. government began scrutinizing individuals and groups that appeared to be raising money for terrorist organizations. The now-defunct Holy Land Foundation for Relief and Development (HLF) was based in Richardson, Texas. At its zenith, it was the largest U.S. Muslim charity. During its prosecution of the HLF for providing funding to a terrorist organization, the Justice Department said, "From its inception, HLF existed to support Hamas." The DOJ further stated that its case "included testimony that in the early 1990s, Hamas' parent organization, the Muslim Brotherhood, planned to establish a network of organizations in the U.S. to spread a militant Islamist message and raise money for Hamas." In 2008, the Holy Land Foundation and five of its members were convicted of providing material support to a designated terrorist organization.

Former federal prosecutor Andrew McCarthy wrote a book titled, *The Grand Jihad: How Islam and the Left Sabotage America*. McCarthy proposed that the U.S. has an insidious problem. For years, our government has engaged in the active appeasement of Islamist ideology. McCarthy says there are willing accomplices to this agenda both inside and outside of government. Islamists aren't merely interested in fueling terrorism, he argues. They've spawned Islamic enclaves in our midst, intending to gradually foist sharia law and Islamic ideology on unwitting Americans. One of McCarthy's greatest concerns is Hillary Clinton's personal assistant Huma Abedin, whose family members have extensive ties to the Muslim Brotherhood.

Huma Abedin

In 2012, five members of the U.S. House of Representatives asked if Huma Abedin's family connections to the Muslim Brotherhood should be considered a red flag. They suggested it might be prudent to evaluate whether her family ties rendered her unsuitable for a position that involves access to classified information about the Muslim Brotherhood.

Nov 3 2017
What data just dropped?
Why is this relevant?
HUMA.
HUMA.
HUMA.
Where is HUMA?
Who is HUMA connected to?
What organization?
What is HUMA's family history?
How did HUMA meet HRC?
What did HRC say about HUMA that demonstrates how close they are?
Why are D's dropping HRC all of a sudden?
Were deals made w/ select D's?
Can we expose every crooked politician?
70%.
HUMA.
Follow HUMA.
Alice & Wonderland.

Huma Abedin was born in Kalamazoo, Michigan, but is of Indian descent. Her father was a Muslim scholar. At the age of two, her parents moved to Saudi Arabia, where she was raised. She returned to the United States at the age of 18 and attended George Washington University. While there, she began working as an intern in the White House. In 1996, she was assigned to then-First Lady Hillary Clinton. For several years, Abedin served as the back-up to Clinton's personal aide, officially taking over as Hillary's aide and personal advisor during the successful 2000 U.S. Senate campaign in New York. Huma later worked as her traveling chief of staff during Clinton's unsuccessful campaign for the White House in 2008. Hillary Clinton has described Abedin as being like her "second daughter."

The Institute of Muslim Minority Affairs is a London-based institute that advances the study of Muslims in non-Muslim nations. It was founded in 1978 by Huma Abedin's father, Syed Abedin, and was backed by the Saudi government and the Muslim World League. Andrew McCarthy called the Muslim World League "perhaps the most significant Muslim Brotherhood organization in the world." The Institute publishes the *Journal of Muslim Minority Affairs*. Its editor in chief is Huma Abedin's mother, Dr. Saleha Abedin. Huma worked for the journal from 1995 through 2008. She was also a member of the executive board of the Muslim Students Association (MSA) while at George Washington University.

The Muslim World League helped the Muslim Brotherhood establish the Muslim Students Association. Andrew McCarthy observed, "The MSA is the foundation of the Brotherhood's American infrastructure, the gateway through which young Muslims join the Brotherhood after being steeped in the supremacist writings of Brotherhood theorist Hassan al-Banna." McCarthy noted that it was through the MSA that Mohammed Morsi joined the Muslim Brotherhood. Morsi's wife, Nagla Ali Mahmoud, became a leader of a group known as the "Muslim Sisterhood." Huma Abedin's mother is a member of the same group.

Huma Abedin's brother, Dr. Hassan Abedin, was a fellow at the Oxford Center for Islamic Studies in Great Britain. At the time he was there, Yusuf al-Qaradawi was on the Center's board of trustees. Qaradawi is an Egyptian Islamic scholar and the spiritual leader of the Muslim Brotherhood. He's known for his militant religious teachings which support acts of terrorism and repression of women. Omar Naseef was also on the board of trustees. Naseef served as Secretary-General of the Muslim World League and the founder of the Rabita Trust—a Pakistani designated terrorist organization.

Given the associations of the Abedin family, is it any wonder people were concerned that Huma might be influenced by the Muslim Brotherhood?

In the following post, Q brought up Huma Abedin's former husband, disgraced Congressman Anthony Weiner.

Oct 29 2017
Huma
Husband in jail.
HRC, Muslim Brotherhood, or child?
What would you do? Kiss your child goodbye and leave without a mother or father for Clinton?
Where is Huma today?
Was she with HRC on her book tour?
◆◆◆

Huma Abedin was married to Anthony Weiner, a New York Congressman who was forced out of office and sentenced to federal prison for transferring obscene material to a minor girl. Huma and Anthony had a child together. Their son was five years old when Anthony went to prison. Q submits the idea that Huma had an important decision to make, and he seems to be questioning her choices and priorities. Was her allegiance to Hillary Clinton, the Muslim Brotherhood, or her child? Q asks: What would you do (if you were in Huma's position)? Would you leave your child (without a mother and father) and travel with Clinton on her book signing tour? News reports show that Huma was with Hillary at her Union Square book signing event in mid-September of 2017 in New York. Huma has a Union Square apartment, so perhaps it was easy for her to be at that event. There are reports that Huma skipped a Clinton book signing date in New Jersey due to a stressful 24-hour period after her husband's September 25th sentencing hearing. Another report from a local radio station said Huma was in attendance at a Costco book signing in Brookfield, Connecticut.

Q asked the question: Where is Huma *today?* This question was posted on October 29th, 2017, which was a Sunday. Headlines show that Huma was reportedly seen (along with other prominent Democrats) at Hillary's surprise birthday party held in Washington D.C. on October 29th. The news about the party didn't hit the headlines until the next day, October 30th, 2017. Another report said Huma was with Hillary in Winnetka, Illinois, on October 30th—another stop on the book tour.

To the casual observer, it might seem like Weiner and Abedin's marriage was serendipitous. Q suggests Abedin's relationship with Anthony Weiner and Hillary Clinton was not a coincidence, but a well-planned operation by the Saudis to control a couple of U.S. politicians.

On November 2nd, 2017, the interim chair of the Democratic National Committee (DNC), Donna Brazile, dropped a bombshell report about the fact that Hillary Clinton's campaign took over control of the DNC during the 2016 Presidential election. The same day, Q mentioned her in the following post.

Nov 2 2017
Follow Huma.
What just broke w/ Huma?
What did HRC instruct Huma to do re: Classified markings?
Why is this story just now coming out?
What relevance does it have?
Why is Donna running for cover?
Was a deal granted in exchange for something?

Who made the deal?
Do we care about Donna or those who instructed her to violate the law?
Why is this being leaked v. simply prosecuted privately?
Who is attempting to change the narrative and soften the acts that are
forthcoming this weekend?

Was Donna Brazile given a deal in exchange for an opportunity to tell the truth publicly? Democrats would never have believed the story had it not come from one of their trusted DNC leaders.

Q continued dropping crumbs about Huma Abedin during the first week of November, asking what organization she was connected to. An anon posted a quote from an article by Kenneth Timmerman, which brought up more concerns about Huma.

Anonymous • Nov 2 2017

http://thehill.com/blogs/pundits-blog/presidential-campaign/292310-huma-abedins-ties-to-the-muslim-brotherhood

The Clinton campaign is attempting once again to sweep important questions under the rug about top aide Huma Abedin, her family ties to the Muslim Brotherhood and to Saudi Arabia, and her role in the ballooning Clinton email scandal.

Her mother, Saleha Abedin, sits on the Presidency Staff Council of the International Islamic Council for Da'wa and Relief, a group that is chaired by the leader of the Muslim Brotherhood, Sheikh Yusuf al-Qaradawi.

Perhaps recognizing how offensive such ties will be to voters concerned over future terrorist attacks on this country by radical Muslims professing allegiance to Sharia law, the Clinton campaign on Monday tried to downplay Ms. Abedin's involvement in the Journal and the Muslim Brotherhood.

The Clinton surrogate group Media Matters claimed predictably there was "no evidence" that Ms. Abedin or her family had ties to the Muslim Brotherhood, and that Trump campaign staffers who spoke of these ties were conspiracy theorists.

To debunk the evidence, Media Matters pointed to a Snopes.com "fact-check" piece that cited as its sole source... Senator John McCain. This is the same John McCain who met Libyan militia leader Abdelkarim Belhaj, a known al Qaeda associate, and saluted him as "my hero" during a 2011 visit to Benghazi.

Q responded.

Senator McCain and others roundly criticized Rep. Michele Bachmann in 2012 when she and four members of the House Permanent Select Committee Intelligence and the House Judiciary Committee cited Ms. Abedin in letters sent to the Inspectors General of the Department of Defense, Department of State, Department of Justice, Department of Homeland Security, and the Office of the Director of National Intelligence, warning about Muslim Brotherhood infiltration of the United States government.
Why is this relevant?
Who took an undisclosed trip to SA?
What was the purpose of a f2f v phone call?
Alice & Wonderland

Michelle Bachman was one of the five members of Congress who accused Abedin of having inappropriate ties to the Muslim Brotherhood. John McCain defended Abedin and Hillary Clinton against the accusations.

On October 31st, 2017, Q predicted that Huma Abedin would be indicted the following week.

Oct 31 2017 22:00:47 (EST)
♦♦♦
11.3 - Podesta indicted
11.6 - Huma indicted
♦♦♦

During the first week of November in 2017, Q posted several messages assuring readers that Huma Abedin, Hillary Clinton, and John Podesta were about to be arrested. That same week, news outlets reported that more than a dozen anti-Trump protests were planned in major U.S. cities for November 4th. People grew concerned about potential violence and civil unrest. Around 2 am eastern time, on November 2nd, Q posted the following message.

Nov 2 2017 02:01
These crumbs are not meant to scare anyone but merely inform.
Resistance will be dealt with swiftly. The core focus is removing
entrenched and fortified bad actors within our federal govt (past and
present) as well as others. Simply be diligent - phone numbers will
be provided if you witness an uprising or other domestic violence (in
addition to 911). Any military seen is for your protection as well as to
demonstrate our resolve. Watch for confirmations tomorrow.

Remember that at this time, those who were following Q did not know whether
the posts predicting the arrests of U.S. political figures were credible. Q had
only been posting for a few days. He had not yet provided information that
established him as a credible source.

We should also keep in mind that on November 2nd, no one would have known
whether the protests planned for the 4th would turn violent.

At 6:07 pm eastern, Q posted the following message, which predicted problems with Twitter.

Nov 2 2017 18:07
Please refer back and collect my crumbs.
As discussed, we've anticipated the Twitter and other social media
blackouts.
Rogue agents/programmers.
Per sealed Federal orders, we quickly tracked and reinstated.
Expect outages periodically (infiltrated).
If this doesn't signal what I've been saying I don't know what will.
Q

An hour later, Q posted this.

Nov 2 2017 19:07:18
:::::Flash Traffic:::::
Three letter agency embedded tracking/up-channel into POTUS'
Twitter to specifically target through specialized geo and send his
location.
We anticipated this (see post a few hours ago).
It has begun.
Perhaps more posts to follow as expected imminent departure.
Q

An anon responded.

Anonymous
Let's be clear - you're telling us POTUS is currently under attack by our own intelligence agencies?

Q replied.

Let's be real clear.
The CIA just attacked the Command and Chief which was immediately detected by NSA/MI and alerted to POTUS.
Re-review all my crumbs including today/yesterday/weekend.
What does this mean?
What actions are immediately occurring?
If this leaks, or the immediate action ongoing at Langley, you'll have your verification ahead of schedule.
Q

On the following day, November 3rd, President Trump wrote a tweet about his Twitter account malfunction.

Donald J. Trump (from his Twitter account):
My Twitter account was taken down for 11 minutes by a rogue employee. I guess the word must finally be getting out-and having an impact.
3:51 AM - 3 Nov 2017

The protests on November 4th turned out to be smaller than anticipated and there were few reports of violence. Huma Abedin, Hillary Clinton, and John Podesta were not arrested, but members of the Saudi royal family were.

Some confusion developed among those who followed Q because of references he made to both a person by the name of Huma, and an organization named HUMA. Research by anons revealed the organization to be Harvard University Muslim Alumni (HUMA). In a post on the day after the arrest of Saudi princes, Q connected a number of people, organizations, and recent events.

Nov 5 2017
Important Context:
What have you learned about HUMA?

What organization is HUMA?
Which US President is affiliated w/ HUMA?
Why is this relevant?
What year(s) did this occur?
Who funded on behalf this President?
Why is this relevant?
What year(s) did this occur?
What just happened in SA?
Who was arrested?
Funds frozen.
Why would this former President be funded pre-political days?
Repeat.
Important.
Why would this former President be funded pre-political days?
Why is the relevance?
Was the MB affiliated to any of these organizations/people?
Fast forward.
Why are the events in SA so important?
Why was JK in SA recently?
Why was POTUS' last Tweet re: SA prior to the happening?
Why was POTUS' Twitter taken down days before under cover of a rogue employee?
Refocus again.
Who was arrested in SA?
Any ownership stakes in US co's?
Why is this relevant?
Twitter.
Las Vegas.
Recent events.
Why would investment be made in a former President pre-political days?
What year(s) did this occur?
What faith does HUMA represent?
What faith does the MB represent?
What faith does Huma represent?
Who are the bad actors?
Who funds majority of US 'senior' politicians?
Fantasy land.
Fantasy land.

Was the former President of the United States groomed to be
Command in Chief?
Is this possible?
Is the US political / election system corrupt?
Who owns poll machines?
Soros?
Why is this relevant?
They never thought she would lose.
They never thought she would lose.
Fantasy land.
Fantasy land.
The complete picture would put 99% of Americans (the World) in a
hospital.
POTUS is our savior.
Pray.
Operators are active.
We are at war.
Goodnight BO.
Snow White.
Godfather III.
Q

Q tied Barack Obama to Alwaleed bin Talal through their shared affiliation
with Harvard University and the assertion that Alwaleed helped fund Obama's
education. Alwaleed was a majority shareholder of Twitter stock when President
Trump's Twitter account was targeted. Alwaleed owned several floors of the
Mandalay Bay Resort and Casino, the site of the Las Vegas shooting. He was
arrested the previous day, and his assets were frozen. Q implied that Huma
Abedin was one of several Muslim Brotherhood operatives sent to infiltrate
the U.S. government.

In the above post, Q referred to George Soros and voting machines. Let me
explain that reference.

Lord Malloch Brown is chairman of the board of directors of SGO Corporation Limited, a holding company whose primary asset is the voting machine
manufacturer Smartmatic. He has been a longtime companion and confidant
of George Soros.

Working for Refugees International, he was part of the Soros Advisory
Committee on Bosnia in 1993–94, formed by George Soros. He has since kept
cordial relations with Soros, and rented an apartment owned by Soros while

working in New York on UN assignments. While serving as United Nations Development Fund Administrator, Malloch Brown spoke beside Soros in 2002, suggesting that the United Nations and Soros' Open Society Institute, as well as other organizations, work together to fund humanitarian functions.

In May 2007, Soros' Quantum Fund announced the appointment of Malloch Brown as vice-president. Also, in May 2007, he was named vice-chairman of Soros Fund Management and the Open Society Institute, two other important Soros organizations.

On December 15, 2006, he was named a visiting fellow at the Yale Center for the Study of Globalization. He announced plans to focus on writing a book on changing leadership in a globalized world while in residence during the spring semester.

Although George Soros doesn't have controlling power over a company that makes voting machines, he does have significant influence with a man who does.

On November 11, 2017, Q posted again about HUMA.

Nov 11 2017
Why were the events in SA extraordinary?
Who was arrested?
What will bank records provide?
List names, family history, investment/ownership stakes, and point-to-point contacts.
EX: Alwaleed HUMA BO Citigroup US Control
Why is this relevant?
House of Saud.
House of Saud US Control
Follow the money.
What power shift recently occurred?
Was a new King appointed?
Coincidence?
Dark to LIGHT.
Why is this relevant?
One side of the triangle removed (1st time in history).
Other sides falling.
+++
++
+
Q

In the above post, Q pointed out that the bank records of the Saudi princes would provide a wealth of information to the FBI as they investigate money laundering. Q tied Prince Alwaleed to the Harvard University Muslim Alumni, Barack Obama, and Citigroup.

In 2008, the year Barack Obama was first elected President, Prince Alwaleed bin Talal was the majority shareholder of Citigroup, a U.S. multinational bank and financial services corporation. As revealed in John Podesta's emails—which were published by *WikiLeaks*—Michael Froman, an executive at Citigroup, wrote an email to Podesta on October 6th, 2008, (a month before the Presidential election) with the subject "Lists." He attached three documents, one of which outlined 31 cabinet-level positions and who would fill them. The list ended up naming many people who were appointed to positions in Obama's cabinet. Some of the names found on the list and their positions were: Eric Holder as Attorney General, Janet Napolitano as Director of Homeland Security, Robert Gates as Secretary of Defense, Rahm Emanuel as chief of staff, Peter Orszag as the Director of the Office of Management and Budget, Susan Rice as U.S. Ambassador to the United Nations, Arne Duncan as Secretary of Education, Eric Shinseki as Director of Veterans Affairs, Kathleen Sebelius as Director of Health and Human Services, Melody Barnes as Chief of the Domestic Policy Council. For Secretary of the Treasury, three possibilities were on the list: Robert Rubin, Larry Summers, and Timothy Geithner. Obama ultimately chose Geithner.

The fact that the list was sent before Obama chose his cabinet raises serious questions. Did he select members of his cabinet from a list submitted by an entity owned by Alwaleed bin Talal?

Q's previous post closed with a list of plus signs. The arrest of corrupt Saudi princes (+++) effectively removed one side of the power triangle that controls world governments. As of today, only the Rothschilds (++) and George Soros (+) remain.

The Las Vegas Shooting

On the night of October 1st, 2017, a gunman opened fire on a crowd of concertgoers at the Route 91 Harvest music festival in Las Vegas Strip, Nevada. The FBI reported that Stephen Paddock killed 58 people and wounded 413. The panic caused by the shooting increased the total number of people injured to 869. I read the FBI's report on the incident. Many questions remain unanswered. The FBI never determined the shooter's motive. Q has suggested that there was more to the Las Vegas shooting than was reported by the media. Below is a post from November 5th, 2017.

Nov 5 2017
Seth Rich only mentioned because it directly relates to SA.
Las Vegas.
What hotel did the 'reported' gunfire occur from?
What floors specifically?
Who owns the top floors?
Top floors only.
Why is that relevant?
What was the shooter's name?
What was his net worth?
How do you identify a spook?
What can historical data collection reveal?
Was there any eye witnesses?
Who?
Was he registered as a security guard?
Why is MS13 important?
What doesn't add up?
Was there only one shooter?
Why was JFK released?
What do the JFK files infer?
Was there only one shooter?
Who was in LV during this time?
What was the real mission?
Speculate.
Why are survivors dying randomly?
What do each of these survivors have in common?
Did they talk on social media?
What did they say?
Were they going to form a group?
Why is this relevant?
How did they die?
What CIA report was released by WK?
What can control a car?
How did the (2) of the survivors die?
Car crash?
How does this connect to SA?
What just happened in SA?
Who owns the top floors of the hotel?
What happened today in SA?

To who specifically?
Was POTUS in LV that night?
Yes/no?
Why was he there?
Who did he have a classified meeting with?
Did AF1 land at McCarran?
What unmarked tail numbers flew into McCarren that night?
Trace AF1 that entire day.
What do you notice?
Classified.
Q

The shooter, Stephen Paddock, was described as a loner and a high stakes gambler. Q suggested his income may indicate that he was a spy. The gunfire was reported to have originated from the 32nd floor of the Mandalay Bay Resort and Casino. The Four Seasons Hotels & Resorts operates as a hotel within a hotel, occupying the top five floors (those above the 35th floor) of the Mandalay Bay Resort and Casino. Alwaleed bin Talal's Kingdom Holding Group was a major shareholder of the Four Seasons at the time of the shooting.

The lone witness to Paddock's activities was Jesus Campos—a man reported to be an unarmed security guard who discovered Paddock just before the shooting began. Campos was reported to have suffered a gunshot wound to the leg when Paddock fired about 200 rounds through the hotel room door at him. The official timeline of the shooting of Campos changed several times, placing it either just before Paddock opened fire on the crowd, or just afterward. Campos made only one TV appearance (on *The Ellen DeGeneres Show*) a couple of weeks after the incident happened. He seemed reluctant to discuss the event in any detail. DeGeneres did most of the talking, praising him as a hero. DeGeneres did something odd during the interview. Speaking on behalf of Campos, she explained to the audience that he would never again discuss the shooting publicly. Campos quickly disappeared from public view. All the interviews that had been scheduled with various news networks were canceled. After the incident, Campos stayed in his home in a Las Vegas suburb and was watched around the clock by security guards. An article by *The Los Angeles Times* on October 16th, 2017, reported that a man in a truck had been posted outside Campos residence with the assignment of keeping the media from making contact with him.

Regarding the eyewitness, Q asked, "Why is MS13 important? What doesn't add up?" Q has hinted that MS-13 gang members are used as disposable assets to assist in operations where secrecy is required.

Q asked if there was only one shooter and what the release of the JFK files infer. The JFK files strongly suggest that President Kennedy was killed by two shooters who fired from different angles. Several eyewitnesses to the Las Vegas shooting reported seeing or hearing several different shooters who were located at different hotels.

Q asked many other questions in his November 5th post. Let's explore some of them in detail.

♦♦♦

Who was in LV during this time?
What was the real mission?
Speculate.

♦♦♦

Q mentioned the assassination of JFK, the Saudi royal family, and hinted at a coverup. I have no way of confirming this, but if I had to speculate, I would guess that Mohammad bin Salman was in Las Vegas that night and that he was the target of an attempted assassination by his opponents inside the Saudi royal family. Speculating further, I would guess the attempted assassination happened at one of the nearby hotels, but not the Mandalay Bay Resort and Casino. The assassination attempt failed. Was the shooting at the Mandalay Bay Resort and Casino a diversion—an attempt to draw attention away from the real mission?

Q asked about survivors of the shooting. Several survivors posted stories about the shooting on social media. These stories conflicted with the account provided by law enforcement agencies and the media. Several of the witnesses died shortly after the shooting. One eyewitness, Roy McClellan, was killed on November 17th, 2017, while walking on the roadway about 60 miles west of Las Vegas. McClellan was struck by a car that fled the scene.

Two eyewitnesses, Dennis and Lorraine Carver, were killed in a freak car accident on October 16th, 2017. Their car caught fire after striking a brick pillar in their own neighborhood about a quarter of a mile from their home. Q hinted that the collision might not have been an accident. The CIA has the ability to take over the control of automobiles. This was disclosed in documents made public by *WikiLeaks*. (Notable from the news reports on that incident was the fact that it took firefighters about an hour to put out the car fire, which is highly unusual.)

Kymberley Suchomel, 28, was one of the more vocal eyewitnesses to the shooting. She insisted there was more than one shooter. Eight days after the shooting, her grandmother found her dead in bed. Although she took medication for a pituitary tumor, her grandmother said she was otherwise in good health.

Q then returned to the subject of Saudi Arabia, asking what had just happened there, and to what person specifically. Was Q drawing our attention to the arrest of the Saudi princes, and in particular, Prince Alwaleed bin Talal? Were the arrests of members of the royal family Mohammad bin Salman's way of dealing with opponents who tried to remove him from power?

Q then asked if President Trump was in Las Vegas the night of the shooting and if he had a classified meeting with someone.

♦♦♦

Was POTUS in LV that night?
Yes/no?
Why was he there?
Who did he have a classified meeting with?
Did AF1 land at McCarran?
What unmarked tail numbers flew into McCarren that night?
Trace AF1 that entire day.
What do you notice?
Classified.
Q

Military and commercial air traffic can be tracked on a number of publicly accessible websites. Air Force One flight logs do not conclusively show the President making a trip to McCarran airport in Las Vegas on October 1st, 2017. It's possible that Air Force One's transponder was turned off if there was a flight to Las Vegas. If the transponder *was* turned off, there would be no data available by which to track the flight. That may be what Q was hinting at when he said, "Trace AF1 that entire day. What do you notice?"

Q suggested more than one aircraft flew into McCarran with unmarked tail numbers. I would assume if this was the case, these measures were taken to ensure privacy. President Trump could have taken an aircraft other than the Boeing 747 he normally uses. Did he take a military flight?

The shooting in Las Vegas happened at around 10 pm local time. That corresponds to 1 am the next day on the east coast. On the afternoon of October 1st, POTUS was at the President's Cup golf tournament in Bedminster, New Jersey. After the tournament, he returned to Joint Base Andrews at 7:34 pm eastern and then, at 7:50, took a short flight on Marine One back to the White House.

Public Pool is an automated feed of White House press pool reports. This was the report from the evening of October 1st, 2017:

Air Force One touched down at Joint Base Andrews at 7:34pm after an uneventful flight. No gaggle or POTUS remarks on plane.

10 minutes later Trump deplaned, but answered none of the shouted questions about tweets and Puerto Rico.

At 7:50 pm he lifted off on Marine One, bound for the White House.

By the time the President returned to the White House the night of October 1st, the shooting had not yet happened. On Monday morning, October 2nd, the President received his daily briefing at 10 am as reported by *Conservative Daily News.*

10:00 AM Receive daily intelligence briefing – Oval Office
10:30 AM THE PRESIDENT gives remarks – Diplomatic Room [Live Stream]
11:00 AM Lead a deregulation summit – East Room [Live Stream] CANCELED
11:35 AM Meet with the governors of Kentucky, Mississippi, Maine, and New Hampshire – Oval Office

If the President did visit Las Vegas the night of October 1st, he may have arrived before the shooting happened. Q said the details of the President's trip are classified. At least for now.

CHAPTER 14

Snow White

ONE OF THE MORE ENTERTAINING aspects of decoding Q's posts is assigning meaning to his "signatures." As we saw in the chapter on Saudi Arabia, the phrase "Alice and Wonderland" was a signature indicating a person and a nation. Hillary Clinton was "Alice." Saudi Arabia was "Wonderland." Q wants researchers to understand his signatures, so he helped them decode that one. It's up to us to decrypt the rest of his signatures; many more need to be unraveled. New signatures are still being introduced by Q.

The easiest way to determine the meaning of a signature is to search for all the posts that contain a particular signature phrase, then pay attention to the subjects and people the posts have in common. Fortunately, the websites that display Q's posts have built-in search capabilities. We'll walk through a decode of the signature "Snow White" by looking at a handful of posts containing that phrase. On November 5th, 2017, Q posted the following message.

Nov 5 2017
Why is MS13 a priority?
Could people pay such gangs to kill opponents and why / how to insulate against exposure?
The truth is mind blowing and cannot fully be exposed. These people

are evil.

Why wasn't HRC prosecuted for the emails?

Put simply, Obama ultimately OK'd by using the non govt email addy to communicate w/ Clinton. Obama also had an alias along with each of his cabinet members. Therefore indicting HRC would lead to indicting Obama & his cabinet etc which could never happen.

Remember he lied about knowing but that ultimately came out in the dump. Poof!

Snow White

Godfather III

Q

This post concludes with the signature "Snow White." This post mentioned the gang, MS-13, and suggested the gang may be used by corrupt politicians to intimidate and silence enemies. It also pointed out the fact that Hilary Clinton wasn't prosecuted for her misuse of emails because it would lead to the prosecution of Barack Obama and members of his cabinet.

The next post focuses on the top shareholders of major social media platforms.

Nov 5 2017

Social media platforms.

Top 10 shareholders of Facebook?

Top 10 shareholders of Twitter?

Top 10 shareholders of Reddit?

Why is SA relevant?

MSM.

Controlling stakes in NBC/MSNBC?

Controlling stakes in ABC?

Controlling stakes in CBS?

Controlling stakes in CNN?

Investor(s) in Fox News?

Why is this relevant?

What is Operation Mockingbird?

Active?

Who is A Cooper?

What is A Cooper's background?

Why is this relevant?

Snow White.

Godfather III.
Speed.
Q

Saudi Prince Alwaleed bin Talal was a major shareholder of Twitter stock at the time of the post, but that changed after he was arrested. Q asked why Saudi Arabia (SA) was relevant. Did Saudi princes own controlling shares of U.S. media companies? Operation Mockingbird was a covert operation by the CIA to infiltrate the mainstream media with CIA operatives, and have media executives on the agency's payroll. Anderson Cooper is a CNN news anchor who spent two summers as a CIA intern.

The two previous posts suggest that Snow White may have something to do with the CIA. A January 13th, 2000, *Chicago Tribune* article reported that the CIA named its supercomputers after the seven dwarves. From that, we may infer that Snow White could indeed refer to the CIA.

Next, we'll examine a message that requires a bit of decoding. I'll summarize some of the key points following the post.

Q !ITPb.qbhqo   Nov 9 2017
1510280445405.jpg
Trip added.
[C]oordinated effort to misdirect.
Guide to reading the crumbs necessary to cont[I]nue.
Attached gr[A]phic is correct.
Linked graphics are incorrect and false.
Graphic is necessary and vital.
Time stamp(s) and order [is] critical.
Re-review graphic (in full) each day post news release.
Learn to distinguish between relevant/non-relevant news.
Disinformation is real.
Disinformation is necessary.
Ex: US ML NG (1) False SA True
Why was this necessary?
What questions were asked re: SA prior to SA events?
Why is this relevant?
Think mirror.
Look there, or [here], or there, truth is behind you.
What is a map?
Why is a map useful?

What is a legend?
Why is a legend useful?
What is a sequence?
Why is this relevant?
When does a map become a guide?
What is a keystone?
Everything stated is relevant.
Everything.
Future provides past.
Map provides picture.
Picture provides 40,000ft. v.
40,000ft. v. is classified.
Why is a map useful?
Think direction.
Think full picture.
Who controls the narrative?
Why is this relevant?
What is a spell?
Who is asleep?
Dissemination.
Attention on deck.
There is an active war on your mind.
Be [p]repared.
Ope[r]ations underway.
Operators [a]ctive.
Graphic is essential.
Find the ke[y]stone.
Moves and countermoves.
They never thought she would lose.
Snow white.
Godfather III.
Iron Eagle.
Q

Q added a tripcode (Q !ITPb.qbhqo) as part of his login credentials. He posted an updated graphic and said a guide to reading his crumbs (a map) was necessary to continue. He noted that his attached graphic was correct, but that linked graphics were incorrect. He reiterated that having a correct graphic, including the accurate chronological order of posts according to timestamps, was critical. He said anons needed to learn to distinguish between relevant and non-relevant news because disinformation was being provided by people with both good and bad intentions. Q asked readers to reflect on the disinformation he posted regarding the deployment of the National Guard (NG) and indicated that it was *true* for Saudi Arabia, but *false* for the United States. This was done to confuse enemy agents who monitor Q's posts. They would have used any valid information to thwart the arrests that were planned in Saudi Arabia. Disinformation is like a mirror: Look there, or [here], or there; the truth is behind you.

Q asked why a map is useful, what a legend is, and what a sequence is. A map helps you know where you're going. A legend helps interpret symbols on a map. A sequence is information provided in successive messages. If we learn to read Q's posts, interpret his language, and connect successive messages, it will help us understand what's *really* happening behind the scenes.

Q uses brackets for many purposes. In this post, two separate messages can be decoded by putting together the words and letters found inside the brackets. Note the bracketed letters and words that spell out a secret message [C][I][A] [is] [here]. Also note another message: [p][r][a][l][y].

The following post discusses the NSA and its access to the big picture.

Nov 12 2017
Patriots don't sleep.
40,000ft. v. necessary to understand [US]/SA/global events.
Paint the picture.
Decrease altitude (we will not fly that high again).
Higher the altitude greater the [risk] of conspiracy ST.
Many cannot/will not swallow.
What is No Such Agency - Q group?
Who has clearance to full picture?
Important.
SIS is good.
+++Adm R+++
What agency is at war w/ Clowns In America?
How does POTUS shift narrative?
(New) Age of Enlightenment.
80% covert.
20% public.
What has occurred over [th]e last several months?
C-info leaks?

Operations (think SA + ???)?
CNN sale?
What co's rec large cash injections by Clowns In America (public)?
Why???
Who does [i]t hurt?
Who control[s] the MSM?
Primary objective from beginning: POTUS discredit MSM.
[W]hy is this relevant?
How is information transmitted?
How are people inform[e]d?
Why was Sarah A. C. attacked (hack-attempt)?
Why was Op[e]ration Mockingbird repeated?
Why was Jason Bourne (CIA/Dream) repeated?
Think social media platforms.
Who are the Wizards & Warloc[k]s?
What council do the Wizards & Warlocks control?
Think Snowden (inside terms dropped).
Alice & Wonderland – understood.
Snow White – understood.
Iron Eagle?
Godfather III?
Speed?
Everything has meaning.
Disney is a distraction.
Senate & Congress = puppets (not all)(power shift).
For [GOD & COUNTRY].
For HUMANITY.
GERONIMO.
Q

In this post, Q asked what the NSA Q group is and suggested they—along with Admiral Mike Rogers—had access to the full picture of global events by virtue of their ability to access signals intelligence (SIS). Q asked why the CIA was at war with the NSA, and suggested U.S. media companies were receiving cash infusions from the CIA (Clowns in America) to keep them solvent. Q hinted that independent reporter Sara Carter was hacked in an attempt to silence her (likely because her reports challenge the mainstream narrative). On several occasions, Q has pointed anons to a Jason Bourne film, which portrays a Facebook-like social media platform called Deep Dream. In the movie, Deep Dream was set up by the CIA to spy on citizens and circumvent surveillance laws. Q suggests that this closely mimics how Facebook was actually established and how it currently operates. The phrase "Wizards and Warlocks" has been mentioned by Q on a number of occasions, implying they are a group inside the NSA. Q confirmed his signatures that had been correctly decoded (Snow White and Alice & Wonderland), and those which had not been decoded (Iron Eagle, Godfather III, and Speed). He closed with what *could* be another signature (Geronimo), which, at the time this book was published, only appears in this post.

By November 25th, 2017, the 4chan board /pol/ had become unusable due to infiltration by the opposition, so Q moved the conversation to 8chan.

Nov 25 2017
Test
Test
4Chan infiltrated.
Future posts will be relayed here.
Q

On November 29th, the CIA (Snow White) attempted to take down Q's communications.

Nov 29 2017
Snow White utilized/activated to silence.
This was not anticipated.
Control / protection lost.
Routing through various networks ('jumpers') randomly has created connection/sec issues.
Working to resolve.
Select people removed.
Stay strong.
We are winning.
More to follow.
Q

The following day, Q posted this coded message referencing the CIA's attempts to disable communications, and the decision to move from 4chan to 8chan.

Nov 30 2017
_Start_IP_log_4ch_y

_Conf_y_
_Lang_v_US_jurid_y
Snow White Pounce.
_Conf_actors_1-9999999_per_condition_89074-b
No nets.
Re_8ch_carry_good_
Q

On December 15th, 2017, due to sustained attacks by the CIA, Q posted the following message suggesting he'd lost the ability to maintain safe and secure communications.

Dec 15 2017
We may have exhausted our ability to maintain safe-comms.
Snow White.
Rig for silent running.
Unknown return.
Godspeed, Patriots.
Q

Q did return. Attacks by the CIA have been a constant source of trouble. Their malicious activity has forced Q to move from one board to another to maintain secure communications. This chapter is not an exhaustive examination of what Q has written about the CIA. It is intended to help decode the signature "Snow White." Other posts related to the CIA and Snow White will be covered in future volumes.

CHAPTER 15

Q and the Mainstream Media

BEFORE RUNNING FOR PRESIDENT, DONALD Trump was generally respected by most members of the media. As the host of a successful TV show, he garnered acclaim from Hollywood and TV personalities and was treated well by most in the industry. Several media reports can be found online about how Donald Trump worked with Jesse Jackson's Rainbow/PUSH coalition in the late 1990s. There are videos on www.c-span.org of Jackson praising Trump while introducing him at a 3-day forum about minority involvement in American business and Wall Street. Trump was not considered a racist. But then he did the unthinkable. He ran for the highest office in the land.

Donald Trump had no prior political experience. He was an outsider to the Washington D.C. scene. The media may have thought his bid for the White House a prank, but politicians took his promise to drain the swamp as a threat to their existence. Washington is run by people who know how to find the weakness of an opponent and exploit it. With few exceptions, according to Q, the Presidents of the last half-century were allowed into the oval office because they were vulnerable to those who could control them. During the 2016 Presidential campaign, Donald Trump's opponents dug feverishly to find dirt on him. Even with access to the NSA's database, Trump's enemies found nothing that could be used to blackmail or control him.

Years ago, the elites of the world, in their infinite wisdom, created an intelligence apparatus that gathers personal information on everyone, including them. Such information is invaluable for learning about the weakness of opponents who need to be controlled. But that information must be carefully guarded, and it could never fall into the hands of someone who could not be controlled—into the hands of an outsider. If that ever happened, and if the one who gained access were interested in justice, corrupt politicians would surely hang from nooses.

Knowing the threat an outsider posed to their house of cards, politicians and their allies in the media developed a plan to make sure Donald Trump would never be elected. Needing to account for the slim possibility that he might win, they also developed an insurance policy.

Ever since he came down the escalator at Trump Tower and announced his intent to run for President, the media's job has been to portray Donald Trump in the most negative light possible. During the 2016 campaign, they claimed he couldn't be nominated. When he won the nomination, they insisted that a racist, misogynist, hateful man like him could never be elected President.

Reporters have known Trump for decades. They're aware that the things they say about him are false. Although MSNBC hosts Joe Scarborough and Mika Brzezinski play along with the media narrative that Trump is a racist, Joe made a confession one day on the air. "We saw him for twelve years behind closed doors. Never, ever once—I'll say it under oath. I'll put it in an affidavit—never once heard him say anything close to being racially insensitive. Never once."

A few months after Donald Trump was inaugurated, Robert Mueller was appointed as Special Counsel to investigate allegations that Trump colluded with Russia during the 2016 election. With few exceptions, the mainstream media spent the next two years warning, and in some cases, promising their viewers that Trump's demise was imminent. He and his family would be indicted. Every desperate tweet was a sign that the orange-haired dictator would soon be removed from office. They said the evidence was overwhelming. The walls were closing in. It was only a matter of time. In March of 2019, after two years and tens of millions of dollars spent, Robert Mueller's investigation abruptly ended. Mueller found no evidence that Trump or anyone in his campaign had colluded with Russia. The Justice Department concluded there was no obstruction by Trump of Mueller's investigation.

What do we conclude about an entire industry (save for a few exceptions) that didn't just get the story wrong, but seemed too emotionally invested in the outcome to have a chance at getting it right?

On August 15th, 2019, *Slate* published an article based on a leaked audio recording of an employee town hall meeting where the executive editor of

The New York Times, Dean Baquet, laid out his vision for the paper's future. Speaking of their coverage of the Trump-Russia story, Baquet said, "We built our newsroom to cover one story, and we did it truly well. Now we have to regroup and shift resources and emphasis to take on a different story." And he said, "We'll... write more deeply about the country, race, and other divisions." After Mueller failed to deliver on Russian collusion, *The New York Times* realized its only hope of stopping Trump was to push the narrative that he's a racist and to emphasize perceived divisions in the country.

Q has had much to say about the mainstream media (MSM) noting in the following post that they're tools of the CIA and that they will, at some point, be exposed.

Nov 5 2017
MSM.
CIA counter-ops.
Will all fall down.
Q

Consider the following post.

Nov 2 2017
◆◆◆
Who controls the narrative?
Why are left wing organizations beginning to report on DNC/D corruption?
Does the CIA have operators inside the MSM?
What happens if exposed?
What happens if tied back as 'knowing' to execs?
What does this have to do with 'leaking'?
What if it can be verified no sourced stories (made up) were in fact (and approved) to be published?
The wormhole goes deep.

Q asked some pointed questions: Does the mainstream media attempt to control the public narrative? Why were liberal news organizations beginning to report on corruption in the Democratic National Committee? Does the CIA have operators in the mainstream media? What would happen to the credibility of the press if this were exposed? What would happen if it could be proven that media executives knowingly hired CIA operatives? Would leaks from intelligence agencies to news outlets have anything to do with this? What if it could be proven that reporters had no sources and were making up their stories? What would happen if executives knew about and approved fictional news stories? Would the CIA benefit from stories that created a narrative but had no sources?

Jan 19 2018
MSM is FAKE NEWS.
Propaganda.
Talking points [4am] - private email addresses.
Paid contractors.
JUDGEMENT DAY.
Q

Q suggested that some journalists are, in fact, paid contractors who receive orders at 4am (via private email addresses) about the narrative that is to be pushed on a given day.

In 1977, Watergate investigator Carl Bernstein revealed that more than 400 of his fellow journalists were secretly working for the Central Intelligence Agency. According to Bernstein, members of the press had "provided a full range of clandestine services—from simple intelligence gathering to serving as go-betweens with spies in Communist countries." It wasn't just beat reporters for small newspapers who were hired by the CIA. The agency developed extensive working relationships with *The New York Times*, CBS, and Time Inc. Their collaboration with the American press has been more extensive than previously acknowledged, either publicly or to Congress.

Operation Mockingbird was an experiment to see if the CIA could infiltrate the news media and influence public opinion. The program succeeded, and although the agency officially denies that it uses such tactics today, Q often reminds us that the mainstream media is, to a large degree, controlled by the Central Intelligence Agency.

If, as Q has suggested, a handful of wealthy elites control society to serve their purposes, harnessing the power of the media would be critical to their success. Is there evidence that wealthy people control the media?

An October 2015 report from CNBC said that Saudi Prince Alwaleed bin Talal was the second-largest holder of Twitter stock with a 5.2% stake in the company. (By comparison, CEO Jack Dorsey only held 3.2% at the time). According to a November 2017 story by *The Guardian,* Alwaleed at one point owned a 6% stake in 21st Century Fox, making him the second-largest stakeholder. He also was a significant shareholder in the Rupert Murdoch company, News Corp, which at one time owned the Fox Entertainment Group, *The Sun, The Times,* and *The Wall Street Journal.*

Decades ago, print media and news networks held tight control over the narrative that shaped our perception of the world. Social media changed all of that. Today, the world gets its information from Twitter, Facebook, YouTube, Instagram, Snapchat, Reddit, and other social media sites. Donald Trump and those who are interested in shaping culture are active on Twitter because news and opinions that impact the public narrative are shared more on Twitter than any other social media platform.

What would wealthy people gain by controlling news outlets and social media platforms? If you're involved in questionable practices, controlling the public narrative about those practices would be important. It would provide cover and concealment of your activities.

Q asked why there is often a terrorist attack or mass shooting following a news cycle that casts Democrats in a negative light. Why, after such an event, is there typically a lengthy debate on social media about gun control?

Nov 6 2017
Why, by coincidence, is there a terrorist attack (or mental health c-level attack) within a short time post negative D news?
Do you believe in coincidences?
They think you are stupid. Puppets w/o power. They want your guns.
Why? No power left.
♦♦♦
Why is controlling the narrative important?
Do most people investigate for themselves or simply follow?
Why is the MSM so hostile towards POTUS?
Who controls the MSM?
Why, each and every day, is the MSM pushing a particular topic?
Coordinated?
Who sets the narrative for the day?
How is the narrative communicated to the MSM?
♦♦♦
Q

Those who wish to control the public narrative (at least in the U.S.) have found a way to end negative news cycles and begin new ones where they control the narrative. Mass shootings provide an opportunity to discuss gun control. Since many patriots are passionate supporters of the second amendment, they'll argue for days on social media over their right to keep and bear arms. Although Democrats generally support limitations on gun rights, Q suggested these discussions are really a distraction—a way to end a news cycle that was causing problems for one political party.

Freedom of the Press Foundation, the CIA, and the Media

It's one thing to claim that the CIA provides a carefully constructed narrative to the media, but it's another thing to explain *how* they do it. According to Q, Edward Snowden has played a key role in helping the CIA communicate with mainstream journalists.

After illegally leaking the NSA's spy tools to the media, Edward Snowden flew to Russia, where he has remained a political asylee. Snowden currently sits on the board of directors of the Freedom of the Press Foundation, which describes itself as a non-profit agency that helps journalists report on public corruption and malfeasance. They specialize in deploying technology that helps journalists communicate with government whistleblowers.

John Perry Barlow co-founded the Freedom of the Press Foundation, which was initially set up to help facilitate donations to support Julian Assange and *WikiLeaks*. Eventually, they stopped processing donations to *WikiLeaks*, and Julian Assange was removed from the Board of Directors. In 2014, Edward Snowden was added as a board member.

John Perry Barlow was an enigmatic man with many interests and talents. He was a lyricist with the Grateful Dead and an unofficial founder of the annual Burning Man Festival. Barlow believed the internet held the potential to solve many of society's problems, without creating more of them. In addition to the Freedom of the Press Foundation, he also co-founded the Electronic Frontier Foundation.

On January 27th, 2018, Q posted the following message, which was directed at Edward Snowden, whose Twitter handle is @Snowden.

Jan 27 2018
@Snowden.
The clock is ticking.
How's Russia?
[Mr. Contractor]
Freedom of the Press.
John Perry Barlow.
https://freedom.press

SecureDrop [Whistleblowers]?
SecureDrop>Clowns In America.
NOBODY IS SAFE.
Q

Q reminded Snowden he will eventually be brought back to the states (most likely to face espionage charges). Since Snowden was a contractor with the CIA and NSA, Q referred to him as "Mr. Contractor." His name appears in brackets. Q then named John Perry Barlow and Freedom of the Press and posted a link to the latter's website. Q mentioned SecureDrop, a communication platform developed by Freedom of the Press Foundation. SecureDrop is used by intelligence sources to submit documents to journalists anonymously. There is a suggestion by Q that although SecureDrop claimed to be a safe platform for government whistleblowers, it was (at the time of Q's post), under the control of the CIA.

An anon replied to Q with a link to an article about the death of one of the developers of SecureDrop. James Dolan was found dead in a Brooklyn hotel in December of 2017. Dolan was the second member of the SecureDrop team to commit suicide. (Co-creator Aaron Swartz took his life in 2013.)

Q replied to the anon with a single word.

Jan 27 2018
SPOOKY.
Q

The implication was that spooks (spies) may have been involved in Dolan's death. Q then replied to his own post on the same day.

Happy Hunting Anonymous.
Set the TRUTH FREE.
Q

About an hour later, Q posted the following message.

:Heart attacks can be deadly.
Q

Eleven days later, on February 7th, an anon *reposted* Q's message from January 27th about Snowden, John Perry Barlow, and SecureDrop. The anon included a screen capture and link to an obituary for John Perry Barlow, who had just died of an apparent heart attack.

Q responded to the anon, reminding them of his post on January 27th, about heart attacks.

Heart attacks can be deadly.
Q

Q's response seemed to imply that Barlow may not have died of natural causes and that his death was known in advance. How could this be possible?

In 1975, during the Church Committee hearings (a Senate select committee that investigated intelligence agency abuses), the existence of a secret assassination weapon came to light. The CIA had developed a poison that caused its victims to suffer cardiac arrest. The poison could be frozen into the shape of a dart and then fired at high speed from a pistol. The gun was capable of shooting the projectile with enough velocity to penetrate clothing and leave a tiny red mark on the skin. Once inside the body, the frozen poison would melt and be absorbed into the bloodstream and cause the victim's heart to stop beating. The poison was developed to be undetectable by modern autopsy procedures.

On February 13th, 2018, Zack Whittaker, a security editor for TechCrunch, posted a message on Twitter about Italy's Anti-Corruption Authority adopting the Tor network.

Zack Whittaker (from his Twitter account):
I wish we had more of this. No reason why official government whistleblower or watchdog organizations don't adopt Tor services to help report wrongdoing and corruption —just like SecureDrop, which journalists use already.
2:38PM - 13 Feb 2018

Edward Snowden retweeted Zack Whittaker. Q posted the following message.

Feb 15 2018
@Snowden
Thank you for showing the world how Clowns pass the narrative to journalists @ 4am.
Re_read crumbs re: SecureDrop.
John Perry Barlow.
Q

Q suggested the CIA (clowns) pass along the day's narrative to journalists at 4 am via SecureDrop.

An anon responded to Q with a list of related people and subjects.

Anonymous • Feb 15 2018
James Dolan. Dead suicide
Aaron swartz. Dead suicide
Kevin Paulson. Turned over securedrop to Freedom of the Press
Securedrop freedom of the press
Freedom of the press. John Barlow/Snowden/assange/John Cusack/
Daniel Ellsberg/Glenn Greenwald/Laura Poitras
Snowden/Cusack. Things that can and cannot be said
Daniel Ellsberg Pentagon papers
Glenn Greenwald/Snowden The Guardian
Laura Poitras/ Snowden. The Program. William Binney
John Barlow VP Algae Systems treating waste water
Barlow/Clark burning man
Gen Clark anti Trump. WestPAC supports Clintons
I think the KEY is the media changing the narrative using securedrop.
Which is dictated heavily by Snowden
The big question who controls Snowden

Q responded to the anon by picking out the relevant people from the list and connecting them.

>James Dolan. Dead suicide
>Aaron swartz. Dead suicide
>Kevin Paulson. Turned over securedrop to Freedom of the Press
John Perry Barlow - 187 post name [DROP].
@Snowden
You are now a liability.
Q

187 is the California penal code for homicide and is often used by Q to suggest someone was murdered. In this case, Barlow died shortly after Q "dropped" his name. Q suggested that Edward Snowden was the key player in the way the CIA controls the media's narrative and that he had become a liability to those who protected him.

On March 10th, 2019, Q responded to a tweet by Edward Snowden that attempted to smear newly appointed CIA Director, Gina Haspel.

Mar 10 2019

♦♦♦

Banking on HRC to win?

You never thought she would lose.

Banking on BRENNAN to bring you home?

You never expected a new DIR to be appointed.

Agency rogue elements still in control of OP?

No.

GINA (EX_UK_DIV_) open attacks?

[3uD_hq]

WHAT DO YOU HAVE LEFT TO SELL TO RUSSIA TO RETAIN YOUR SAFETY AND SECURITY?

WELCOME HOME, @SNOWDEN.

Q

Edward Snowden was stranded in Russia without support from the CIA since Gina Haspel took over as Director from John Brennan, and removed rogue operators from the original operation (OP) who helped him.

On October 1st, 2018, Q replied to an anon who was trying to understand the threat John Perry Barlow posed to the CIA and their control of the mainstream media. Q's reply suggested that his public exposure of their use of SecureDrop to control the media's narrative *coincidentally* caused the operation to be closed and cleaned of bad actors.

Oct 1 2018

Simple.

We made it public.

Operation closed and cleaned.

Coincidence post drop?

♦♦♦

WWG1WGA!

Q

Q has explained that the U.S. government is negotiating for the return of Edward Snowden. In December of 2019, Q seemed to predict that he will be returning to the U.S. in 2020.

Dec 15 2019
@Snowden
#HOMECOMING2020
Q

All for a LARP

A few weeks after Q's operation started, the mainstream media began publishing articles stating that Q was a ridiculous conspiracy that no sane person would take seriously.

Nov 20 2017
Coordinated effort to silence.
It will only get worse.
All for a LARP right?
Q

The media's loathing of Q reached a high water mark at the end of July 2018. For several months, the President had been holding political rallies around the country. During the rallies, POTUS occasionally pointed to Q supporters, many of whom posted their pictures on social media. On July 31st, Donald Trump held a rally in Tampa, Florida. Some Q supporters wore their Q t-shirts to the rally. One person was singled out by the President. Q told that individual to post their picture or video on social media so he could repost it.

Jul 31 2018
To the person holding the "Q" cut out:
Please post your pic/vid as POTUS specifically pointed at you moments ago.
We will scrub the web to find the source no matter where posted.
WE ARE Q.
Q

The anon posted a picture they took at the rally. Q located the picture and reposted it.

Anonymous • Jul 31 2018
I know it's a bit late, but thank you Q for the IRL (You).
Watching a rally on TV does not come anywhere near the atmosphere

of a rally in person and up front. I had a blast and to tippy top it off, I found out i was a Q drop. Best day ever!

Q responded.

We saw you, Patriots.
God bless!
WWG1WGA!
Q

The media have suggested that for all we know, Q might be lone individual posting from his mother's basement. How is it possible that Q can search the internet and find a photo posted on social media without knowing the name of the person who posted it, or the platform on which it was posted?

In the 48 hours that followed the rally, more than 50 news outlets around the world published negative stories about Q. Even conservative outlets like *Fox News* bashed Q as a dangerous internet conspiracy. To date, we know of no mainstream articles published that take a positive or even a neutral stance on Q. The handful of positive articles that have been published about Q have come from independent sources. What are the odds that news outlets around the world would suddenly, without coordination, publish dozens of articles warning readers about the dangers of Q?

Jul 30 2018
Obvious MSM coordination?
Independent?
POTUS coordinated attacks.
Q coordinated attacks.
Who/what else is under coordinated attack by the MSM?
Logical thinking.
What do they know?
Why won't they ask the obvious question?
All for a conspiracy?
Enjoy the show.
Q

Q asked if the attacks seemed independent or coordinated. Who else besides Donald Trump receives nearly unanimous negative coverage? Q asked anons why the media refused to ask the President to confirm or deny knowledge of him.

Jun 28 2018
We are waiting for a reporter to ask the ultimate question.
What are they waiting for?
They can end this at any time simply by asking POTUS, right?
We may have to 'force' this one.
Q

An anon replied:

Anonymous
I almost hope they don't ask. It would be fun to watch them try to
manage the spin when 90% of the country is aware of you and all that
you've been shining a light on, while the MSM still can acknowledge it.

I can see them squirming now..

Q responded:

It must happen.
Conspiracy no more.
Think of every post made.
It would force us to prove everything stated to avoid looking crazy,
correct?
What do they fear the most?
Public awakening.
If they ask.
They self destruct.
They know this is real.
See attacks.
The build is near complete.
Growing exponentially.
You are the frame.
You are the support.
People will be lost.
People will be terrified.
People will reject.
People will need to be guided.
Do not be afraid.
We will succeed.

Timing is everything.
Think Huber.
Think DOJ/FBI reorg.
Think sex/child arrests / news.
Think resignations (loss of control).
How do you remove evil in power unless you reveal the ultimate truth?
It must be compelling to avoid a divide (political attack/optics).
We are the majority (growing).
WW.
Sheep no more.
TOGETHER.
Q

The mainstream media have access to the President, and they can ask the question, but they're in a catch 22. They can continue writing negative articles as long as Trump hasn't publicly confirmed Q. If they ask the question and Q is confirmed, every article they've written is immediately discredited, and what remains of their reputation is destroyed.

By August of 2018, the Q movement was growing rapidly. Mainstream news articles attacking Q were regularly published. One reporter asked then-Press Secretary Sarah Sanders about Q, but she deflected the question. Q had finally gone mainstream.

Aug 1 2018
Mainstream = when you are now the news.
Mainstream = when a WH pool reporter asks about you.
Mainstream = when coordinated attacks (waves) against you continue to occur.
Game Theory.
Q

Going mainstream was, of course, the plan from the very beginning. Q provides evidence to skeptics. He provides feedback and tips at no cost. He encourages us to do our own research and come to our own conclusions. And he does it anonymously. Why wouldn't millions of people follow Q?

The President and Q have pulled back the curtain and revealed the dishonesty of the mainstream media and the corruption of politicians. That spectacle can't be unseen. It has been burned into the psyche of an entire generation, and it will not be forgotten.

CHAPTER 16

The Clinton Foundation

IT'S COMMON FOR U.S. POLITICIANS to have non-profit organizations named after them. But the money collected by a nonprofit doesn't belong to the individual for which it is named. It belongs to the nonprofit, and there are restrictions on how it may be received and spent. Donations may not be received (legally) as payment for political favors. Money that has been received cannot be used for personal expenses. It must only be used for legitimate expenses of the organization.

Since bribery of elected officials is illegal, some have theorized that to get around bribery laws, politicians who wish to make their services available for a fee have embraced the practice of establishing non-profit foundations. Their foundations receive donations. Then, so the theory goes, a complex series of transfers are made through other people and organizations, and the money finds its way into the pockets of politicians.

It's easy to point to examples where there appears to be impropriety on the part of politicians, but it's generally difficult to prove that they've taken money in exchange for political favors or that they've used the money from a foundation for personal use. With that background, we turn to the operations of the William Jefferson Clinton Foundation, named after former President Bill Clinton. (In this book, it is simply referred to as the Clinton Foundation.)

In his posts, Q often ties former Secretary of State Hillary Rodham Clinton (HRC) and the Clinton Foundation (CF) to Saudi Arabia (SA).

Nov 4 2017
Follow HUMA.
Who connects HRC/CF to SA?
Why is this relevant?
♦♦♦

After Hillary lost the 2016 Presidential election, donations to the Clinton Foundation dried up. The Foundation fired most of its staff and closed its doors. Although it is claimed that the Clinton Foundation doesn't sell political favors, the fact that few people donated to the Foundation after Hillary's Presidential election loss suggests otherwise. If the Foundation engaged in purely benevolent purposes, and there was no expectation of political favor in exchange for a donation, why would millions of dollars be donated just before an election but not afterward?

Heavy criticism has been leveled against the Clinton Foundation for its operations in Haiti. In the aftermath of the 2010 earthquake, foreign governments and foreign companies were awarded construction deals in Haiti in exchange for donations to the Clinton Foundation. The Foundation's reports show that the Brazilian construction firm OAS and the InterAmerican Development Bank (IDB) have donated between $1 billion and $5 billion.

The IDB received funding from the State Department, some of which was diverted to OAS for contracts to build roads on the island. An IDB auditor, Mariela Antiga, said the contracts were padded with "excessive costs" to build roads that "no one needed."

The Clinton Foundation selected Clayton Homes, a construction company owned by Warren Buffett's Berkshire Hathaway, to build temporary shelters in Haiti. Buffett is a member of the Clinton Global Initiative who donates to the Clinton Foundation. The contract was supposed to be awarded through the normal United Nations bidding process, with the contract being awarded to the lowest bidder. UN officials said the contract was never competitively bid for. It was awarded to Clayton Homes, who built "hurricane-proof trailers" that were structurally unsafe, with high levels of formaldehyde fumes emitting from the walls. The walls were improperly insulated; the high temperatures inside made Haitians sick, and many of the trailers were abandoned.

On January 29, 2010, Laura Silsby was arrested with nine American missionaries while attempting to smuggle 33 children out of the country. Many of the children were not orphans; they had families. This was not the first time Silsby had attempted to traffic children out of Haiti. Haitian police acting on a tip had intercepted Silsby in an earlier attempt to remove 40 children from the country. In that incident, she was turned back at the border.

On February 7th, 2010, *The Sunday Times* reported that Bill Clinton helped negotiate a deal with the Haitian government, securing the release of all co-conspirators except Silsby. Prosecutors ultimately sought a six-month sentence on charges that were reduced from conspiracy and child abduction to "arranging irregular travel." Silsby escaped a harsh sentence with the help of the Clintons.

Mar 6 2018
So much is open source.
So much left to be connected.
Why are the children in Haiti in high demand?
How are they smuggled out?
'Adoption' process.
Local 'staging' ports friendly to CF?
Track donations.
Cross against location relative to Haiti.
Think logically.
The choice, to KNOW, will be yours.
Q

Q implied that children have been trafficked from Haiti as orphans under cover of adoption and that the Clinton Foundation is involved. Much of the information needed to connect the dots is open source.

On November 5th, 2017, an anon created an updated graphic of Q's posts. Q replied.

Nov 5 2017
Thank you Anon.
FBI/MI currently have open investigation into the CF.
Why didn't Comey drop this?
Who was the FBI director during the Haiti crisis? How many kids disappeared?
How much money was sent to CF under disguise of Haiti relief and actually went to Haiti?
What countries donated big money to CF?
SA?

Why is this relevant?
Snow White
Q

Q asked why FBI Director James Comey didn't halt the ongoing FBI investigation into the Clinton Foundation (CF). Robert Mueller was FBI Director when
the Clinton Foundation provided relief to Haiti. (Mueller was also FBI Director
when Uranium One was sold to Rosatom, and he signed off on the deal.) Q said
there was an open military intelligence (MI) investigation into the Clinton
Foundation. The signature "Snow White" in this post indicates some level of
CIA involvement.

One scandal that has the potential to take down many corrupt people is
the sale of Uranium One and its subsidiaries to the Russian energy company
Rosatom. As reported by *The New York Times* on April 23, 2015, the only publicly reported donation made to the Clinton Foundation by Uranium One CEO
Ian Telfer, amounted to $250,000. That donation was made in 2007, several
years before the proposed sale of Uranium One was in the works. But a review
of Canadian tax records, where Mr. Telfer has a charity called the Fernwood
Foundation, shows that he donated millions of dollars more, during and after the
time when the U.S. government was reviewing his proposed deal with Rosatom.

Telfer's donations to the Clinton Foundation through the Fernwood Foundation included $1 million in 2009, the year his company appealed to the American
Embassy to help keep its uranium mines that were located in Kazakhstan. In
2010, the year Rosatom sought majority control of the company, $250,000 was
donated to the Clinton Foundation. $600,000 was donated in 2011, and $500,000
was donated in 2012. These donations were not initially disclosed by the Clinton
Foundation; they were uncovered upon inspection of Fernwood's filings.

Telfer said that his donations were unrelated to his business dealings, and
he had never discussed Uranium One with the Clintons.

In June of 2010, Bill Clinton was invited to speak in Moscow. It happened to
be at the same time Rosatom was making its bid for majority control of Uranium
One. The $500,000 speaking fee Clinton received was paid by Renaissance
Capital, a Russian investment bank with ties to the Kremlin. Renaissance
hyped Uranium One's stock, assigning it a "buy" rating and stated in a July 2010
market report that it was "the best play" in the uranium markets at the time.
The Clinton Foundation has denied allegations of pay-for-play with respect to
the sale Uranium One.

Investigators for *The New York Post* found evidence of a mysterious off-the-
books branch of the Clinton Foundation in the emails of John Podesta that were

published by *WikiLeaks*. The Haiti Development Fund, an LLC incorporated in Delaware in August 2010, was created by the Clinton Foundation with an initial endowment of $20 million by Canadian mining billionaire Frank Giustra and Mexican billionaire Carlos Slim. The fund was set up ostensibly to provide capital to Haitian businesses after the 2010 earthquake. Investigators found only one project that it funded using a fraction of the start-up cash. Since the fund was incorporated as a private company instead of a nonprofit, it was not subject to the same disclosure rules as a public charity, and the Clinton Foundation never disclosed it as a "related entity" on its tax filings. It was only disclosed later after the Clinton Foundation—under mounting scrutiny and media pressure—refiled five years' worth of tax returns in 2015 that the fund appeared on the forms.

"This cries out for an audit or an investigation," said Ken Boehm, chairman of the National Legal and Policy Center, a Virginia-based watchdog group. "Its director was in bankruptcy and there's almost nothing in the public record showing what happened to the millions of dollars it supposedly was going to use to help poor Haitians." Did the money from Carlos Slim and Frank Giustra end up in the pockets of the Clintons?

In January of 2018, Q asked how much money Australia and Saudi Arabia donated to the Clinton Foundation.

Jan 6 2018
How much did AUS donate to CF?
How much did SA donate to CF?
Compare.
Why is this relevant?
What phone call between POTUS and X/AUS leaked?
List the leadership in AUS.
IDEN leadership during Hussein term.
IDEN leadership during POTUS' term.
Who controls AUS?
Who really controls AUS?
UK?
Why is this relevant?
Q

Former Australian Foreign Minister Alexander Downer helped arrange a $25 million donation from Australia to the Clinton Foundation. The FBI has stated that it was Downer's conversation with George Papadopoulos that led to the opening of its investigation into Russian interference in the 2016 Presidential election. Q asked why the phone call between President Trump and Australia's Prime Minister was leaked to the press. There is a suggestion that it was done to embarrass Trump and that the decision came from the UK, which really controls affairs in Australia.

The Clinton Foundation records show that the Kingdom of Saudi Arabia donated between $10 million and $25 million to them. I would imagine the Saudis expected a return on their investment after Hillary became President. Why would they donate such a large sum of money? They never thought she would lose.

Q asked anons to research the net worth of politicians who have non-profit foundations or institutes.

Nov 2 2017
Review BO's financial disclosure when he submitted pre-D election campaign.
What is the annual salary of a sitting US President?
What home(s) were just purchased by BO?
How much did it cost?
How does it reconcile?
What is the net worth of Pelosi?
How does it reconcile?
What is the John M Institute?
Notice any patterns relating to the CF?
Where did John M obtain his surgery?
Why is that relevant?
What surgery did he supposedly have?
How many days until he was back in Congress and sitting on the OS comm?
What is John M's net worth?
How does it reconcile?
What is MW's net worth?
How does it reconcile?
You can play this game with most D's and many R's.
What does swamp refer to?
What does money buy?
Alice & Wonderland.

Q asked about Barack Obama (BO), House Speaker Nancy Pelosi, Maxine Waters (MW), the Clinton Foundation (CF), and former Senator John McCain who quickly returned to his position on the oversight (OS) committee after having surgery. In May of 2017, Barack and Michelle Obama purchased a home in a suburb of Washington D.C. for $8.1 million. In 2019, they purchased a home on Martha's Vineyard for $11.75 million.

The day the Saudi princes were arrested, Q asked if Hillary Clinton owed money to Saudi Arabia, and if so, how it was repaid.

Nov 4 2017

♦♦♦

What happened when HRC lost the election of 2016?
How much money was provided to the CF by SA during 15/16?
HRC lost.
Loss of access/power/control.
Does repayment of funds to SA occur? If so, how?
Why did BO send billions in cash to Iran?
Why wasn't Congress notified?
Why was this classified under 'State Secrets'?
Who has access to 'State Secrets'?
Where did the planes carrying the cash depart from and land?
Did the planes all land in the same location?
How many planes carried the cash?
Why is this relevant?

♦♦♦

Q suggested that the Saudis fronted Hillary Clinton money for her 2016 Presidential campaign, and when she lost the election, she had to repay it. An anon discovered what he believed to be the repayment to the Saudis.

Anonymous • Nov 5 2017
Obama sent 221 million to Palestinians right before leaving office. The payout..
http://www.breitbart.com/big-government/2017/01/23/report-obama-gave-221-million-palestinians-last-hours/

Q confirmed the anon's discovery.

Amazing how things make sense once you are asked a question.
That's the entire point of this operation.
It's up to you all to collect, archive (safely), and distribute in a graphic

that is in order with the crumb dumbs.
It will all make sense.
Once it does, we look to you to spread and get the word out.
Time stamps will help you validate authenticity.
Your President needs your help.
He wants full transparency for the great people of this country.
Everything stated is for a reason.
God bless, Patriots.
Q

Let's look again at this post about Uranium One.

Nov 22 2017
U1 - CA - EU - ASIA - IRAN/NK
Where did it end up?
What was the purpose?
Who was suppose to win the election of 2016?
Why was the Iran deal kept from Congress and placed at the highest level of classification?
Meaning, a United States Senator could NOT review the deal but other foreign powers could.
How much money was hand delivered by plane(s)?
Why in cash?
Where did the plane(s) actually land?
What was the cover?
Who paid for BO to attend Harvard?
Why would this occur pre-political days?
Who was the biggest contributor to the CF?
The graphic is the key.
Why does the MSM push conspiracy w/o investigation?
Who controls the MSM?
What does the word 'conspiracy' mean to you?
Has the word 'conspiracy' been branded to mean something shameful in today's society?
The world cannot handle the truth.
This pill cannot be swallowed by most.
Risk in painting this picture.
THE SUM OF ALL FEARS.
Q

Q intimated that some of the details of the Iran deal were classified at the highest level to keep Congress and U.S. citizens from knowing about them. He asked if the term *conspiracy theory* had been used to shame those who question official explanations. Indeed, it has. The term conspiracy theory was developed and popularized by the CIA after the Kennedy assassination and used to shame those who questioned official explanations of current and historical events. Q provides a counter-narrative to the official explanation of those events.

Q ended the above post with the signature "THE SUM OF ALL FEARS," which is the title of Tom Clancy's tale of a plot by a sociopath to trick the U.S. and Russia into starting a nuclear war. In the film, the plan was to get the two superpowers to destroy one another then set up a fascist superstate in Europe.

Q's signatures use familiar stories to convey hidden truths. We might consider whether there was an actual plot to destroy Russia and the U.S. for the purpose of establishing a post-war super state. In January of 2018, Q posted a lengthy message which provided details of such a plan. We'll explore that post next, but I'd like to preface that discussion with the following observation:

There are many world leaders who believe that war results from the existence of independent nation-states. Their assertion is that nations must wage war in order to exert their national sovereignty. The solution they propose is to have all independent nation-states surrender their national sovereignty to a global government. Their goal is to eradicate international borders and create a borderless, global community. That goal necessitates either the willing submission or the forced subjugation of individual nation-states. Two nations, in particular, have historically caused problems for those who pursue this goal. The United States and Russia have strongly resisted the demand to surrender their national sovereignty.

With that in mind, let's look at a post that outlines what Q said was the 16-year plan to destroy America. Here is the post. A section by section interpretation will follow.

Jan 21, 2018
♦♦♦
[The 16 Year Plan To Destroy America]
Hussein [8]
Install rogue_ops
Leak C-intel/Mil assets
Cut funding to Mil
Command away from generals
Launch 'good guy' takedown (internal remove) - Valerie Jarrett (sniffer)

SAP sell-off

Snowden open source Prism/Keyscore (catastrophic to US Mil v. bad actors (WW) +Clowns/-No Such Agency)

Target/weaken conservative base (IRS/MSM)

Open border (flood illegals: D win) ISIS/MS13 fund/install (fear, targeting/removal, domestic-assets etc.)

Blind-eye NK [nuke build]

[Clas-1, 2, 3]

Blind-eye Iran [fund and supply]

Blind-eye [CLAS 23-41]

Stage SC [AS [187]]

U1 fund/supply IRAN/NK [+reduce US capacity]

KILL NASA (prevent space domination/allow bad actors to take down MIL SATs/WW secure comms/install WMDs) - RISK OF EMP SPACE ORIG (HELPLESS)

[CLAS 1-99]

HRC [8] WWIII [death & weapons real/WAR FAKE & CONTROLLED] [population growth control/pocket billions]

Eliminate final rogue_ops within Gov't/MIL

KILL economy [starve/need/enslave]

Open borders

Revise Constitution

Ban sale of firearms (2nd amen removal)

Install 'on team' SC justices> legal win(s) across spectrum of challengers (AS 187)

Removal of electoral college [pop vote ^easier manipulation/illegal votes/Soros machines]

Limit/remove funding of MIL

Closure of US MIL installations WW [Germany 1st]

Destruction of opposing MSM/other news outlets (censoring), CLAS 1-59

[]

Pure EVIL.

Narrative intercept [4am].

Sessions/Nunes Russian OPS.

Repub distortion of facts to remove Mueller.[POTUS free pass].

Shutdown Primary Reasons.

Distract.

Weaken military assets.

Inc illegal votes.

Black voters abandoning.
"Keep them starved"
"Keep them blind"
"Keep them stupid"
HRC March 13, 2013 [intercept].
The Great Awakening.
Fight, Fight, Fight.
Q

Next, we'll examine parts of the post with an explanation provided below each section.

Jan 21 2018
◆◆◆
Hussein [8]
Install rogue_ops
Leak C-intel/Mil assets
Cut funding to Mil
Command away from generals
Launch 'good guy' takedown (internal remove) - Valerie Jarrett (sniffer)
◆◆◆

Barack Obama (Hussein) was given eight years to accomplish certain strategic goals. Since the U.S. military plays a key role in protecting our national sovereignty and our borders, under Obama, the military would be weakened and compromised. Rogue operators would be installed in key government positions. Classified intelligence would be leaked that would harm military assets. Military funding would be cut. The leadership ability and decision making of military leaders would be undermined. Patriots in the military (good guys) would be targeted for removal. Valerie Jarrett would be used to help identify those targets.

◆◆◆
SAP sell-off
◆◆◆

The 16-year plan included weakening the military by selling Special Access Programs (SAPs) to foreign nations. (SAPs were described in an earlier chapter.) A *Fox News* article from April 18 of 2016 reported that Hillary Clinton's unsecured, private email server held Special Access Programs.

◆◆◆
Snowden open source Prism/Keyscore (catastrophic to US Mil v. bad actors (WW) +Clowns/-No Such Agency)
◆◆◆

The leak by Edward Snowden of the NSA's spy tools gave the public a greater understanding of government surveillance. While the leak accomplished that goal, Q warned that Snowden's leak had a nefarious objective, of which the public is ignorant. The real purpose was to harm the credibility of military intelligence and give the CIA an upper hand.

◆◆◆
Target/weaken conservative base (IRS/MSM)
◆◆◆

The Obama IRS was found to have engaged in targeted harassment of conservative organizations. It seems this was part of a coordinated effort that included attacks by the liberal mainstream media in an effort to discourage and demoralize conservatives.

◆◆◆
Open border (flood illegals: D win) ISIS/MS13 fund/install (fear, targeting/removal, domestic-assets etc.)
◆◆◆

Democrats running for President in 2020 have made open borders one of their major priorities. Q said their goal is to flood the nation with illegal immigrants and give them voting rights since most will vote for Democrats. Allowing gangs like MS-13 and terror groups like ISIS into the country would help remove opposition through violence and intimidation.

◆◆◆
Blind-eye NK [nuke build]
[Clas-1, 2, 3]
Blind-eye Iran [fund and supply]
Blind-eye [CLAS 23-41]
◆◆◆
U1 fund/supply IRAN/NK [+reduce US capacity]
◆◆◆

The Obama administration turned a blind eye while North Korea and Iran developed weapons of mass destruction. Worse, Q said the money sent to Iran helped them develop their weapons programs, and the Obama administration allowed the sale of Uranium One to deplete our own production capacity. We previously learned that the uranium from the sale of Uranium One may have been diverted to Iran and Syria to help them build weapons of mass destruction, the goal of which was to precipitate a third world war.

Q has access to both open source and classified information. While he is free to provide open source information, national security laws prevent the release of classified information. When Q writes the term "CLAS" as in [CLAS 23-41], I believe it indicates that there is related information that is classified.

◆◆◆
Stage SC [AS [187]]
◆◆◆

Q has put forth the possibility that Supreme Court Justice Antonin Scalia (AS) was murdered to stage a liberal takeover of the Supreme Court (SC). 187 is the California penal code section for homicide. There was no autopsy performed after Scalia was found dead.

◆◆◆
KILL NASA (prevent space domination/allow bad actors to take down MIL SATs/WW secure comms/install WMDs) - RISK OF EMP SPACE ORIG (HELPLESS)
[CLAS 1-99]
◆◆◆

Q suggested the Obama administration allowed NASA to languish so that corrupt people could gain space dominance by taking down military satellites and putting their own in orbit, which would disrupt secure communications worldwide. It would also facilitate the deployment of weapons of mass destruction in space, leaving good people helpless to defend themselves against bad actors.

◆◆◆
HRC [8] WWIII [death & weapons real/WAR FAKE & CONTROLLED]
[population growth control/pocket billions]
Eliminate final rogue_ops within Gov't/MIL
KILL economy [starve/need/enslave]

Open borders
Revise Constitution
Ban sale of firearms (2nd amen removal)
Install 'on team' SC justices> legal win(s) across spectrum of
challengers (AS 187)
Removal of electoral college [pop vote ^easier manipulation/illegal
votes/Soros machines]
Limit/remove funding of MIL
Closure of US MIL installations WW [Germany 1st]
Destruction of opposing MSM/other news outlets (censoring),
CLAS 1-59

◆◆◆

The plan was intended to continue if Hillary Clinton managed to serve two terms (eight years) as President. Under her reign, more patriots in the military would be identified and eliminated. More corrupt operatives would be installed in government. The economy would be decimated, making the population completely dependent on the government for survival. Borders would be opened, allowing the country to be flooded with immigrants. The constitution would be revised. Private ownership of firearms would be banned, leaving citizens defenseless against government tyranny.

The Supreme Court would be revamped to support the globalist agenda. The constitution would be revised to eliminate the electoral college. The outcome of Presidential elections would be determined by popular vote, making it easier to manipulate elections through fraud.

Military funding would continue to decline, and overseas military bases would be closed, beginning with the U.S. base in Germany. Conservative news outlets would be destroyed. The voices of independent conservative commentators would be censored. The globalist propaganda campaign via the mainstream media would continue.

In this scenario, Hillary's eight years would culminate in a third world war after the successful attainment of weapons of mass destruction by rogue nations. The war would put billions of dollars in the pockets of corrupt people and reduce the global population. A post-war global community would be established that prohibited international borders and eliminated national sovereignty. The world's population would be easily controlled, having been massively reduced by the devastation of war.

Because Donald Trump was elected President, and because he has help from patriots in the military, we averted the 16-year plan to destroy America.

When Can We Expect Arrests?

Some people were disappointed or confused, having expected that the release of the Department of Justice IG report on FISA abuse would lead to the arrest of corrupt people in government. That was never a realistic expectation. The prosecution of those who have committed crimes is one step in a complex process that must be allowed to unfold in its entirety if corruption is to be permanently removed from our government.

The removal of corruption has many steps. If the process is to be effective, each step must be taken at a precise time and in the prescribed order. Permanently removing corruption is more than merely a matter of arresting people for criminal behavior. Measures must be put in place to make sure this type of corruption never happens again.

Some have objected to what they perceive to be unnecessary delays that cause continued human suffering.

Anonymous • Dec 19, 2017
Q, where are the children?
Seriously. Where are the children?
Love,
TlinOKC

Q responded.

3,000+ saved by the raids in SA alone.
WW lanes shut down.
Bottom to TOP.
[HAITI].
[RED CROSS]
[CLASSIFIED]
High Priority.
Q

The corruption crackdown in Saudi Arabia alone rescued 3,000 people. Other actions have eliminated human trafficking lanes worldwide (WW). The operators involved consider this to be one of their highest priorities.

The Justice Department could arrest thousands of corrupt people tomorrow if they wanted to. But if the problems in our two-tiered system of justice aren't fixed first, the guilty may be arrested, but they would not be convicted.

Corrupt people must first be removed from the system of justice. That is going to take time.

Soon after he was appointed, then-Attorney General Jeff Sessions began removing corrupt people from the FBI and DOJ. Some employees left under cover of retirement or resignation, but Q indicated they were forced out or fired.

Feb 12, 2019
https://www.foxnews.com/politics/newly-released-emails-show-fbi-scrambling-to-respond-to-clinton-lawyer-amid-weiner-laptop-review
Shall We Play a Game?
Where are they now?
[Ref: public optics: 'retired''left' refers to 'fired/forced']
FEDERAL BUREAU OF "INVESTIGATION"
James Comey, Director – FIRED
Andrew McCabe, Deputy Director - FIRED
Jim Rybicki, Chief of Staff and Senior Counselor – FIRED
James Baker, General Counsel – FIRED
Bill Priestap, Director of Counterintelligence (Strzok's boss) – FIRED
Peter Strzok, Deputy Assistant Director of Counterintelligence – FIRED
Lisa Page, Office of General Counsel – FIRED
Mike Kortan, Assistant Director for Public Affairs – FIRED
Josh Campbell, Special Assistant to Comey – FIRED
Michael Steinbach - Head of NAT SEC Div - FIRED
John Glacalone – (Predecessor to Steinbach) – Head of NAT SEC Div - FIRED
James Turgal – Assistant Director - FIRED
Greg Bower – Top Congressional Liaison - FIRED
Trisha Anderson – Principle Deputy General Counsel - FIRED
Randy Coleman - Assistant Director of Counterintelligence Div – REMOVED
Coleman Authored:
(1) Anthony Wiener [sic]
(2) [Unrelated]
(3) Wiener [sic] – texting 15 yo – Sexually Explicit
9/26 – Federal SW – IPhone/IPAD/Laptop
Initial analysis of laptop – thousands emails
Hillary Clinton Foundation
Crime Against Children
Kevin Clinesmith – track follow

Tashina Gauhar – track follow
Sally Moyer – track follow
Jason V. Herring – track follow
Nothing being done?
FAKE NEWS?
Q

Randall Coleman is notable for his meeting with James Comey to discuss what was found on Anthony Weiner's laptop when it was confiscated by the NYPD. That meeting was mentioned in the 2017 IG report on the FBI's handling of Hillary's email investigation. Coleman wrote a note about things found on Weiner's laptop, including two items: "Hillary Clinton Foundation" and "Crime Against Children."

Kevin Clinesmith is the FBI attorney who changed a CIA email confirming that Carter Page was one of their sources. Clinesmith's alteration stated Page was *not* a CIA source. That email was used to obtain a FISA warrant to spy on Page.

The successful prosecution of corruption requires changes to federal courts. As of the end of 2019, Donald Trump had added two supreme court justices, 50 circuit court judges, and 133 district court judges. Trump's nominees now comprise about a fifth of all federal judgeships and nearly a third of circuit court judgeships, with more appointments yet to be confirmed.

If we hope to avoid civil war as a reaction to the arrest of corrupt politicians, the public must first see evidence of the crimes they've committed. Perhaps more importantly, if the public isn't made aware of *how* political corruption happens—at a later time, it will happen again. Educating the public is essential to preventing corruption from reoccurring. Thanks to a dishonest press, a majority of citizens are still uninformed about the true nature and extent of political corruption.

The release of the IG report on FISA abuse was one step in the process of making the public aware of how elected officials and career government employees commit crimes. Unfortunately, public awareness of corruption won't happen overnight. It will take time for the public to process the IG report and come to conclusions different from what they currently believe. Attorney General Barr will declassify documents that will further expose corruption. If my understanding of the process is correct, declassification is the next step. Again, it will take time for the necessary documents to be released and for the public to process them. Only then will they realize how entrenched corruption is and how adversely it affects us.

Once the public has been made aware of how corruption happens, they'll demand changes. Members of Congress, judges, and Executive Branch officials will then make the necessary changes to the various systems of government.

The next step is the prosecution of those who illegally surveilled the Trump campaign. At this point, the work of U.S. Attorney John Durham will be revealed. Because the media have distorted the actions of the guilty and the innocent, the crimes perpetrated against Donald Trump and others will be difficult for the average person to understand. It will be necessary to bring the public up the learning curve at a manageable pace. Once the prosecution has commenced for those who spied on President Trump, the DOJ can move to the next step in the process.

The Clinton Foundation and the Uranium One scandals are far more complex. In addition to corruption in the government, the public will learn about corruption in foreign governments, corporations, and non-profit organizations. Corruption related to the Clinton Foundation and Uranium One will be exposed once the public understands the crimes that took place during the 2016 election. The prosecution of crimes related to Hillary Clinton will reveal the work that U.S. Attorney John Huber has been doing.

The fact that no information has leaked from Huber's investigation since its inception has caused some to conclude that he has been doing nothing. Since there were no news reports on the progress of his investigation, articles were published claiming his investigation never began or that he had not bothered to interview key witnesses. These reports caused some to doubt Q's insistence that Huber was investigating corruption.

Anonymous • Dec 12, 2018
So HUBER is a HEADFAKE? If so, BRILLIANT Q!

Q replied.

FALSE.
HUBER will bring SEVERE PAIN TO DC.
SESSIONS' forced release of name [HUBER] to House created another variable.
Use Logic.
Why would we tell you the plan if in doing so also alerts those who we are actively engaged in HUNTING?
You are witnessing, first-hand, the demise of those in power [OLD GUARD].

Those who push simply have no grasp of reality.
Those who push simply do not understand warfare tactics.
Emotions cloud judgement.
Emotions cloud logic.
You have more than you know.
♦♦♦

In June of 2018, Q provided this update.

Jun 18th 2018
IG email investigation (weakest of set).
Opened door to:
Weiner HRC / Others - crimes against children.
Noose.
Ref to Huber?
Non public.
CF investigation ongoing.
Connected.
Ref to Huber?
+FBI protection of HRC.
+FBI criminal acts.
Ref to Huber?
What about DOJ texts/emails?
Why did the intel comm rate sections of the IG report @ highest level of NAT SEC?
What does it involve?
DOJ?
WH?
Tarmac?
Ref to Huber?
[[RR]]
IG report release does not coincide with true start date (info push to) of Huber re: above.
Scope Size biggest in history.
Grand Jury in place?
Q

According to Q, the FBI's investigation of Hillary's emails provided evidence of far worse crimes that were referred to John Huber. They included attempts to protect Hillary from prosecution and other criminal acts committed by FBI & DOJ employees. Q mentioned crimes against children related to the Clinton Foundation. Also mentioned were matters discussed in the 2016 IG report on the FBI's handling of Hillary's email investigation. The DOJ intelligence community (intel comm) rated these matters at the highest level of national security. Q said this pertained to the now-famous tarmac meeting between Bill Clinton and Loretta Lynch.

Feb 22,2019
The Deal of a Lifetime?
[Tarmac] meeting not planned according to [LL] [BC]?
Security reports indicate USSS (sec detail [BC] FBI (sec detail [LL])
planned for meeting?
SC/[LL] deal presented by BC?
What actions did [JC] take days after?
Less than a week after the tarmac meeting, [JC] announced that the
FBI would not recommend an indictment against [HRC]?
Returning to the news?
Q

The official story on the tarmac meeting was that it was unplanned, however, Secret Service agents say there was communication ahead of time to arrange the meeting. Q asked if Bill Clinton (BC) offered Loretta Lynch (LL) a Supreme Court (SC) position if she would arrange for Hillary not to be prosecuted over her email scandal. Less than a week later, James Comey (JC) announced that she would not be prosecuted.

Huber's criminal investigation may turn out to be the biggest in history. Q has suggested that grand juries were empaneled long ago and that sealed indictments are waiting to be unsealed. In an interview on May 30, 2019, Attorney General Barr confirmed that Huber has been investigating matters related to Hillary Clinton. At that time, he said Huber's investigation was "winding down" and that they hoped to be bringing those matters to fruition soon.

If you're looking for a time frame, I can offer you this: In an interview on December 10th, 2019, Attorney General Barr said he expects Durham's investigation will be "reaching an important watershed in late spring or early summer" of 2020. Will there be indictments before then? It's impossible to say for sure.

CHAPTER 17

Bunker Apple Yellow Sky

THIS CHAPTER IS AN EXERCISE in learning to decode some of Q's more cryptic posts. Messages like the ones we'll look at in this chapter don't give us much to go on. We see what appears to be a meaningless string of letters and numbers and a few unrelated words. When we find a cryptic post, if we wait and if we consider the subjects related to Q's mission, a future news event will usually shed light on it. These odd posts are markers in time—beacons that, at a precise moment, will draw our attention and provide a bridge to help us see the truth behind the news story. The key to decoding them is waiting for more information and putting that information together with what clues have already been given.

On November 15th, 2017, Q posted the message that follows. This was the only message posted that day. It's worth noting that there were four posts the previous day and none the following two days, but Q made one post three days later on November 18th. These facts are relevant because sometimes, sequential posts are related.

Nov 15 2017
_Conf_D-TT_^_v891_0600_yes
_green1_0600

Bunker Apple Yellow Sky [... + 1]
Yes
Godspeed.
Q

On November 18th, Q posted a message that simply contained two plus signs.

Nov 18 2017
++

At this point, we might develop a hypothesis that the post from the 15th is related to the one on the 18th. We don't know this to be true, but it's a possibility that's worth exploring. Time will either prove us right or wrong. Next, we need to know what the two plus signs might represent. Q discussed this in previous posts. On November 6th, 2017, he posted a message immediately after the arrest of Saudi princes.

Nov 6 2017
Nothing is random.
Everything has meaning.
+++
Q

The following day, Q posted the message below.

Nov 7 2017
+++
++
+
Q

That message was somehow deleted from the board, so Q posted it again.

Nov 7 2017
Previous was deleted. Curious.
+++
++
+
Q

The next message that we'll consider was posted on November 11th, 2017. Q said this information would be difficult for many people to accept as true, but his mission had reached a point where it was necessary for us to understand these facts.

Nov 11
Hard to swallow.
Important to progress.
Who are the puppet masters?
House of Saud (6+++) - $4 Trillion+
Rothschild (6++) - $2 Trillion+
Soros (6+) - $1 Trillion+
Focus on above (3).
Public wealth disclosures – False.
♦♦♦

The post names the three wealthiest families in the world. According to Q, their publicly stated net worth is incorrect. They control events on the geopolitical stage by virtue of their money and power. They control politicians from the shadows. They're represented in Q's posts by plus signs; the Saudi royal family is represented by +++, the Rothschilds by ++, and George Soros by +.

We've previously discussed the Saudi royal family. Now it's time to consider the Rothschilds. The Rothschilds are a wealthy family descended from Mayer Amschel Rothschild (1744–1812), who started a family business in Europe in the 1760s. Mayer Rothschild bequeathed his wealth to his descendants and established an international banking family through his five sons who settled in London, Paris, Frankfurt, Vienna, and Naples. During the 19th century, the Rothschild family possessed the largest private fortune in the world. In my research of the Rothschilds, I was struck by how much of the family's wealth came from making loans to kings who needed money to pay for wars.

Two days after the previous message, Q posted this:

Nov 13 2017
Distress cal[L]s to others will [d]o you/family no good at this stage.
We know whe[R]e you/the family are at all times and can hear you breathing.
Q
_D7g^-_%19FZBx_decline

Note the bracketed letters [L][d][R] in the above post, which could indicate either Lynn or Lord De Rothschild.

Now, let's return to the Bunker Apple Yellow Sky message. The post that followed it on November 18th had two plus signs, which we now know signifies the Rothschild family. If our hypothesis is correct, then we would expect to see a news story related to the Rothschilds and perhaps to other elements found in that post.

It just so happened that there was a mid-air collision over the Rothschild's estate the previous day, November 17th. According to news reports, four people were killed in a collision between a helicopter and a small airplane flying from an airfield where air traffic control had been suspended due to "staff shortages." Debris from the wreck landed about a mile from the former home of the Rothschild family at Waddesdon Manor in Buckinghamshire around noon local time. News reports said members of the Rothschild family reported hearing a "loud bang" and that a plume of smoke could be seen above trees.

On November 18th, *The Telegraph UK* reported the names of those who died in the crash. Among them was a helicopter pilot named Mike Green. By November 21st, no one had yet made the connection between the crash and the Bunker Apple Yellow Sky post, so Q provided a reminder:

Nov 21 2017
Expand your thinking.
Captain Mike Green.
_Conf_D-TT_^_v891_0600_yes
_green1_0600
Bunker Apple Yellow Sky [... + 1]
Yes.
Who countered?
Do you believe in coincidences?
Learn how to read the map.
Q

Q asked a few questions about the Bunker Apple Yellow Sky stringer and implied that some "key" words were intentionally included in it to prove that he had foreknowledge of the event:

Nov 21 2017
What was posted prior to the stringer?
What keywords were within the stringer?

Why would keywords be left in the stringer?
Future shows past.
Learn to read the map.
Everything has meaning - EVERYTHING.
Q

Anons were still not picking up on Q's clues, so he asked them to consider specific keywords—*green* and *sky*—and asked what they might signify. He asked about the two plus signs that were posted before the air collision and if they might be connected. He asked if the Rothschilds made a counter move.

Nov 21 2017
Keywords:
Confirm.
Green.
Sky.
Why were keywords added in the stringer?
What was the purpose?
What was previously stated?
To who specifically?
++
Who countered?
Learn to read the map.
Missing critical items.
Graphic is key.
Ordering is critical.
Q

Anons still didn't make the connection between the pilot (Mike Green), the aircraft crash (the "Sky" event), and the Rothschilds (Lord d R and ++), so Q posted this message.

Nov 21 2017
Archive immediately.
Stringer = code = command.
What stringer was provided (2) days prior to event?
What were the keywords in the stringer?
Confirm.
Green (Yes).

Sky.
Why were keywords provided?
Guide to reading map?
Lord d R.
What was previously stated?
++
Who was the pilot of the plane?
Bad actor?
Who was the pilot of the helicopter?
Green?
What was countered?
Who was on the ground (outside) shortly before the collision?
Who was in the home shortly before the collision?
Learn to read the map.
We may have overestimated your ability.
Q

Q explained that the code was actually a command to green-light the operation. Lord d R and ++ were connected. Green was a go signal and also the name of one of the pilots. He asked who was in the house and who was outside of it. He told anons to archive all information.

An anon reposted the individual lines from Q's post and responded to each one:

Spreadsheet Anon AT • Nov 21 2017

>What stringer was provided (2) days prior to event?
_Conf_D-TT_^_v891_0600_yes
_green1_0600
Bunker Apple Yellow Sky [... + 1]

confirm 0600 (time) yes
Green 0600 (time)
Base Green Yellow (condition yellow?) Air

>What were the keywords in the stringer?
confirm
green
Yellow

Sky

>Guide to reading map?
legend, past provides the future, questions provide the answers

>Lord d R.
++
target

>Who was the pilot of the plane?
Green

>What was countered?
Unknown to us

>Who was on the ground (outside) shortly before the collision?
"Unnamed" Rothschild

>Who was in the home shortly before the collision?
Unknown to us now, was "dog grooming event"

>Learn to read the map.
trying really hard, is like herding kittens in here sometimes

>We may have overestimated your ability.
you came to us for certain strengths but there are weaknesses as well,
some being exploited
not enough focus

answer the questions
build the big picture
break it back down
make memes for the normies to calm & educate
so we'll be ready for the Storm

Q responded to the anon that same day.

Shadow war.
Act II, Scene IV.

(Movie idea – thoughts?)
(Characters)
Good guy (pilot of helicopter).
Bad guy (pilot of plane).
Targets (on ground and in home).
(Story)
Upon receipt of the 'go' code - Good guy flies during a blackout window provided by unknown agency w/ unknowns (ordinary people by the look of it) to a select location (re: highly classified mission) who was given the 'go' order by 'x' to execute (delivery – (3) for care_). Bad guy intercepts message due to rogue operator embedded in tactical observation unit and takes out Good guy by top down invisible attack.
Mission failure.
Encore: What has since occurred by Targets?
Q

Mike Green was a good guy on a mission. Q hinted that the Rothschilds discovered the mission and sent an airplane to take down Green's helicopter.

An anon responded:

Anonymous
CONFIRM GREEN SKY = giving an order to Captain Green to do something to the Rothschilds.
Q gave us this crumb beforehand, and also wrote a message to LdR (we can hear you breathing).
This was a map. Q told us that future shows the past meaning that a future event (Captain Mike Green doing something with a helicopter to Rothchilds) will explain these keywords and confirm that Q knows top secret information.
Green, obviously a good guy, had a mission. We don't know what exactly he was supposed to do. But it had to be something very serious because bad guys countered very seriously and killed several people. Mission failed.

Q responded again, on the same day:

You are learning.
You needed a push.

Godspeed.

Q

Several months later, in a tweet, Donald Trump accused Adam Schiff of leaking confidential information from Congressional committees:

Donald J. Trump (from his Twitter account):
Little Adam Schiff, who is desperate to run for higher office, is one of the biggest liars and leakers in Washington, right up there with Comey, Warner, Brennan and Clapper! Adam leaves closed committee hearings to illegally leak confidential information. Must be stopped!
5:39 AM - 5 Feb 2018

The same day, Q posted this:

Would POTUS make a serious accusation if the TRUTH wasn't about to come to LIGHT?
Black Forest.
Austria.
Rothschild.
FIRE sale days after post?
What went on there?
Dopey.
You have more than you know.
Q

Langau is the name of a large hunting estate in Austria that had been owned by the Rothschild family for 143 years. On December 21st, 2017, Donald Trump signed an executive order allowing the U.S. Treasury to seize the assets of people and organizations known to be involved in corruption, human rights abuse, or human trafficking. One month later, on January 31st, 2018, the Rothschilds put the estate up for auction. Q suggested the sale was to liquidate assets because the family had fallen upon hard financial times.

In the above post, Dopey is a reference to Saudi Prince Alwaleed bin Talal. On December 11th, 2015, Donald Trump tweeted about Prince Alwaleed attempting to control U.S. politicians:

Donald J. Trump (from his Twitter account):
Dopey Prince @Alwaleed_Talal wants to control our U.S. politicians with

daddy's money. Can't do it when I get elected.
10:53 PM - 11 Dec 2015

Eleven months before Trump was elected, he called his shot. He warned the puppet masters they would no longer be able to control U.S. politicians when he became President. Trump is succeeding where others have failed. But the battle to remove corrupt people from power is real. The campaign is waged on a variety of fronts that go unreported by the media. Q reminded us that operators involved in the battle have paid with their lives. One such operator was Mike Green.

Apr 29 2018
Statements today needed to be made.
Operators have died.
They approach the field of battle w/o fear.
They lay down their lives for YOU.
They are SELFLESS.
They are fighting for our FREEDOM.
They fight unconditionally because they hold a core value, a value that we should all live in FREEDOM.
We HONOR them.
We must do better to protect them.
WWG1WGA.
Q+
Patriots.

On the anniversary of the attack on Pearl Harbor, Q ended the discussion of Bunker Apple Yellow Sky.

Dec 7 2017
For Green.
Q
—end—

ABOUT THIS SERIES

Q Chronicles is a series that explores the topics and signatures of Q as well as news relevant to the "Great Awakening."

ABOUT THE AUTHOR

Dave Hayes is a teacher, public speaker, and author. He has written more than a dozen books on faith and the spiritual life under the pen name Praying Medic.

GLOSSARY

Because Q's posts include terms you may not be familiar with, I've provided a glossary to help decode abbreviations, acronyms, symbols, names, and agencies. The decodes I've provided are not to be taken as the only possible correct ones. There are, no doubt, valid decodes I have not considered and have not included. Some abbreviations have been confirmed by Q to have multiple meanings. As Q's mission continues, some abbreviations that have been used in one way may later be used in a different way. In such cases, the context of a particular post should be used to determine the best interpretation. The terms in this glossary are not exclusive to posts found in this book. They pertain to the entirety of Q's operation to date.

Note: names and initials are alphabetized as they appear in Q posts which is usually the first name followed by the last name.

/calmbeforethestorm/ or **/CBTS/** — An 8chan board where Q has posted messages.

/greatawakening/ or **/GA/** — A read-only board on 8chan where Q has posted.

/patriotsfight/ or **/pf/** — An 8chan board where Q has posted messages.

/pol/ — Boards on 4chan and 8chan where Q has posted messages.

/projectdcomms/ — A read-only board on 8kun where Q posts.

/qresearch/ — Boards on 8chan and 8kun where anons can interact with Q.

/thestorm/ — An 8chan board where Q has posted messages.

/_ — A three-sided shape used by Q to illustrate the power structure of the three wealthiest and most politically influential families in the world; the Saudi royal family (removed from power in 2017) the Rothschilds, and George Soros. Q's mission involves the gradual removal of all three sides of the triangle, representing the removal of these families from power.

@jack — Jack Dorsey, who is the CEO of Twitter, a social media platform, and the CEO of Square, a mobile payment processing company.

#2 — Andrew McCabe, Deputy Director of the FBI from February 2016 to January 2018. Later, McCabe became Acting Director of the FBI briefly—May 9th to August 2nd, 2017—after Director James Comey was fired, but McCabe then returned to his Deputy Director position until he was fired by Jeff Sessions in March of 2018.

#FLY# — Q uses the word FLY along with a name and pound sign (#) to indicate a person whose influence has been neutralized or a politician who has been removed from office.

#FlyCoatsFly# — Signified the removal of Dan Coats as President Trump's Director of National Intelligence.

#FLYJOHNNYFLY — Signified the resignation of John Conyers from the United States Congress.

##FLYMAYFLY## — Signified the announcement by Teresa May that she would step down as the Conservative party leader and Prime Minister of the UK.

#FLYROTHFLY# — Signified the reduction of political influence by the Rothschild family.

#FLYSIDFLY# — Two possibilities. This may have signified the end of Arizona Senator John Sidney McCain's time as a U.S. Senator, or it may signify the removal of the influence of Sidney Blumenthal, a trusted associate of Hillary Clinton.

#FLYALFLY# — Signified the resignation of Al Franken from the U.S. Senate.

#FLY[RR]FLY# — Signified the resignation of Rod Rosenstein as U.S. Deputy Attorney General.

[] — Brackets indicate different things depending on the context. Q answered an anon's inquiry by indicating that brackets signified a "kill box" but sometimes brackets are used to highlight letters that spell out a message hidden within a post, for example, [p], [r], [a], [y]. Brackets can also be used to disrupt computer programs used by opponents that search Q's posts for key words.

[30] — A time interval, typically 30 days or one month. In some cases, it will signify 31 or 28 days, depending on the number of days in the month.

[93   dk] — 93 dark seems to be a prediction of the 93 days between August 1st and November 2nd of 2019 that Q would not post after 8chan went offline and before its replacement, 8kun, went live.

[E] — Gate E at Terminal 2 in Shanghai Pudong International Airport (PVG).

[F] — Foreign

[R] — Several meanings. Used once to refer to the Republican party, and once to refer to the name Rothschild. Used multiple times to indicate Barack Obama, whose Secret Service code name was "Renegade." Obama was referred to by the single letter R in text messages between former FBI employees Lisa Page and Peter Strzok.

[T2] — Terminal 2 at Shanghai Pudong International Airport (PVG).

(6+) — George Soros, a hedge fund billionaire who is known for using his wealth to fund his own brand of political activism. Recipients of his philanthropy appreciate his money, but those who oppose his political views see him as a creator of chaos around the world, and a destabilizing force on economies and societies. Some countries have either banned Soros or restricted his organizations from operating within their borders. These countries include Pakistan, Poland, Turkey, Russia, Soros' home country of Hungary, and the Philippines. The Israeli government has said Soros is not welcome there.

(6++) — The Rothschilds, an influential banking family that exerted economic and political influence over Europe during the 18th and 19th centuries and over the world during the 20th and 21st centuries.

(6+++) — Saudi Arabia, a nation ruled by a hereditary monarchy—the House of Saud. The king serves as head of state and the head of the government.

(You) — When viewing posts on 4chan, 8chan, or 8kun, the word "you" is displayed in parenthesis to indicate that you are viewing your own post.

+ — George Soros, a hedge fund billionaire who is known for using his wealth to fund his own brand of political activism. Recipients of his philanthropy appreciate his money, but those who oppose his political views see him as a creator of chaos around the world—a destabilizing force on economies and societies. Some countries have either banned Soros or restricted his organizations. These countries include Pakistan, Poland, Turkey, Russia, Soros' home country of Hungary, and the Philippines. The Israeli government has said Soros is not welcome there.

++ — The Rothschilds, an influential banking family that exerted economic and political influence over Europe during the 18th and 19th centuries and over the world during the 20th and 21st centuries.

+++ — Saudi Arabia, a nation ruled by a hereditary monarchy—the House of Saud. The king serves as head of state and the head of the government.

187 — California penal code for murder. Often found in criminal gang tattoos.

1+1 = 2 or 2 + 2 = 4 — When the facts of a story as reported don't add up or make sense, Q will use a math equation to suggest that the facts must be carefully evaluated or interpreted logically.

4-10-20 — Initials of Donald John Trump when the numbers are replaced with the corresponding letters of the alphabet.

15-10-5 or [5] [10] [15] — Q and the President occasionally post with predetermined time intervals (deltas) between their posts. In this case, Q had posted within five minutes of the President, and anons caught it. Q was directing them to find two past posts where the President tweeted a message 10 and 15 minutes from the time of his post.

302 — An FD-302 form is used by FBI agents to summarize the interviews they conduct. A 302 contains information from the notes taken during the interview by the non-interviewing agent (there are supposed to be at least two agents present, one to interview and one to take notes).

470 Investigators — Department of Justice Inspector General Michael Horowitz is reported to have a staff of 470 investigators, attorneys and other personnel. Horowitz is coordinating with U.S. Attorney John Huber, giving Huber access to a staff considerably larger than that of a Special Counsel

4chan — An internet message board where users can post anonymously.

5 Eyes or Five Eyes or FVEY A multilateral intelligence-sharing alliance that includes Australia, Canada, New Zealand, the United Kingdom and the United States.

7 Dwarves — According to the Michael Kilian article Spy vs. Spy published in 2000 by *The Chicago Tribune*, the CIA has seven supercomputers named after the seven dwarves; Doc, Dopey, Bashful, Grumpy, Sneezy, Sleepy and Happy.

7th Floor — According to an October 17th, 2016 article published by *The New York Post*, "The 7th Floor" was a group of U.S. State Department officials who met regularly on the 7th floor of the Harry S. Truman Building in Washington, D.C. The group's activities came to light in the fall of 2016 and appeared to have formed in support of Hillary Clinton during her email investigation. The FBI referred to them as the "shadow government" inside the State Department, which briefly attracted the attention of mainstream media. Most, if not all, members were terminated by Rex Tillerson in February of 2017.

5:5 — "Five by five" is military jargon signifying loud and clear, or understood. Radio transmissions are rated for signal clarity and strength on a scale from 1-5 with 1 being the lowest and 5 being the highest. 5:5 indicates the signal is loud and clear.

8chan — An internet message board where users can post anonymously.

8kun — An internet message board where users can post anonymously. Created in 2019 after 8chan was de-platformed.

A321 — The Airbus A321 is a member of the Airbus A320 family of short-to medium-range, narrow-body, commercial passenger twin-engine jet airliners manufactured by Airbus.

A or A's — Agency, agencies, intelligence agencies.

Adam Schiff — Democrat representative from California, and Chair of the House Select Committee on Intelligence.

Adm R — Admiral Michael Rogers, Director of the National Security Agency from 2014 to 2018. Rogers is a former U. S. Navy Admiral who served as the second commander of the U.S. Cyber Command.

AF1 — Air Force 1, the call sign designator for the airplane in which the President of the United States travels, regardless of which particular airplane it happens to be.

AG — U.S. Attorney General

Agnes Nixon — TV soap opera pioneer who created the shows *One Life to Live* and *All My Children*.

AJ — Alex Jones, founder of InfoWars, a conservative media outlet operated by Free Speech Systems LLC.

AL — Senator Al Franken, who formerly represented the state of Minnesota, but resigned in 2017 after multiple women accused him of sexual impropriety and unwanted advances.

AL-Q — Al-Qaeda, a militant Sunni Islamist organization founded in 1988 by Osama bin Laden.

Alan — Alan Dershowitz, a lawyer, author, and Harvard law professor. Although he is a registered Democrat, Dershowitz has supported President Trump against those who have criticized him.

Alice and Wonderland — A signature phrase that Q helped anons decode. Alice is Hillary Clinton. Wonderland is Saudi Arabia. Q says Saudi Arabia has been the source of funding for many U.S. politicians.

Alphabet — The parent company of Google, YouTube, and others subsidiaries.

Alice — Hillary Clinton, as she was referred to in emails from Marty Torrey (published by *WikiLeaks*), who went by the moniker "Hatter."

AM — Andrew McCabe, Deputy Director of the FBI from February 2016 to January 2018. Later, McCabe became Acting Director of the FBI briefly—May 9th to August 2nd, 2017—after Director James Comey was fired, but McCabe then returned to his Deputy Director position until he was fired by Jeff Sessions in March of 2018.

AMB Matlock — Ambassador Jack F. Matlock was appointed by President Reagan to be the U.S. ambassador to USSR. Matlock has defended the Trump's transition team's contacts with Russian officials as normal diplomatic relations.

Amanda Renteria — A political aide who has worked for U.S. Senators Dianne Feinstein and Debbie Stabenow. In 2018, she announced her candidacy for Governor of California but lost in the primary to Gavin Newsom.

Anderson Cooper — CNN News Anchor who previously served as chief international correspondent for Channel One News, where he reported and produced his own stories. Cooper graduated from Yale University in 1989 with a BA in political science. During college, he spent two summers as an intern at the Central Intelligence Agency.

Angela Dorothea Kasner — Angela Dorothea Merkel neé Kasner, Chancellor of the country of Germany.

Anne Wojcicki — The co-founder and CEO of 23andMe, a genetic testing company. She is married to Sergey Brin, the co-founder of Google. Her sister is Susan Wojcicki, the CEO of YouTube.

Anon or **Autist** — Anonymous people who monitor and post messages on 4chan, 8chan, or 8kun. Many are researchers. The autist label refers to the fact that "autists" can become hyper-focused on their research.

Antifa — An American militant movement that embraces a far-left political ideology. Members employ a variety of tactics, including online activism, damaging personal property, inflicting physical violence, and harassing those they deem to be fascists, racists, or politically far-right.

APACHE — A term that has multiple meanings. It may refer to the internet domain that hosts SecureDrop, a platform that journalists use to communicate anonymously with their sources. It could also refer to the open source software used on computer servers. Or it may refer to Apache Co. (NYSE:APA), an oil and exploration company. The Rothschild's Family Trust divested 30 percent of their interest in the company in late January of 2018.

ARM or **ARM/MSM** — The context of its use would seem to indicate ARM is a group connected to the mainstream media, who oppose the agenda of President Trump. (Q has not confirmed an exact decode.)

As the World Turns — A television soap opera that aired on CBS for 54 years. When President John F. Kennedy was assassinated in 1963, the news story about the assassination interrupted the show's broadcast.

AS — There are three possible decodes. It has been confirmed as the initials of Antonin Scalia, the Supreme Court Justice, who died mysteriously in 2016. Alternately, it may refer to Adam Schiff, the Democrat representative from California. In November of 2018, Abigail Spanberger was elected as the representative of Virginia's 7th congressional district. Spanberger is a former CIA agent. Context determines the best decode.

ATL — Hartsfield-Jackson Atlanta International Airport

ATL -> IAD — Atlanta Airport to Dulles International Airport

AUS — The country of Australia.

Autist or **Anon** — Anonymous people who monitor and post messages on 4chan, 8chan, or 8kun. Many are researchers. The autist label refers to the fact that "autists" can become hyper-focused on their research.

AW — Anthony Weiner, disgraced ex-congressman from New York who served time in prison, and former husband of Huma Abedin.

Awan — Family name of the Pakistani brothers Imran, Abid and Jamal, who operated an IT company that was hired by more than 40 Democratic members of Congress. Imran Awan pled guilty to bank fraud charges but a Department of Justice case regarding him is currently open.

AZ — Arizona, a state in the U.S.

B2 or **B(2)** — The B-2 Spirit, also known as the Stealth Bomber. An American military bomber featuring radar-evading aircraft shapes and built with radar-resistant materials. Q has used the term to refer to someone who seems unthreatening but is working covertly.

Bad actor — A person who has engaged in criminal acts or corrupt behavior.

Bakers — Slang term for anons who assemble 4chan, 8chan, or 8kun posts (crumbs) into threads (breads) for discussion.

BB — U.S. Attorney General William (Bill) Barr.

BC — Bill Clinton, 42nd president of the United States from 1993 to 2001.

BDT — Several possibilities: Blunt & Direct Time, Bangladeshi Taka (Bangladesh's currency). Bangladeshi Terrorist or a Bulk Data Transfer.

Betsy D or **Betsy DeVos** — Secretary of Education under President Trump, and sister of Erik Prince.

Biblefag — Slang term for a 4chan, 8chan, or 8kun user who posts scripture verses.

BIDEN/CHINA — Robert Biden (son of former Vice President Joe Biden) partnered with John Kerry's stepson, Chris Heinz, to form Rosemont Seneca Partners, LLC. The firm signed a billion-dollar deal with the government-owned Bank of China following a diplomatic trip to that country by then-Vice President Joe Biden.

Bilderberg Group — Variously referred to as the Bilderberg Group, Bilderberg conference, Bilderberg meetings or Bilderberg Club, it is a group of 120 to 150 elite members of society including individuals from governments, business, media, and academia from Europe and the United States, which meets annually to promote the concept of "Atlanticism," which is an agenda that supports the mutual interests of Europe and the U.S.

Bill Priestap — Director of FBI Counterintelligence from 2015 to 2018.

Black ops — Black budget operations. Government operations (typically military or intelligence) that are not publicly acknowledged and not under congressional oversight. Some of these operations are funded through the official federal budget. Some are funded by siphoning money from approved programs, some by money made through illegal activities, and some are funded privately.

Blackwater — Blackwater USA is an American private military company founded in 1997 by former Navy SEAL officer Erik Prince. It was renamed as Xe Services in 2009 and is now known as Academi after the company was acquired by a group of private investors.

Blockade — Q indicated that Robert Mueller's investigation into 2016 election interference was designed by the enemies of Donald Trump to serve as a blockade to his success.

BO — There are three confirmed decodes: Bruce Ohr (former U.S. Associate Deputy Attorney General), former President Barack Obama, or Board Owner.

BOB — Robert Mueller, former FBI Director who served as Special Counsel in the 2016 Trump-Russia investigation.

BOD — Board of Directors

Bolton — An American attorney, political commentator, and Republican consultant. Bolton was President Trump's National Security Advisor from March 2018 until September 2019. He also served as the U.S. Ambassador to the UN from August 2005 to December 2006.

BOOM — As in "Lower the Boom." Chastisement, punishment, to deliver a knockout punch.

Bots — Internet 'crawler' programs used to find and analyze data and run coded routines. May also be used as a derogatory term for people with a certain belief system, i.e., "Russian bots" or "Soros' bots."

Bottom to top — An order of operations that begins at the lowest level and proceeds toward the upper levels. These operations, because of their nature, take time to complete.

BP — There are two decodes: Border Patrol, or Bill Priestap (FBI former Chief of Counterintelligence).

Bridge — A term found in Q's posts that indicates someone who acts as a go-between for others. It has also been used in at least one post that discusses a "central" social media algorithm that helps track users. The word has other uses that are still not confirmed by Q.

Bring the thunder — Artillery/aircraft controller term for final authorization of a fire/ bombing mission.

Bruce Ohr — Former U.S. Associate Deputy Attorney General, who was demoted for his role in the surveillance of President Trump. Husband of Nellie Ohr, an employee of Fusion GPS.

Bump — A comment that forces a conversation thread to rise to the top of a particular board.

Burner phone — A cheap, disposable phone used by those who do not wish to be tracked by intelligence agencies.

BUZZF — Buzzfeed, an American internet media company.

CA — In most cases, it refers to California, but when used in a stringer with Uranium One (U1), it refers to Canada.

C-Info — Confidential or Classified Information.

C_A — Central Intelligence Agency, A civilian foreign intelligence service of the U.S. federal government.

C Wray — Christopher Wray, Director of the FBI who began serving in that capacity in 2017. From 2003 to 2005, he was the Assistant Attorney General in charge of the Criminal Division in the George W. Bush administration.

Carter Page — Briefly served as a staffer on candidate Donald Trump's 2016 Presidential campaign. Page became the target of an FBI investigation as a possible foreign agent, and then became the center of a controversy surrounding the surveillance of Trump's campaign.

Castle — Secret Service code name for the Executive Mansion or the White House.

CBTS — Calm before the storm.

CC — Chelsea Clinton, daughter of Bill and Hillary Clinton.

CF — The William Jefferson Clinton Foundation

CFR — Council on Foreign Relations, a United States nonprofit think tank specializing in U.S. foreign policy and international affairs.

CHAI — Clinton Health Access Initiative. In 2010, the Clinton Foundation's HIV/AIDS Initiative became a separate nonprofit organization called the Clinton Health Access Initiative (CHAI).

Chair — Likely a reference to what the Catholic Church considers to be the throne of St. Peter on which the current Pope sits.

Chatter — Conversations between politicians, media and intelligence operatives that are detected by agencies like the NSA.

CIA — Central Intelligence Agency, a civilian foreign intelligence service of the U.S. federal government.

Clapper — James Clapper, former Director of National Intelligence under Barack Obama.

CLAS or [CLAS 1-99] — Q has access to both classified and non-classified information. These terms refer to the names of people, agencies, and organizations that are currently classified.

Clock — Some believe the word clock is a reference to a clock diagram, "the Q clock" that pinpoints and predicts events in Q's mission. The clock image has been posted on Q's board many times, and anons have asked for confirmation, but Q has not confirmed the clock diagram yet.

My theory about references to a "clock" takes into consideration that Q and the President post close to each other in time—often less than 10 minutes apart. A clock is necessary to track the time intervals (deltas), showing the relationships between their posts. Graphics can then be made showing the time intervals.

Clowns — The U.S. Central Intelligence Agency.

CLOWN DIR — Former CIA Director John Brennan

CM — Code Monkey, the administrator who provided technical support for Q's board on 8chan, and the current administrator of 8kun.

Coats — Dan Coats, former Director of National Intelligence under President Donald Trump.

CoC — Two confirmed decodes: Chain of Command, and Chain of Custody.

Cohen — Michael Cohen, former personal attorney for Donald Trump.

Cohn — Gary Cohn, President Trump's former Chief Economic Advisor.

COMM — An abbreviation for committee or community.

COMMS — Communications

Corsi — Jerome Corsi is an author and political commentator. He was an avid Q supporter early in the mission but became the center of a controversy in the spring of 2018 when he claimed that Q had been compromised, and Q's posts could no longer be trusted.

CoS — Chief of Staff

Crop or **[crop]** — A euphemism used by Q to taunt former FBI Director James Comey about his pending prosecution. (Comey has often posted photos of himself standing in a cornfield.)

Crossfire Hurricane — The codename for the FBI's counterintelligence investigation of Donald Trump's campaign prior to the appointment of Special Counsel Robert Mueller.

CrowdStrike — A tech company contracted by the Democratic National Committee to investigate their computer system for alleged hacking during the 2016 Presidential election.

Crumb — Slang term for a single post on 4chan, 8chan, or 8kun. Crumbs, when brought together, make a bread (thread).

CS — Several confirmed decodes: Senator Charles Schumer, former British spy Christopher Steele, or the tech firm CrowdStrike that was used by the Democratic National Committee. Context determines the best decode.

D5 — The metric used to rate the potential danger an avalanche poses on a scale from D1-D5, with D5 being most severe. Q uses it as a metaphor to convey the idea that a coming avalanche of justice will devastate corrupt people.

D or D's — Democrats

Dafna Linzer — Since October of 2016, she has been the managing editor of NBC/MSNBC politics.

DAG — U.S. Deputy Attorney General.

David Laufman — Former Chief of the U.S. Justice Department's Counterintelligence and Export Control Section.

DC — Washington, District of Columbia.

DC-CAP — Washington D.C., Capitol of the United States.

DDoS — Distributed Denial of Service, an attack used by hackers to take down a website or network by causing server overload. "Distributed" means the attack comes from multiple users and machines that overtax a website's resources.

DE_POTUS — Democratically elected President of the United States.

Dead Cat Bounce — An investing term for a temporary recovery in a prolonged decline or bear market that is followed by the continuation of the downtrend. The name "dead cat bounce" illustrates the idea that even a dead cat will bounce if it falls far enough and fast enough.

Declas or DECLASS — The declassification of documents that will shed light on corruption.

Deep Dream — A reference to a Jason Bourne film in which a social media company named Deep Dream gathered personal information from subscribers and secretly funneled it to the Central Intelligence Agency.

DefCon — Defense Condition which is indicated by a number 1 through 5. DefCon 5 is a state of low alert. DefCon1 is a state of high alert. Q has used the term in some unorthodox ways. Look for context to determine the correct application.

Delta — Several possible uses: The U.S. Defense Department uses four conditions to indicate the relative level of a terrorist threat (Threatcon). Alpha is the lowest Threatcon level, bravo is higher and delta is the highest. In chemistry, delta (Δ) is used to indicate the change in a system during a reaction. For fighter pilots, it indicates a change to a later time, either minutes or hours depending on the context. ("Delta 10 on your recovery time" means the jet is now scheduled to land 10 minutes later.)

In most of Q's posts, the term "delta" indicates the time interval between one of Q's posts and a tweet by the President.

DF — Dianne Feinstein, a Democrat U.S. Senator from California.

DHS — U.S. Department of Homeland Security, which is a cabinet department of the U.S. federal government with responsibilities in public security.

DJT — Donald John Trump, the 45th President of the United States. Before entering politics, he was a businessman and television personality.

DNC — Democratic National Committee, the governing body for the United States Democratic Party.

DNC BREACH — In 2016, files from the Democratic National Committee were transferred to and made public. The incident was widely attributed to a Russian hacking operation, but Q has suggested the information was given to by a DNC staffer.

DOD — U.S. Department of Defense, which is part of the Executive Branch of the federal government that handles functions of national security.

DOE — U.S. Department of Energy, a cabinet-level department of the federal government, concerned with energy and safe handling of nuclear material.

DOJ — U.S. Department of Justice (also known as the Justice Department), which is a federal executive department of the U.S. government responsible for the enforcement of the law and administration of justice in the U.S.

Donna — Donna Brazile, who, in 2016, served as the interim Chair of the Democratic National Committee after the resignation of Debbie Wasserman Schultz.

Dopey — In a tweet, Donald Trump referred to Saudi Prince Alwaleed bin Talal as "Dopey Prince Alwaleed." Q has also referred to Alwaleed as Dopey.

DOSSIER — A collection of documents assembled by former British spy Christopher Steele, used to obtain a warrant to surveil Carter Page and the Trump campaign.

Durham — John Durham, U.S. Attorney from Connecticut. Tasked by former Attorney General Jeff Sessions to investigate government corruption.

DWS — Debbie Wasserman Schultz, a Representative from Florida who resigned as chair of the DNC after emails were published by that revealed DNC staff favoring Clinton over Sanders.

E — Two confirmed decodes: The rapper known as Eminem, or emergency.

Eagle — Secret Service code name for President Bill Clinton.

EC — This usually signifies Electronic Communication, as in email, instant messaging, or other communications. In more recent posts, it refers to Eric Ciaramella, a CIA analyst and former National Security Council staffer. Ciaramella is believed to have filed the whistleblower complaint used to impeach Donald Trump.

Ed O'Callaghan — The former Principal Associate Deputy Attorney General for Rod Rosenstein.

EG — Abbreviation for Evergreen, Hillary Clinton's Secret Service code name.

EH — Eric Holder, former U.S. Attorney General under Barrack Obama.

EM — Elon Musk, CEO of Tesla and SpaceX.

EBS — Emergency Broadcast System

EMP — Electromagnetic Pulse

EMS — Emergency Messaging System

EO — Presidential Executive Order

ES — Two confirmed decodes: Eric Schmidt (ex-CEO of Alphabet/Google) or Edward Snowden, a former CIA employee and NSA contractor. Snowden is usually indicated by @snowden but on rare occasions by ES. Context determines which is correct.

EU — European Union

Epstein Island — Little Saint James Island, an approximately 75-acre island in the U.S. Virgin Islands, owned by American financier and convicted child sex offender Jeffrey Epstein from 1998 until his death in 2019.

Erik Prince — Former U.S. Navy SEAL officer best known for founding the government services and security company, Blackwater USA. He served as its CEO until 2009. Prince supported Donald Trump in his bid for President.

Epstein — Jeffrey Epstein, an American financier and convicted child sex offender who died in his jail cell in 2019 while awaiting trial.

Evergreen — Hillary Clinton's Secret Service code name.

Eyes in the SKY — Drone or satellite surveillance.

Eyes On — To watch or observe.

Ezra Cohen-Watnick — National security advisor to the U.S. Attorney General, and a former Senior Director for Intelligence Programs for the United States National Security Council (NSC).

F + D — Foreign and Domestic.

F2F — Face-to-face meeting.

F9 — Two uses: SpaceX Falcon 9 is a two-stage medium-lift space launch vehicle. F9 is also a Facebook surveillance algorithm.

Facebook — A popular social network founded on February 4th, 2004—the same day the Pentagon's DARPA Lifelog Project was shut down. Lifelog was designed to track the same life events as Facebook.

Fag — Slang term for an anon. It is sometimes combined with areas of interest, i.e. biblefag, planefag, lawfag, etc.

Fakewood — Hollywood

Fantasy Land — A Q signature indicating a truth that is too wild for the average person to believe. Cognitive dissonance is caused by information that challenges a programmed way of thinking.

FB — Facebook

FED — Federal Reserve System, a private banking corporation that controls the U.S. money supply.

FED G — Federal Government

FF — False Flag. A secret operation that is intended to deceive. The deception creates the appearance that a particular party, group, or nation is responsible for some type of activity, while the actual source of the activity is concealed. The term originally referred to pirate ships that flew flags of countries as a disguise to prevent their victims from fleeing or preparing for battle. Sometimes the flag would remain, and the blame for the attack would be laid incorrectly on another country.

FISA — The Foreign Intelligence Surveillance Act, which permits the surveillance of foreign citizens or U.S. citizens suspected of being foreign agents.

Five Eyes — Often abbreviated FVEY, it is an intelligence-sharing alliance that includes Australia, Canada, New Zealand, the United Kingdom, and the United States.

FOIA — The Freedom of Information Act. It allows individuals to request government documents on particular subjects and requires compliance within certain guidelines.

Follow the Pen — A pen photograph has appeared in a number of Q's posts. Sometimes the images precede a Presidential Executive Order or declassification of documents.

Fox Three — Military aviator jargon for firing an active radar-guided air-to-air missile.

Future Marker — A reference in a post by Q intended to mark a topic that will be discussed in greater detail at a future time.

Future proves past — A phrase suggesting that information contained in a current post will be proven true at a future time.

G — Google

Game Theory — The study of conflict and cooperation by opponents within a competitive game environment.

Gang of 8 — A term used to describe the eight leaders in the United States Congress who are briefed on classified intelligence matters. It includes the leaders of both parties from the Senate and House of Representatives, and the chairs and ranking minority members of both the Senate and House Intelligence Committees.

Gardens by the Bay — A nature park in central Singapore, adjacent to the Marina Reservoir. Kim Jong-un explored the park on his first night in Singapore preceding the Summit meeting with President Trump on June 11th, 2018.

GCHQ — An acronym for the Government Communications Headquarters, an intelligence and security organization responsible for providing signals intelligence (SIGINT) and information to the UK government and armed forces.

General K — President Trump's former Chief of Staff General John F. Kelly.

GEO — A reference to geographic location.

GEO-T or GEO-T/L — Geological tracking, and location. Tracking a person's location by using global positioning satellites.

GEOTUS — Acronym for God-Emperor of the United States. A meme used to aggravate those who despise Donald Trump.

Gina Haspel — Director of the Central Intelligence Agency under President Trump.

GITMO — Guantanamo Bay Naval Base, a military prison and detention camp.

Gloria V — Gloria Vanderbilt, an American artist, author, actress, fashion designer, heiress, and socialite.

Godfather III — A Q signature that connects posts containing this phrase to a film from 1990 about the Corleone crime family's involvement with the Vatican.

GREEN_CASTLE — Q confirmed this was a reference to the U.S. Army Corps of Engineers who have an office in Green Castle, Indiana.

G v E/R v W — Good versus evil. Right versus wrong.

GOOG — Google

GS — George Soros, a hedge fund billionaire who is known for using his wealth to fund his own brand of political activism. Recipients of his philanthropy appreciate his money, but those who oppose his political views see him as a creator of chaos around the world—a destabilizing force on economies and societies. Some countries have either banned Soros or restricted his organizations. These countries include Pakistan, Poland, Turkey, Russia, Soros' home country of Hungary, and the Philippines. The Israeli government has said Soros is not welcome there.

GWB — Former U.S. President George W. Bush.

GZ — Ground Zero

H Report — One of several reports released by the U.S. Department of Justice Inspector General Michael Horowitz.

H — Two decodes: Haiti, or in rare cases, Hillary Clinton, who is known to sign letters and emails with the letter H.

H-relief — Haiti earthquake relief.

Hatter — Marty Torrey, as he was referred to in emails from Hillary Clinton (published by *WikiLeaks*), who went by the nickname "Alice."

Hillary Clinton — Former Secretary of State under Barack Obama. Democratic Presidential Candidate in 2016. Wife of President William Jefferson Clinton.

HK — Hong Kong

Honeypot — A scheme used to lure people into behaviors that are unethical, immoral, or illegal. Their participation can be recorded and used as leverage to control them.

Holder — Eric Holder, former U.S. Attorney General under Barrack Obama.

HRC — Hillary Clinton, former Secretary of State under Barack Obama. Democratic Presidential Candidate in 2016. Wife of President William Jefferson Clinton.

HS — U.S. Department of Homeland Security

Huma — Huma Abedin, Hillary Clinton's Chief of Staff, and ex-wife of Anthony Weiner.

HUMA — Harvard University Muslim Alumni

Hunter — Q often uses this as a euphemism for those who are hunting criminals and bringing them to justice. It can also refer to Hunter Biden, the trouble-prone son of former U.S. Vice-president Joe Biden.

Hunt for Red October — Multiple meanings including, but not limited to, the film by that title and a steel plant in Stalingrad, Russia, which appears on a CIA document, for which Q provided a link. Note: Q removed "the Hunt for," and in October of 2018, a new theme "Red October" appeared.

Hussein — Barack Hussein Obama, the 44th President of the United States.

Hussein's PL — Barack Obama's Presidential Library

HW — Hollywood

H-wood — Hollywood

Hannity intruder — Sean Hannity's wife found a man trespassing in their home on Long Island. The intruder claimed to be writing a book about the Fox News host and was arrested.

I — The letter I has been used at least once to refer to criminal indictments.

IBOR — Internet Bill of Rights, a set of ideas proposed by California Representative Ro Khanna that would guarantee the rights of internet users.

IC — Intelligence Community

ICBM — Intercontinental Ballistic Missile

ID/IDEN — Identification, or to identify an individual.

IG — Inspector General. Every U.S. government agency has an Inspector General. In most cases, the reference is to the Department of Justice Inspector General Michael Horowitz.

In-Q-Tel — A venture capital firm that invests in tech companies for the sole purpose of keeping the Central Intelligence Agency and other intelligence agencies equipped with the latest in information technology. The name "In-Q-Tel" is an intentional reference to Q, the fictional inventor who supplied technology to James Bond.

Insurance Policy — According to publicly released text messages between FBI agent Peter Strzok and FBI attorney Lisa Page in 2016, a plan was developed to prevent Donald Trump from being elected. A backup plan (an insurance policy) was put in place to remove him from office if he were to be elected.

Intelligence A — Intelligence Agency

IP-Ghost — Using a device or software to conceal your IP address.

IRL — In real life, as opposed to online.

IRON EAGLE — A 1986 movie starring Lou Gossett Jr. about a retired Air Force Colonel and an 18-year-old whose father had been shot down in the Middle East and was sentenced to death. The two men obtained a pair of F-16 fighter jets and managed to fly to the Middle East for a rescue mission for the young man's father. Iron Eagle is a Q signature.

IRS — U.S. Internal Revenue Service, a government agency that is a bureau of the Department of the Treasury.

ISIS — Islamic State in Iraq and Syria. Listed as a terrorist group by the U.S. State Department.

JA — Julian Assange, founder of *WikiLeaks,* a watchdog organization that publishes leaked documents.

Jack — Jack Dorsey, CEO of the social media platform, Twitter. He is also the CEO of the mobile payment processing company Square.

James Alefantis — Named in GQ magazine as one of Washington D.C.'s 50 most influential people. He is a American chef and restaurateur.

James Baker — Former FBI Chief Counsel.

James Dolan — From 1999 to 2006, Dolan served with the U.S. Marines in the Iraq war. He helped develop SecureDrop, an open source whistleblower submission system that eventually came under the control of the Freedom of the Press Foundation. Dolan's death at the age of 36 on December 27th, 2017, was thought to be a suicide and was followed by the death of John Perry Barlow in February of 2018.

Jared Cohen — A businessman who serves as the CEO of Jigsaw (previously Google Ideas) and an Adjunct Senior Fellow at the Council on Foreign Relations (CFR). Previously, he served as a member of the Secretary of State's Policy Planning Staff and as an advisor to Condoleezza Rice and later, Hillary Clinton.

Jason Bourne — A fictional agent and hero in a series of books and films. Bourne was the subject of a CIA mind-control experiment that made him into the perfect asset for the Agency.

JB — At least two confirmed decodes: former FBI Chief Counsel James Baker, or former CIA Director John Brennan. Context determines the correct one.

JC — At least two confirmed decodes: former FBI Director James Comey, or former Director of National Intelligence James Clapper. Context determines the correct one.

J C or **J_C** — John P. Carlin, former Director of the National Security Division of the U.S. Department of Justice.

JD — Jack Dorsey, the CEO of Twitter, a social media platform, and the CEO of Square, a mobile payment processing company.

Jim Jordan — Representative from Ohio's 4th congressional district and member of the House Freedom Caucus. He has been the ranking member of the House Oversight Committee since 2019.

Jim Rybicki — Former FBI Chief of Staff.

JK — Two confirmed decodes: In Q's earlier posts, JK refers to Jared Kushner, senior advisor to his father-in-law, President Donald Trump. In later Q posts, JK refers to John Kerry, Secretary of State under Barack Obama.

JFK — Two confirmed decodes: John Fitzgerald Kennedy, 35th President of the United States, or President Trump's former Chief of Staff General John F. Kelly.

JFK JR — John Fitzgerald Kennedy, Jr. was the son of the 35th President John F. Kennedy Sr. He was a lawyer, journalist, magazine publisher, and actor. Kennedy died on July 16th, 1999 (along with his wife, Carolyn, and sister-in-law Lauren Bessette) when his small plane crashed into the Atlantic Ocean near Martha's Vineyard.

JL — John Legend, singer, songwriter, musician, actor, and philanthropist. Legend participated in a telethon to benefit Haiti victims.

John Durham — U.S. Attorney from Connecticut. Tasked by former Attorney General Jeff Sessions to investigate government corruption.

John M — John McCain, U.S. Senator from Arizona. He served as a senator from January 1987 until his death in 2018.

John McCain — U.S. Senator from Arizona who served from January 1987 until his death in 2018.

John P. Carlin — Former Director of the National Security Division of the U.S. Department of Justice.

John Perry Barlow — Poet and essayist, cattle rancher, and a cyber-libertarian, political activist, and lyricist for the Grateful Dead. Founding member of the Electronic Frontier Foundation and the Freedom of the Press Foundation. Barlow died in February, 2018.

Johnny — John Conyers, U.S. Representative from Michigan who resigned from Congress in 2017 after multiple allegations of sexual harassment. Now deceased, he was the longest-serving black member of Congress in history.

Josh Campbell — Former FBI agent, appointed Special Assistant to former FBI Director James Comey. Contributor for CNN.

JP — John Podesta, White House Chief of Staff under President Bill Clinton, and Counselor to President Barack Obama. Chairman of Hillary Clinton's 2016 Presidential campaign. Currently serves as Chair of the Center for American Progress, a think tank based in Washington, D.C.

JPC — John P. Carlin, former Director of the National Security Division of the U.S. Department of Justice.

JS — John Solomon, investigative journalist, reporter, and Editor in Chief of *Just the News.*

KANSAS — Mike Pompeo, former CIA director and current Secretary of State. Pompeo also served as a U.S. Congressman from Kansas.

Kashyap Patel — Indian American lawyer Kashyap "Kash" Patel, who was the primary author of the House Intelligence Committee memo that was critical of the FBI and Justice Department handling of the investigation into alleged collusion between Donald Trump and Russia.

Kek — Laughter or amusement. Synonymous with "lol" (laughing out loud). Kek had its origins in World of Warcraft, where one faction's "lol" was translated as "kek" by the other.

Keith Raniere — Co-founder of NXIVM, a multi-level marketing company based near Albany, New York, that offered personal and professional development seminars through its "Executive Success Programs." NXIVM leaders were prosecuted for sexual abuse and sex trafficking of members.

Kim — Kim Jong-un is a North Korean politician who has been the Supreme Leader of North Korea since 2011 and chairman of the Workers' Party of Korea since 2012.

Kerry — John Kerry, a former U.S. Senator and Secretary of State under President Barack Obama.

Keystone — Several uses: decoded by Q to indicate the power given to average citizens when they're assisted by the President, the military, and its intelligence apparatus. Information is the *key*. The executive branch and military are the *stone*. Together, they form the *keystone*. Also refers to a trapezoidal-shaped building stone found at the apex of some arches and doorways.

KKK — Ku Klux Klan, a hate group that became a vehicle for southern post-Civil War resistance against freedmen and the Republican Party leaders who sought to establish equality for blacks. As a secret, masked vigilante group, the Klan aimed to restore white supremacy by using threats and violence, including murder.

Klaus Eberwein — A former Haitian government official who was found shot to death just before he was scheduled to expose Clinton Foundation fraud before an anti-corruption committee.

Knowingly — Used by Q as a reminder that many actions taken by corrupt people were not done negligently, but knowingly. Negligence is generally not prosecuted. Certain acts, when done knowingly, are.

LARP — Live Action Role Play. On 4chan, 8chan and 8kun, it refers to a phony.

Lawfag — A slang term for an anon who has a background in law.

LdR or LDR — Two possible decodes. Lord de Rothschild or Lynn de Rothschild (aka Lady de Rothschild)—both members of the Rothschild banking family.

LifeLog Project — A project of DARPA, the Defense Department's research arm. The goal of the LifeLog Project was to get citizens to voluntarily provide their private information to a military database. The program ended on February 4th, 2004—the same day Facebook was launched.

Lisa Page — Former FBI attorney, and legal advisor to then-FBI Deputy Director Andrew McCabe. Page became the focus of media attention for her role in the surveillance of Donald Trump's 2016 Presidential campaign.

Little St. James Island — Little Saint James Island, an approximately 75-acre island in the U.S. Virgin Islands, owned by American financier and convicted child sex offender Jeffrey Epstein from 1998 until his death in 2019.

LL — Loretta Lynch, served as U.S. Attorney General under Barack Obama. Lynch came under scrutiny when she met secretly with former President Bill Clinton on a tarmac at an airport in Arizona during an active investigation of Hillary Clinton.

Login Devices — Various secure computers, tablets, or mobile phones that Q uses to connect to the internet to post messages.

LOOP — In most cases, a reference to Loop Capital Markets, a Chicago-based investment firm. There may be other uses.

Lord d R — Lord Jacob de Rothschild of the Rothschild banking family.

Lurk — To read a 4chan, 8chan, or 8kun board without posting a comment. Lurking is not only acceptable, but recommended. If you make a bad or unoriginal post, someone will likely ask you to "lurk more" (sometimes written "lurk moar") before posting again.

LV — Las Vegas, a city in Nevada.

Mack — Allison Mack, a Hollywood actress who played the part of Chloe Sullivan in the TV show *Smallville*. Mack pleaded guilty to racketeering and conspiracy as a member of the NXIVM sex cult that was founded by Keith Raniere. As part of her guilty plea, Mack admitted to extortion and forced labor.

M — Used at least once to refer to Moloch, the biblical name of a Canaanite god associated with child sacrifice.

Macron — Emmanuel Macron, elected President of France on May 7th, 2017.

MAGA — "Make America Great Again," Donald Trump's 2016 Presidential campaign slogan.

Maggie Haberman — White House correspondent for *The New York Times* and a former political analyst for CNN. Emails published by indicated that Haberman was particularly useful in releasing political talking points friendly to Hillary Clinton. She was also reported by to be one of many reporters who colluded with Hillary's campaign and the DNC during the 2016 election.

Maggie Nix — The daughter of Sarah Nixon and granddaughter of actress and TV soap opera writer and producer Agnes Nixon.

MagikBOT — A *Wikipedia* bot that makes automated or semi-automated edits to *Wikipedia* entries that would be difficult to do manually.

MAKE IT RAIN — Military jargon for the detonation of explosive ordnance (bomb), which sends a shower of debris on those who are nearby.

Manafort — Paul Manafort, a businessman, lobbyist, and member of Donald Trump's 2016 Presidential campaign. He was convicted of money laundering, tax evasion and failing to register as a foreign agent.

Mariah Sunshine Coogan — One of six people killed in a plane crash near Scottsdale, Arizona, on a flight to Las Vegas, Nevada, on April 9th, 2018.

Marine 1 — The President's helicopter operated by the U.S. Marines.

Marker — A reference in a post by Q intended to mark a topic that will be discussed in greater detail at a future time.

MAP — A graphic that displays Q's posts.

Master — The identity of the "Master" is uncertain. In a discussion about the Pope and the Rothschilds, Q wrote:
The "Chair" serves the Master
P = C.
Who is the Master?

May — Theresa May, served as the Prime Minister of the United Kingdom and Leader of the Conservative Party from 2016 to 2019.

MB — Muslim Brotherhood, a political and military group based in Egypt. The government of Egypt banned the group and named it a terrorist organization.

MBS — Mohammad bin Salman, Crown Prince of Saudi Arabia, Muslim reformer, and ally of Donald Trump.

McCabe — Andrew McCabe, Deputy Director of the FBI from February 2016 to January 2018. Later, McCabe became Acting Director of the FBI briefly—May 9th to August 2nd, 2017—after Director James Comey was fired, but McCabe then returned to his Deputy Director position until he was fired by Jeff Sessions in March of 2018.

Media Matters — Media Matters for America (MMfA) is a progressive tax-exempt, non-profit organization, with the stated mission of "comprehensively monitoring, analyzing, and correcting conservative misinformation in the U.S. media." MMfA was founded by political activist David Brock and is known for its aggressive criticism of conservative journalists and media outlets. Hillary Clinton and John Podesta were instrumental in helping form MMfA, which receives partial funding from George Soros.

Melissa Hodgman — Associate Director of Securities and Exchange Commission Enforcement Division. Wife of fired FBI Special Agent Peter Strzok.

MI — Military Intelligence

Memo — House Intelligence Committee 4-page memo on the FBI's FISA warrant against Trump campaign staffer Carter Page.

Merkel — Angela Merkel, a politician who has served as the Chancellor of Germany since 2005.

MF — Retired Lieutenant General Michael Flynn, served as the National Security Advisor briefly under President Trump in 2017. Flynn became a target during the SpyGate scandal and entered a guilty plea under pressure from Special Counsel prosecutors. Previously, Flynn served as Director of the Defense Intelligence Agency for two years under the Obama administration and was forced out due to his criticism of Obama's policy on the Islamic State.

Michael Avenatti — The attorney who represented Stormy Daniels in her lawsuit against President Trump. Q has not mentioned him by name but has posted links to his tweets and his website. Avenatti is currently facing charges in New York and California.

Michael Gaeta — The FBI's legal attaché in Rome, Italy.

Mika Brzezinski — MSNBC reporter and co-host of the weekday show *Morning Joe*. Daughter of Zbigniew Brzezinski, President Jimmy Carter's National Security Advisor.

Mike Kortan — Former FBI Assistant Director for Public Affairs, an influential position that controlled media access. He also served under Robert Mueller in the 2016 Trump-Russia probe.

MIL SATs — Military Satellites

Mitch McConnell — Mitch McConnell, U.S. Senator from Kentucky is also the Senate Majority Leader. Elected to that position unanimously by his Republican colleagues in 2014, 2016, and 2018, he is the longest-serving Senate Republican leader in the history of the United States.

MKUltra — CIA mind-control project that involved the use of psychological experiments combined with the use of drugs.

ML — Marshal law, refers to a state where the military assumes control of civilian law enforcement duties.

MLK — The Reverend Martin Luther King, Jr. was the most influential black leader of the 1960s. He was a Baptist minister and an advocate of civil rights in America. He led the peaceful historical boycott of city buses in Montgomery, Alabama, in 1955. King was assassinated in 1968.

mm — Millions

MOAB — an acronym for Mother of All Bombs. The nickname for GBU-43/B Massive Ordnance Air Blast, which, weighing in at over 21,000 pounds, was the largest non-nuclear bomb ever used by the U.S. military. It was dropped on an ISIS-Khorasan camp in Afghanistan in April of 2017.

Moar — Slang term for "more" used on 4chan, 8chan, and 8kun.

Mockingbird — Operation Mockingbird was a CIA operation where the agency recruited news reporters and their managers to disseminate propaganda for the purpose of controlling the masses.

Moloch — The biblical name of a Canaanite god associated with child sacrifice.

MOS — Mossad, an Israeli intelligence agency.

Mr. Contractor — Edward Snowden, a former CIA employee and NSA contractor who illegally leaked information about NSA surveillance programs to the press in 2013.

MS-13 — Mara Salvatrucha, also known as MS-13, is a criminal gang that originated in Los Angeles, California, in the 1970s and 1980s. It was primarily comprised of and helped protect Salvadoran immigrants. The gang's influence has spread throughout the Western hemisphere and Europe. In 2012, the U.S. Department of the Treasury labeled the group a "transnational criminal organization," the first such designation for a U.S. street gang.

MSM — Mainstream Media

Mueller — Robert Mueller, former FBI Director and Special Counsel.

MW — Maxine Waters, a U.S. Representative from California who has served in Congress since 1991. A member of the Democrat Party, she chaired the Congressional Black Caucus from 1997 to 1999.

MX — The country of Mexico.

MZ — Mark Zuckerberg, founder, CEO, and controlling shareholder of the social media platform Facebook.

N_C — National Security Council. Part of the Executive Office of the President of the United States. It is the principal forum used by the President for consideration of national security, military, and foreign policy matters with senior national security advisors and Cabinet officials.

Nancy Pelosi — U.S. Representative from California and Speaker of the House of Representatives.

Nancy Salzman — President and co-founder of NXIVM, a multi-level marketing company based near Albany, New York, that offered personal and professional development seminars through its "Executive Success Programs." NXIVM leaders were prosecuted for sexual abuse and sex trafficking members.

Natalia Veselnitskaya — A Russian attorney who gained notoriety for her meeting with Donald Trump Jr., Paul Manafort, and Jared Kushner prior to the 2016 Presidential election.

NATSEC or **NAT SEC** — National Security

Nellie Ohr — The wife of former Associate Deputy Attorney General Bruce Ohr. Both Ohr's have been implicated in the Obama administration's 2016 surveillance of the Trump Presidential campaign.

Newfag — Slang term for new user on 4chan, 8chan, or 8kun.

NG — National Guard

NK — North Korea, also known as the Democratic People's Republic of Korea (DPRK).

No name — John McCain, U.S. Senator from Arizona. He served as a senator from January 1987 until his death in 2018.

No Such Agency — National Security Agency (NSA) is a signals intelligence agency within the U.S. Department of Defense. It collects and analyzes electronic signals intelligence of interest to the security of the U.S. and protects all classified and sensitive information stored on government information technology equipment. In addition, the NSA supports and contributes to the civilian use of cryptography and computer security measures.

NP — Usually refers to Nancy Pelosi, a U.S. Representative from California and Speaker of the House of Representatives. In a couple of cases (related to George Soros), it stands for non-profit.

NOFORN — Regarding the classification of information by the U.S. government, this designation (meaning "no foreign nationals") is applied to any information that may not be released to any non-U.S. citizen.

Normalfag or **normie** — Slang term for normal members of society who don't share the same interests as those who commonly use 4chan, 8chan, or 8kun boards.

NPO — Non-Profit Organization

NR — Nuclear Reactor

NSA — National Security Agency is a signals intelligence agency within the U.S. Department of Defense. It collects and analyzes electronic signals intelligence of interest to the security of the U.S. and protects all classified and sensitive information stored on government information technology equipment. In addition, the NSA supports and contributes to the civilian use of cryptography and computer security measures.

NSC — National Security Council. Part of the Executive Office of the President of the United States. It is the principal forum used by the President for consideration of national security, military, and foreign policy matters with senior national security advisors and Cabinet officials.

Nunes — Devin Nunes, U.S. Representative from California and ranking member of the House Intelligence Committee.

NV — Natalia Veselnitskaya, a Russian attorney who gained notoriety for her meeting with Donald Trump Jr., Paul Manafort, and Jared Kushner prior to the 2016 Presidential election.

NWO — New World Order, sometimes referred to as a one-world government. A governmental concept where individual nations surrender their political sovereignty to the will of a centralized world governmental power.

NXIVM — A multi-level marketing company based near Albany, New York, that offered personal and professional development seminars through its "Executive Success Programs. NXIVM leaders were prosecuted for sexual abuse and sex trafficking of the group's members.

NYT — *The New York Times*, an American newspaper founded in 1851.

o7 — Used as an online salute. The letter o symbolizes a head. The number 7 is a hand in position to salute.

O-games — The Olympic Games are international sporting events held every four years.

Oldfag — Slang term for a longtime 4chan, 8chan, or 8kun user.

OO — The Oval Office, which is the working office space of the President of the United States, located in the West Wing of the White House.

OP — Usually stands for "original poster," the person who originally published the thread on 4chan, 8chan, or 8kun. Occasionally it stands for "operation" as in a military or intelligence operation.

OPS — An abbreviation for "Operations" such as military or intelligence operations.

OS — Congressional Oversight Committee

Owl — Occult symbol found throughout history.

O-WH — The Obama White House

OCONUS lures — Oconus = Outside Contiguous United States. Lures = spies. The term was found in text messages between FBI agent Peter Strzok and attorney Lisa Page from conversations they had in December of 2015.

P — Multiple uses: may refer to the Pope, but Q suggested it may also refer to the Payseurs—the descendants of the French Royal family who emigrated to the U.S. after the French Revolution. In more recent posts, it seems to indicate FBI agent Joe Pientka, who interviewed General Michael Flynn when he served as President Trump's National Security Advisor.

P_PERS — A personal message from President Trump.

Pain or **[PAIN]** — A reference to the pending prosecution of corrupt individuals.

Paul Manafort — A businessman, lobbyist, and Member of Donald Trump's 2016 Presidential campaign. He was convicted of money laundering, tax evasion and failing to register as a foreign agent.

Paul Nakasone — The Lieutenant General who succeeded Admiral Michael Rogers as the Director of U.S. Cyber Command and NSA.

Pawn — An individual who is used by influential people to accomplish their objectives.

Pay-for-play — Bribery of a public official. Something of value is exchanged for an action taken by a public official.

PEOC — Presidential Emergency Operations Center, an underground bunker-like structure beneath the East Wing of the White House.

Peter Strzok — FBI agent who was involved in the bureau's counterintelligence investigation of Presidential candidate Donald Trump. He was also a member of Special Counsel Robert Mueller's team until it was disclosed that he harbored an excessive bias against Trump. Strzok was one of the FBI agents who questioned Hillary Clinton regarding her emails, and he interviewed Lt. General Mike Flynn regarding his communications with Russian Ambassador Sergey Kislyak.

PG — Pizzagate/PedoGate, an internet controversy that surfaced in 2016, where restaurant owner James Alefantis and John Podesta were accused of pedophilia.

Phase [2] — The second phase of a covert operation that Q mentioned on February 21st, 2018.

Planefag — Slang term for a 4chan, 8chan, or 8kun user who specializes in tracking airplanes by radar.

POTUS — President of the United States. As Q uses the term, it specifically refers to Donald J. Trump.

pp — People

PP — Planned Parenthood, the largest abortion provider in the United States, is a highly controversial organization with ardent supporters as well as staunch opponents.

Pickle Factory — A term used for the CIA.

Pickle — A euphemism that describes a difficult or messy situation with no obvious solution.

Placeholder — A current post that alludes to details which will be disclosed in a future post.

PM — Prime Minister

Prince Al-Waleed — Alwaleed bin Talal, a billionaire and philanthropist who was arrested November 4th, 2017, as part of the Saudi corruption crackdown.

PRO — Meaning "in favor of." Examples: O-PRO is supportive of Barack Obama, PRO-POTUS is supportive of President Trump.

PROJECT DEEPDREAM — A reference to a Jason Bourne film in which a social media company called Deep Dream, gathers personal data from subscribers and secretly funnels it to the Central Intelligence Agency.

PSYOP — Psychological Operations, which convey selected information and indicators to audiences in order to influence their emotions, motives, objective reasoning, and ultimately their behavior.

Punisher skull — Marvel Comics' superhero Frank Castle (The Punisher) typically wears a shirt with a skull emblazoned on the chest. The skull logo was unofficially adopted by some military special operations teams and has been posted by Q.

PVG — Pudong International Airport in Shanghai, China.

Q Clearance — Access to the highest level of classified information in the U.S. Department of Energy. Q suggested in his case; it refers to the highest level of access across all departments.

Q Clearance Patriot — The first appearance of the term "Q Clearance Patriot" was on November 1st, 2017, where Q introduced himself with this name and the initial Q.

Quid Pro Quo — A Latin phrase indicating something given or received for something else. In cases of public bribery, something of value is exchanged for an action taken by a public official.

R — In most contexts, a reference to Renegade, the Secret Service code name for President Barack Obama. Other uses are possible.

R's — Republicans

R+D — Republicans and Democrats

Rachel Brand — United States Associate Attorney General from May 22nd, 2017, until February 20th, 2018. She resigned to take a job as head of global corporate governance at Walmart.

Rapid Fire — A 1992 film starring Brandon Lee and Powers Booth, who battle a Chinese drug lord and corrupt FBI officials.

RBG — Ruth Bader Ginsburg is an Associate Justice of the U.S. Supreme Court. Nominated by Bill Clinton in 1993, she is a liberal noted for her feminist views.

RC — Rachel "Ray" Chandler, photographer who co-founded Midland modeling Agency with Walter Pearce.

RED_CASTLE — A reference to the insignia of the U.S. Army Corps of Engineers.

Red Cross — The International or American Red Cross.

Red October — Multiple meanings including but not limited to the film by that title and a steel plant in Stalingrad, Russia, which appears on a CIA document that Q provided a link to. Note: Q removed "the Hunt for," and in October of 2018, a new theme "Red October" appeared.

Red pill — A reference from the film *The Matrix*. Taking the red pill causes one to awaken to a different reality.

Red Red — The International or American Red Cross.

Renegade — The Secret Service code name for President Barack Obama.

Renee J. James — A technology executive, who was formerly the president of Intel. She is currently Chairman and CEO of Ampere Computing and an Operating Executive with The Carlyle Group in its Media and Technology practice.

Repost Lost — When a post has been deleted from the board, Q will sometimes repost it with this notice.

Rizvi Traverse Management — The secretive New York private equity firm founded by Indian-born Suhail Rizvi. Investments include ICM Talent Agency, Summit Entertainment, Playboy Enterprises, SpaceX, Flipboard, and Square. Rizvi Traverse was the largest initial stakeholder of Twitter and was instrumental in bringing on board other investors like JP Morgan Chase and Alwaleed bin Talal. At Twitter's Initial Public Offering in 2013, Rizvi Traverse held a 15.6 percent stake in the company valued at $3.8 billion.

RM — Robert Mueller, Special Counsel who investigated President Donald Trump. Served as FBI Director from 2001-2013.

RNC — Republican National Committee, the governing body for the United States Republican Party.

Road block — Using the U.S. Military at the Mexico border to prevent the inflow of illegal aliens, drugs, cash, terrorists, trafficked children, and MS-13 gang members.

ROASTED — A reference to President Trump's participation in the Gridiron Roast Dinner on March 4th, 2018.

RR — Former U.S. Deputy Attorney General Rod Rosenstein. He conducted oversight of Robert Mueller's investigation of President Donald Trump.

Robert Byrd — The U.S. Senator from West Virginia. Byrd was the longest-serving U.S. Senator in history. According to *Wikipedia*, in the early 1940s, he recruited 150 of his friends and associates to create a new chapter of the Ku Klux Klan in Sophia, West Virginia. Hillary Clinton said Byrd was her mentor in the Senate.

Rosatom — A Russian state-owned energy company that purchased the North American company, Uranium One, during Barack Obama's presidency.

ROT — Rotation. A different view provided by the rotation of a camera.

ROTH — Rothschild

Rothschild — An influential banking family that exerted economic and political influence over Europe during the 18th and 19th centuries and over the world during the 20th and 21st centuries.

RT — Multiple possible meanings including retweet, real-time, the news outlet Russia Today, and former Secretary of State Rex Tillerson. The context will dictate the best decode.

Ryan — Paul Ryan, former Wisconsin Representative and Speaker of the U.S. House of Representatives.

SA — The Kingdom of Saudi Arabia

SA --> US --> Asia --> EU — A flow chart showing an order of operations. According to Q, the removal of corruption began in Saudi Arabia and will then happen in the United States, followed by Asia, then the European Union, and other nations.

Sage — By entering the word "sage" in the email field on a 4chan, 8chan, or 8kun thread, you can comment on a thread without bumping it to the top of the board. (Typically used to comment on bad threads to avoid giving them more visibility.)

Sally Yates — Served as Deputy Attorney General under Barack Obama, and briefly as Attorney General under Donald Trump but was fired for insubordination.

Sam Clovis — A national co-chair and policy advisor to the Trump campaign in 2016.

SAP — Special Access Program, a security protocol used by the U.S. federal government that provides highly classified information with safeguards and access restrictions that exceed those used for regular classified information.

Sara — Sara A. Carter, a national and international award-winning investigative reporter who is currently a Fox News contributor.

Sauce — Slang term derived from the word "source." When information is provided on 4chan, 8chan, or 8kun that is not common knowledge, the one posting the information will frequently be asked to provide a source (sauce).

SB — Super Bowl, the annual championship game of the National Football League.

SC — Two confirmed decodes: Special Counsel, or the Supreme Court. The context will dictate the correct one.

SCARAMUCCI MODEL — Anthony Scaramucci served as President Trump's White House Director of Communications from July 21st to July 31st, 2017. During those ten days, Sean Spicer and Reince Priebus resigned. The point Q wants us to understand is that a temporary hire can accomplish unpleasant tasks easier that someone in a permanent position.

Schneiderman — Eric Schneiderman, former New York state Attorney General who resigned May 7th, 2018, due to allegations of past sexual assault by four women.

SCI — Sensitive Compartmented Information. A protocol for securing highly sensitive information using control systems approved by the Director of National Intelligence.

SCI(f) or SCIF — Sensitive Compartmentalized Information Facility. An enclosed area that is used to process sensitive and classified information and restrict access to people who do not have the proper security clearance and need to know.

SD — State Department (formally called the U.S. Department of State). The department of the U.S. executive branch responsible for carrying out foreign policy and international relations.

SEALS — Special forces teams of the U.S. Navy tasked with conducting small-unit special operation missions. The acronym comes from "Sea, Air, and Land."

SDNY — U.S Attorney's office for the Southern District of New York.

SEC — In most cases, it refers to "secure" or "security," i.e., NAT SEC (National Security). In some cases, it refers to the Securities and Exchange Commission. The context will provide the correct decode.

SecureDrop — A program that allows intelligence community employees to communicate with journalists securely.

Sergey Brin — Sergey Mikhaylovich Brin, the Russian-born former President of Alphabet (the parent company of Google and YouTube). Brin co-founded the search engine firm Google with Larry Page in 1998.

Sessions — Jeff Sessions, former U.S. Senator from Alabama. Served as Attorney General under President Trump from 2017-2019.

SFO — San Francisco International Airport

SH — Steve Huffman is the founder and CEO of Reddit, an online discussion site. He is also known by his Reddit nickname "Spez."

Shall we play a game? — A line spoken by a computer (WOPR, or War Operation Plan Response) to Matthew Broderick's character David in the 1983 film *War Games*. David thought he'd hacked a software developer and gained access to new games, but he unwittingly hacked into a Department of Defense system and nearly started a global thermonuclear war. Q uses the phrase in some cases to challenge anons and, in other instances, to taunt his enemies.

Shell1/Shell2 — A reference to "shell" companies. A shell company is a business created to hold the funds and manage the financial transactions of another entity. They don't have employees, don't make money, and don't provide customers with products or services. They only manage the assets they hold.

Shooter — A reference to the perpetrator of a mass shooting.

SID — Likely a reference to Arizona Senator John Sidney McCain III. A second possibility is Sid Blumenthal, a longtime confidant to Hillary Clinton.

Sidley Austin — Chicago-based law firm Sidley Austin LLP is the sixth-largest U.S.-based corporate law firm with approximately 2,000 lawyers and annual revenues of more than two billion dollars.

SIG — Special Interest Group, a group of individuals, brought together by a shared belief or interest, often aiming to influence politics or policies.

SIGINT — Signals Intelligence. The interception and decoding of electronic signals, whether used in communication between people or other applications (i.e., radar and weapon systems). Analysts evaluate raw electronic data and transform it into actionable intelligence.

SIS — Secret Intelligence Service, another name for the UK's MI6. This agency is the UK counterpart to the CIA. SIS was also the acronym used for the Signal Intelligence Service, the United States Army's codebreaking division, before World War II. It was renamed the Signal Security Agency in 1943, and in 1945, it became the Army Security Agency. During World War II, its resources were reassigned to the newly established National Security Agency (NSA).

SIT ROOM — Situation Room. Officially known as the John F. Kennedy Conference Room, the "Situation Room" is a conference room and intelligence management center in the basement of the White House run by the National Security Council staff for the use of the President and his advisors to monitor and deal with crises at home and abroad and to conduct secure communications with outside persons.

SKY EVENT or **SKY Event** — Q posted a reference to this twice, but has not confirmed a decode yet.

Sleeper — a term for someone who joins a community pretending to share their values, while secretly opposing them. At a strategic time—when the "sleeper" is signaled to "awaken" or become active—they carry out their covert mission of disruption or sabotage.

Smollett — Jussie Smollett, an American actor and singer, who was indicted on February 20th, 2019, for allegedly paying two Nigerian-Americans to stage a fake hate crime assault on him.

Sniffer or **Sniffers** — Generally, a bot designed to search the internet for specific data on websites. Q has alluded to highly sophisticated artificial intelligence programs that aggregate data and interpret it. Valerie Jarret has also been identified by Q as a "sniffer."

Snopes — A fact-checking organization that produces reports on rumors, urban legends, and odd news stories. Snopes has been criticized for its liberal-progressive bias.

Snowden — Edward Snowden, the former CIA employee and NSA contractor who stole and made public two classified NSA surveillance programs—PRISM and XKeyscore.

Snow White — A signature by Q referring to the CIA, so named because of the Agency's seven supercomputers that are named after the seven dwarves.

Soros — George Soros, a hedge fund billionaire who is known for using his wealth to fund his own brand of political activism. Recipients of his philanthropy appreciate his money, but those who oppose his political views see him as a creator of chaos around the world—a destabilizing force on economies and societies. Some countries have either banned Soros or restricted his organizations. These countries include Pakistan, Poland, Turkey, Russia, Soros' home country of Hungary, and the Philippines. The Israeli government has said Soros is not welcome there.

SOTU — The annual State of the Union speech given by the President of the United States.

SP — Samantha Power, U.S. Ambassador to the United Nations from 2013 to 2017.

Spade — Katherine Noel Brosnahan, known professionally as Kate Spade and Kate Valentine. She was a fashion designer and businesswoman, who founded the designer brand "Kate Spade New York." Spade's death in June of 2017 was ruled a suicide. She was reported to have hung herself from a doorknob using a red silk scarf.

Spartans in Darkness — "Spartans in Darkness: American SIGINT and the Indochina War, 1945-1975" is a report written by Robert J. Hanyok, of the Center for Cryptologic History, National Security Agency. A link to the document was posted by Q as reference material.

Speed — A film starring Keanu Reeves and Sandra Bullock about a bus that had a bomb connected to the speedometer by a villain. If the bus speed dropped below 50 miles per hour, the bomb would detonate. The conundrum for the hero was how to defuse the bomb without stopping the bus. "Speed" is used as a signature by Q to indicate a delicate situation involving corrupt people that is being dealt with by patriots in a way that will avoid unnecessary harm to the public and keep government services open.

Spirit Cooking — (from *Wikipedia*) Marina Abramovic worked with Jacob Samuel to produce a cookbook of "aphrodisiac recipes" called Spirit Cooking in 1996. These "recipes" were meant to be "evocative instructions for actions or for thoughts." For example, one of the recipes calls for "13,000 grams of jealousy," while another says to "mix fresh breast milk with fresh sperm milk." The work was inspired by the popular belief that ghosts feed off intangible things like light, sound, and emotions.

In 1997, Abramovic created a multimedia Spirit Cooking installation. This was originally installed in the Zerynthia Associazione per l'Arte Contemporanea in Rome, Italy and included white gallery walls with "enigmatically violent recipe instructions" painted in pig's blood. According to Alexxa Gotthardt, the work is "a comment on humanity's reliance on ritual to organize and legitimize our lives and contain our bodies."

Abramovic also published a Spirit Cooking cookbook, containing comico-mystical, self-help instructions that are meant to be just poetry. Spirit Cooking later evolved into a form of dinner party entertainment that Abramovic occasionally lays on for collectors, donors, and friends.

SURV — Surveillance

Splash — A Naval aviator term for shooting down an enemy aircraft. An airplane shot down over the ocean will "splash" into the sea.

spy_T — The government spying operation against President Donald Trump.

SR — There are two confirmed decodes: Barack Obama's National Security Advisor Susan Rice, or Seth Rich, the Democratic National Committee staffer who was murdered on July 10th, 2016.

SS — U.S. Secret Service, a federal law enforcement agency under the Department of Homeland Security charged with conducting criminal investigations and protecting the nation's leaders and their families.

Standard Hotel — The Standard Hotels are a group of five boutique hotels in Los Angeles (Hollywood and Downtown LA), New York City, and Miami Beach. Q's references pertain to the Hollywood location.

Stanislav Lunev — A former Soviet military officer who defected to the United States in 1992. He is the highest-ranking GRU (Russian intelligence) officer ever to defect to the United States. He has worked with the CIA and FBI and is currently in the federal witness protection program.

Stormy Daniels — A pornographic actress, stripper, screenwriter, and director. In 2018, Daniels became involved in a legal dispute with President Trump and his attorney Michael Cohen. Daniels claimed that Trump and his surrogates paid $130,000 in hush money to silence her about an affair she says she had with Trump in 2006. Trump's spokespeople have denied the affair and have accused Daniels of lying.

Strike Package — As used by the military, a strike package is a group of aircraft having different weaponry and capabilities that are launched as a unit to perform a single attack mission.

Sum of All Fears — A Q signature and a reference to the Tom Clancy novel and film by that name. The plot: a sociopath develops a plan to get Russia and the U.S. to destroy each other in a nuclear war, paving the way for him to set up a fascist superstate.

Susan Rice — Served as U.S. National Security Advisor for Barack Obama from 2013 to 2017. She also served as U.S. Ambassador to the United Nations from 2009 to 2013.

Swamp — Washington D.C., which is rumored to have been built on a swamp. Research more at Histories of the National Mall: http://mallhistory.org/explorations/show/was-the-national-mall-built-on

T2 — Terminal 2 at Shanghai Pudong International Airport (PVG).

Taken — A 2008 film about a retired CIA agent who traveled across Europe relying on his knowledge of tradecraft to save his estranged daughter, who, along with her girlfriend, was kidnapped by Albanian sex traffickers.

TG — Trey Gowdy, former South Carolina Representative and former federal prosecutor who served as Chair of the House Oversight and Government Reform Committee.

The Analysis Corporation (TAC) — A corporation founded in 1991 in McClean, Virginia, by Cecilia Hayes. TAC works on projects in the counterterrorism and national security industries. John Brennan was appointed TAC President and CEO in 2005.

The Bloody Wonderland — Q's reference to Saudi Arabia, which was notorious in the past for its frequent use of public execution.

TheMagikBOT — A *Wikipedia* bot that makes automated or semi-automated edits to *Wikipedia* entries that would be difficult to do manually.

TP — Tony Podesta, an influential Washington D.C. lobbyist who stepped down from his firm, The Podesta Group, as a result of Special Counsel Mueller's investigation and the firm's unregistered lobbying for the European Centre for Modern Ukraine. Podesta Group failed to file as an agent of a foreign power under the Foreign Agents Registration Act (FARA). Tony is the brother of John Podesta, the chairman of the 2016 Hillary Clinton Presidential campaign.

Trip, Tripcode or **Trip code** — A hashed password used on internet boards like 4chan, 8chan, or 8kun that provides a unique user identity while maintaining anonymity.

TSA — Transportation Security Administration, an agency of the U.S. Department of Homeland Security created as a response to the September 11th attacks. TSA has authority over the security of the traveling public in the United States.

TT — Two confirmed decodes. The context will determine the correct one. It can refer to Trump Tower in New York. It can also be an abbreviation for Tarmac Tapes. According to Q, the NSA has a recording (tape) of the conversation that Bill Clinton had with then-Attorney General Loretta Lynch on the tarmac at Sky Harbor Airport in Phoenix, Arizona, on June 27th, 2016.

T-Tower — Trump Tower. A skyscraper on Fifth Avenue, between 56th and 57th Streets, in Midtown Manhattan, New York City. Trump Tower serves as the headquarters for the Trump Organization.

U1 — A abbreviation for the North American company, Uranium One, which was sold to the Russian energy company, Rosatom.

U1 -> CA -> EU -> ASIA -> IRAN/NK — According to Q, this is the route of travel for uranium transferred when the company, Uranium One, was sold to the Russian company, Rosatom: from Canada, to the European Union, to Asia, to Iran/North Korea.

UBL — Usama bin Laden (AKA Osama bin Laden) was a founder of the pan-Islamic militant organization al-Qaeda.

Uhuru Kenyatta — Kenyan politician and the fourth president of the Republic of Kenya.

UID — User ID for internet connection or specific internet-connected device.

UK/AUS assist/set up — According to Q, the UK and Australia, through the Five Eyes agreement, assisted the Obama administration in surveilling Donald Trump's Presidential campaign.

Unmask — Exposing the concealed name of a U.S. person in surveillance data.

UN — United Nations, an intergovernmental organization responsible for facilitating cooperation in international law, international security, economic development, diplomacy and human rights. It was founded in 1945 to replace the League of Nations.

US Cyber Task Force — In February of 2018, Attorney General Jeff Sessions ordered the creation of the Justice Department's Cyber-Digital Task Force, which "will canvass the many ways that the Department is combatting the global cyber threat, and will also identify how federal law enforcement can more effectively accomplish its mission in this vital and evolving area."

USMC — United States Marine Corps, a branch of the U.S. Armed Forces responsible for conducting expeditionary and amphibious operations with the Navy, the Army, and the Air Force.

US — The United States of America

US-G — United States Government

USSS — United States Secret Service, a federal law enforcement agency under the Department of Homeland Security charged with conducting criminal investigations and protecting the nation's leaders and their families.

Vault 7 — A series of documents published by *WikiLeaks* in 2017 that detail the capabilities of the CIA to perform electronic surveillance and cyber warfare. The files, dated from 2013–2016, include details on the agency's software capabilities, such as the ability to compromise cars, smart TVs, web browsers, and the operating systems of most smartphones, as well as operating systems like Microsoft Windows, MacOS, and Linux.

VIP — Very Important Person. Usually a reference to people who wear Q related shirts at President Trump's rallies. On a few occasions, the President has pointed to these patriots in the crowd. Many VIPs have posted rally photos on Twitter. Q has reposted links to them on the board.

VJ — Valerie Jarrett, a businesswoman and former government official who served as the senior advisor to U.S. President Barack Obama. Jarrett was born in Iran to African-American parents; her family moved to London for a year, and then to Chicago in 1963.

We don't say his name — John McCain, U.S. Senator from Arizona. He served as a Senator from January 1987 until his death in 2018.

Wendy — Nickname for Maggie Nixon. The daughter of Sarah Nixon and granddaughter of actress and TV soap opera writer and producer Agnes Nixon.

Wet Works — Slang for assassination. The term was used in the John Podesta emails published by *WikiLeaks*.

WH — White House, the official residence and workplace of the President of the United States. White House is also used as a metonym for the President and his advisors.

Wheels up — An aviation term indicating an aircraft is taking off, and its landing gear are being retracted. Q used this term as a signal that an individual he referred to as the "stealth bomber" was commencing operations.

Where we go one, we go all — A line from the film *White Squall* which was based on the sinking of a school Brigantine sailing ship in 1961. The phrase "Where we go one, we go all" is a signature found in many of Q's posts.

White Squall — A 1996 coming of age film in which a group of high school and college-aged misfits sign up for training aboard a sailing ship under the instruction of a hard but courageous skipper. Scenes from the film have been highlighted by Q as themes that illustrate different aspects of his mission.

Who performs in a circus? — Clowns, which is a reference to the CIA; an agency also known as Clowns In America.

WikiLeaks — A watchdog organization founded by Julian Assange that publishes documents leaked from various government and corporate sources.

Wizards & Warlocks — An internal name used by NSA employees and contractors—guardians of all electronic information.

WL — *WikiLeaks,* a watchdog organization founded by Julian Assange that publishes documents leaked from various government and corporate sources.

Wray — Christopher Wray, Director of the FBI.

WRWY — We are with you.

WW — World Wide

WWG1WGA — The abbreviation for "Where we go one, we go all," a line from the film *White Squall* which was based on the sinking of a school Brigantine sailing ship in 1961. The phrase "Where we go one, we go all" is a signature found in many of Q's posts.

Y — Generally, refers to the goat head and owl symbolism, images, and icons used by the occult. It has also been used in references to former FBI Director James Come[Y] and with reference to his book, A Higher Loyalty [Y].

YT — YouTube, an American video-sharing platform headquartered in California that now operates as one of Google's subsidiaries.